NAVIGATING SPECIAL EDUCATION:

A Parent's Guide To Rights And Advocacy

By Dana Jonson, MSEd, JD

Navigating Special Education
A Parent's Guide To Rights And Advocacy

by **Dana Jonson**, MSEd, JD

DISCLAIMER
This book provides general information on special education advocacy and rights under the Individuals with Disabilities Education Act (IDEA) and other relevant laws. It does not constitute legal advice. Because special education laws and procedures vary by state, readers should consult a qualified special education attorney regarding their specific situation. This book may reference third-party websites or external resources for informational purposes only. Such references do not imply endorsement or guarantee of accuracy, and the author and publisher are not responsible for the content, legality, or reliability of any external sites. No responsibility is assumed for actions taken based on the information or resources included in this book.

PUBLISHING DETAILS
StarrWay Press
ISBN: 979-8-9988750-0-7
First Edition: 2025

For inquiries, permissions, or additional resources, visit:
specialeducation.guide

STARRWAY
— PRESS —

For my children, my foster children, and every student I have had the privilege of working with—You have taught me more about resilience, determination, and the power of advocacy than I could have ever imagined. This book is for you. ♥

ACKNOWLEDGEMENTS

Writing this book was a journey—one that would not have been possible without the unwavering support, guidance, and inspiration from so many people.

To my **children, foster children, and students**—you are the reason behind every page of this book. Your strength, challenges, and triumphs have shaped my understanding of advocacy in ways no textbook ever could.

To the **parents and caregivers** who fight tirelessly for their children, often in systems designed to wear them down—you are the backbone of change. Your persistence, courage, and refusal to accept "no" as a final answer continue to inspire me.

To the **teachers, therapists, and special education professionals** who believe in inclusion and go above and beyond to support students—thank you for proving that real advocacy happens not just in meetings, but in classrooms, hallways, and quiet moments of understanding.

To my **mentors, colleagues, and fellow advocates**—your wisdom, insight, and shared frustrations (often with a side of much-needed humor) have strengthened my ability to push forward, even when the road has felt impossible.

To my **friends and family**—thank you for the encouragement, for listening when I needed to vent, and for reminding me that sometimes, even advocates need a break.

Finally, to **every parent holding this book,** I see you. I know this road is not easy, but I also know your advocacy is making a difference. Keep going. Your child is lucky to have you in their corner.

With gratitude.

PREFACE

Dear Fellow Maze Runners,

Welcome to the labyrinth of special education—where the rules are complicated, the paperwork never ends, and the stakes could not be higher. It is a maze nobody asks to enter, yet here you are: pushing forward with determination, love, and a fierce commitment to your child's future. You may feel lost, overwhelmed, or even defeated some days. But hear this: you are not lost. You are exactly where you need to be—and this book is here to ensure you do not have to do it alone.

Why This Book?

Special education is a system built on complex laws, endless jargon, and an overwhelming amount of red tape. Parents are often expected to navigate it alone—but that is not how it should be. You deserve clear guidance, practical strategies, and real-world support.

This book is not a legal textbook. It is your survival guide, your flashlight, your map. Whether you are just starting this journey or already deep in the IEP trenches, you will find the tools you need to fight smarter, advocate louder, and stand stronger for your child.

Here is what we will do together:

✓ Decode confusing terms and laws—without needing a law degree.
✓ Learn what to ask for—and how to ask for it.
✓ Break down the process step-by-step—without the jargon.
✓ Arm you with real-world strategies to secure the education your child deserves.

Why I Wrote This

I have sat where you are sitting. I have stared down a mountain of paperwork, felt the gut-punch of a denied service, and celebrated the small (but mighty) victories that come when you refuse to give up. I have spent twenty years as a special education attorney, but I am also a parent to five incredible children—all with different special education needs. Before that, I was a special education teacher and administrator. I know this maze from every angle—and I know you can navigate it too.

You do not have to know everything. You only need to know the next right move. And together, we will make certain your child receives the support and education they deserve.

Deep breath. Grab a coffee. Let's dive in.

LEGAL DISCLAIMERS

⦿ Understanding IDEA And State Laws

The Individuals with Disabilities Education Act (IDEA) is a federal law that sets the baseline for special education rights and protections nationwide. However, each state can expand upon these protections and offer additional rights, services, or dispute resolution options beyond what federal law requires. The IDEA is the floor, not the ceiling. Some states provide stronger protections than IDEA mandates, while others barely meet the minimum requirements.

➤ **What This Means for You:** Always check your state's special education laws and regulations to ensure you are fully aware of the rights and services available to your child. If you are unsure, consult your state's Department of Education website or a local advocacy group for guidance.

⦿ This Book Is Not Legal Advice

I designed this book to provide practical guidance, advocacy strategies, and information on navigating the special education system. However, it is not a substitute for legal advice. Special education laws and enforcement vary by state, and the specifics of your child's situation may require individualized legal guidance.

➤ If you are facing a dispute with your school district, a denial of services, or a due process hearing, consult with a qualified special education attorney—preferably one who primarily practices in this area. An attorney can provide state-specific legal advice and representation tailored to your child's needs.

◉ The U.S. Department Of Education Is Currently A Dumpster Fire

As I write this, the current administration is actively working to dismantle the U.S. Department of Education, gut civil rights enforcement, and roll back key special education protections. What does this mean for parents? No one knows for certain—but history tells us that when federal oversight weakens, schools are less likely to be held accountable.

➤ **What You Can Do:** Stay informed, know your rights, and be prepared to advocate harder than ever. If federal protections disappear, you may need to rely more heavily on state laws, local advocacy groups, and legal action to secure services for your child.

★ **Direct Action Tool:** Want to quickly find your elected officials? Use _myreps.datamade.us_ to locate contact info for your federal, state, and local representatives. Your voice matters—make sure they hear it.

The system may be broken, but your advocacy is not. You are your child's strongest line of defense—and that will never change.

This fight is far from over.

KEY TERMS & ACRONYMS IN SPECIAL EDUCATION

This reference guide combines essential terms and acronyms frequently used in special education. It is designed to support parents, advocates, and educators by simplifying the language of IEP meetings, evaluations, and legal frameworks. Bookmark this section—it will be a useful tool throughout your advocacy journey.

Core Terms

504 Plan
Provides accommodations for students with disabilities who do not need special education services under IDEA.

Accommodations
Adjust how a student learns (e.g., extended time), without changing what they learn.

Modifications
Alter what a student is expected to learn (e.g., simplified content or reduced workload).

Evaluation
Formal assessments and observations used to determine a student's strengths, needs, and eligibility for special education.

Eligibility Determination
The process of deciding whether a student qualifies for services under IDEA.

IEP (Individualized Education Program)
A legally binding document outlining the services, goals, and accommodations for a student with disabilities.

FAPE (Free Appropriate Public Education)
An educational right under IDEA guaranteeing that students with disabilities receive tailored instruction at no cost to families.

LRE (Least Restrictive Environment)
Requires students to be educated with nondisabled peers to the maximum extent appropriate.

Related Services
Support services like speech therapy, counseling, or transportation needed to help a child benefit from special education.

Transition Plan
A required part of the IEP by age 16 that prepares students for post-secondary life, including employment or further education.

Behavior & Discipline

FBA (Functional Behavioral Assessment)
A structured process to identify triggers and functions of challenging behavior.

BIP (Behavioral Intervention Plan)
A personalized strategy to address behavior concerns using positive supports and interventions.

MDR (Manifestation Determination Review)
A meeting held when a student with an IEP is suspended or removed to determine if the behavior was related to their disability.

Dispute Resolution & Legal Rights

PWN (Prior Written Notice)
A written explanation from the school whenever it proposes or refuses a change in a child's educational program.

Due Process
A formal legal procedure to resolve disagreements between parents and schools regarding special education.

IEE (Independent Educational Evaluation)
An evaluation conducted by a qualified professional who is not employed by the school district. There are several ways an IEE can be obtained:

- **School-recommended IEE:** The school selects the evaluator and pays for the evaluation.

- **Privately arranged IEE:** Parents choose an evaluator and pay for the evaluation themselves.

- **Mutually agreed-upon IEE:** Parents and the school agree on an evaluator, and the school pays.

- **Parent-requested IEE at public expense:** If parents *disagree* with the school's evaluation, they may request an IEE, and the school must either approve it (and let the parent choose the evaluator) or initiate a due process hearing to defend its own evaluation.

Child Find
The school's legal duty to identify, locate, and evaluate students who may have disabilities.

RTI (Response to Intervention)
A tiered intervention system used to support struggling students before referring them to special education.

Section 504
A civil rights law that prohibits discrimination based on disability in programs receiving federal funds.

IDEA (Individuals with Disabilities Education Act)
Federal law that governs special education and ensuring FAPE for students with disabilities.

Additional Acronyms & Agencies

ASL – American Sign Language, a visual language used by the Deaf and hard-of-hearing community

ADA – Americans with Disabilities Act, a federal law prohibiting discrimination based on disability (https://www.ada.gov)

ABA – Applied Behavior Analysis, a therapeutic approach often used to support individuals with autism

COPAA – Council of Parent Attorneys and Advocates, a national nonprofit that plays a pivotal role in advancing the civil and educational rights of students with disabilities through legal advocacy, policy influence, and family empowerment (https://www.copaa.org)

DOE – Department of Education, the federal agency overseeing education policy and enforcement (https://www.ed.gov)

LEA – Local Education Agency, typically the local public school district responsible for providing education

NCLD / NDRN – National Center for Learning Disabilities / National Disability Rights Network, national advocacy organizations for individuals with disabilities (https://www.ncld.org / https://www.ndrn.org)

OCR – Office for Civil Rights, a branch of the U.S. Department of Education that enforces civil rights laws in education (https://www2.ed.gov/about/offices/list/ocr)

OSEP – Office of Special Education Programs, a division of the U.S. Department of Education that administers IDEA (https://osepideasthatwork.org)

PTA / SEPTA – Parent Teacher Association / Special Education PTA, school-based groups supporting family-school collaboration (https://www.pta.org)

PTIs – Parent Training and Information Centers, federally funded centers offering guidance to families of children with disabilities (https://www.parentcenterhub.org/find-your-center)

Section 504 – Section 504 of the Rehabilitation Act of 1973, a federal law that protects the rights of individuals with disabilities in programs that receive federal funding (https://www2.ed.gov/about/offices/list/ocr/504faq.html)

SMART – Specific, Measurable, Achievable, Relevant, Time-bound, a framework for setting effective goals

SST – Student Support Team, a school-based team that develops early interventions for struggling students

SSI – Supplemental Security Income, a federal program that provides financial support to individuals with disabilities and low income (https://www.ssa.gov/ssi)

Title I – Title I of the Elementary and Secondary Education Act of 1965, federal aid for schools with high low-income populations (https://www2.ed.gov/programs/titleiparta)

Voc Rehab / VR – Vocational Rehabilitation, state services that help individuals with disabilities prepare for and obtain employment (https://rsa.ed.gov/about/programs/vocational-rehabilitation)

Wrightslaw – A leading resource on special education law and advocacy, created by Attorney Pete Wright, who successfully argued the landmark U.S. Supreme Court case Florence County School District Four v. Shannon Carter (https://supreme.justia.com/cases/federal/us/510/7/ , https://www.wrightslaw.com)

✱ Pro Parent Tip: If a term comes up in an IEP meeting that you do not recognize—ask. Acronyms are only helpful when everyone knows what they mean.

Table Of Contents

INTRODUCTION

Your Special Education Survival Guide

Welcome to your essential guide for navigating the world of special education. If you are here, you probably have questions—many of them. Perhaps your child was just evaluated, and you are staring at an IEP full of acronyms that make little sense. Or maybe you have been advocating for years, yet still feel like you are fighting an uphill battle.

Wherever you are in this journey, this book is here to help. It is not a textbook. It is not a legal manual. It is a practical, no-nonsense guide designed to empower you—not overwhelm you.

What You Will Get from This Guide

✓ Straightforward, real-world advice—not vague, feel good platitudes.

✓ Step-by-step breakdowns of IEPs, 504 Plans, evaluations, accommodations, and more.

✓ Advocacy strategies that help you speak up, push back, and get results.

✓ Legal insights—explained in plain English, so you do not need a law degree to understand your child's rights.

How To Use This Book

The world of special education is not linear—it is a maze. Every parent's path through it is different.

This guide is designed to meet you wherever you are, whether you are just learning about IEPs or already navigating eligibility meetings and service denials. You can:

▶ **Start at** *Chapter 1: Understanding Special Education* for a full, step-by-step breakdown of the special education process.

▶ **Skip directly to a topic**—such as evaluations, accommodations, or discipline—when a specific issue arises.

▶ **Scan the Pro Tips**, scripts, and checklists if you are short on time and need immediate support.

▶ **Flip to the key words or appendices** for quick help with acronyms, legal terms, or sample documents.

This book is your reference, your encouragement, your shortcut, and your toolkit. Use it as you need it—there is no wrong way to begin.

CHAPTER 1:
Understanding Special Education

A. Key Terminology You Need To Know

The world of special education is filled with acronyms, jargon, and legal terms that can be difficult to decode. But knowing these terms is essential—you cannot effectively advocate for your child if you do not speak the language of the system.

So, let's break it down.

Major Laws That Shape Special Education

- **IDEA** (Individuals with Disabilities Education Act) – The federal law that guarantees special education services for eligible children.

- **Section 504** (of the Rehabilitation Act of 1973) – A civil rights law that protects students with disabilities from discrimination and provides accommodations for students who do not qualify for special education under IDEA.

- **ADA** (Americans with Disabilities Act) – Ensures accessibility and non-discrimination in schools, workplaces, and public spaces.

Key Components of Special Education

- **FAPE** (Free and Appropriate Public Education): Schools must provide an education that is free, individualized, and designed to promote progress.

- **LRE** (Least Restrictive Environment): Schools must place students in inclusive settings whenever possible.

- **IEP** (Individualized Education Program): A legally binding plan that outlines a student's learning goals, accommodations, and services.

- **Related Services:** Additional supports, such as speech therapy, occupational therapy, physical therapy, or transportation.

- **504 Plan:** A non-IEP plan that provides accommodations for students who do not need specialized instruction but still require support due to a disability.

Evaluations & Disciplinary Protections

- **Evaluation:** A series of tests and observations used to determine if a child has a disability that affects their learning, how it affects their learning, and whether they qualify for special education. This includes cognitive and academic testing, input from teachers and parents, assessments in related service areas, and sometimes medical or psychological evaluations.

- **Manifestation Determination Review (MDR):** An IEP meeting is held before a student with a disability is suspended for more than 10 days or expelled to determine if their behavior was caused by their disability. MDRs are also necessary if there is a pattern of students being removed from their program.

- **Functional Behavioral Assessment (FBA):** A process used to identify the reasons behind a child's behavior and find patterns that affect learning. It helps determine what triggers the behavior and how to support the child effectively.

- **Behavioral Intervention Plan (BIP):** A personalized plan that outlines strategies, supports, and consequences to help a student manage their behavior in a positive way at school. It is based on the results of the FBA.

B. What Is Special Education?

Special education may sound like an exclusive service—something schools offer at their discretion. It is not. Special education is a legal right for students who learn differently. Special education is not optional, and it is definitely not a favor schools do for students. It is a legal right for children who learn differently—a structured system designed to ensure that all students, regardless of ability, have access to an education that meets their needs.

That sounds great, right? Until you actually have to navigate it.

The moment your child enters the world of special education, you are suddenly drowning in acronyms, paperwork, and school meetings that seem to be conducted in a different language. Terms like "FAPE," "LRE," and "procedural safeguards"—the critical legal protections that ensure parents have a voice in decision-making—are thrown around as if you are expected to have a PhD in education law already. And sometimes, it feels as though you need one just to keep up.

But here is the good news: you do not need to be a lawyer to advocate for your child—you need the right information. Let's start by breaking it down—because the more you know, the stronger your advocacy becomes.

The Law That Makes It Happen: IDEA

The Individuals with Disabilities Education Act (IDEA) is the federal law that guarantees special education services for students who qualify. This law is why special education exists in public schools. It establishes two key rights:

Free Appropriate Public Education (FAPE)

Schools must provide an education that is free (no sneaky fees for required services), appropriate (meaning it meets the child's individual needs), and public (meaning the responsibility falls on the school system).

Least Restrictive Environment (LRE)

Schools must educate students with disabilities alongside their non-disabled peers whenever possible—or to the greatest extent appropriate for that student. If a student needs a self-contained classroom or an alternative setting, that is okay, but there must be a clear reason why that placement is necessary.

✦ **Important Note:** Special education rights under federal law apply specifically to children in public schools. The IDEA requires schools to identify students with disabilities—including those in private schools—but the full range of special education services and protections applies only within the public school system. If your child is homeschooled or attends a private school, they may still have access to evaluations and some limited services, depending on your state. However, the rights and obligations are different. Be sure to consult your local school district, state Department of Education, or a special education advocate or attorney to understand your specific options if your child is outside the public school system.

The Purpose of Special Education

At its core, special education exists because not all children learn the same way.

Some students need extra time to process information, while others require specialized instruction, speech therapy, behavior support, or sensory accommodations to stay engaged in the classroom. Some children struggle with reading or math, while others need help with executive functioning, social skills, or mobility. Special education is not about giving your child a better grade—it is about leveling the playing field so they can actually access the curriculum in the first place.

Special education is not just about accommodations like extra time on tests or homework extensions. It is individualized, specially designed instruction intended to meet each child's unique learning needs, remove barriers, and promote real educational progress.

What special education does is level the playing field.

It does not provide an "advantage." It is not a bonus. Special education is an equity-based system that ensures students with disabilities get the same access to learning as their non-disabled peers.

What Special Education Looks Like in Practice

The first rule of special education: It is not a location (i.e. the special education classroom). It is a collection of services and supports delivered wherever the child needs them—whether in a general education classroom, a resource room, a therapy setting, or another environment entirely, designed to help them thrive.

Some students receive accommodations in a general education classroom. Others require one-on-one support, small-group instruction, or specialized therapy services. Some students benefit from assistive technology, while others need modifications to the curriculum. And some require completely different schools. The "I" in IEP stands for "Individual" for a reason. But more on that later.

➜ *Examples of Special Education in Action*

- A student with dyslexia might receive specialized reading instruction and extra time on tests.

- A student with autism might need a structured routine, social skills training, and sensory supports, all within the regular education classroom.

- A student with cerebral palsy might use assistive technology and receive physical therapy to navigate the school environment.

- A student with ADHD may require movement breaks, a quiet workspace, and support with executive functioning.

Each child's needs are unique, which is why they get an Individualized Education Program (IEP)—a legally binding document that outlines their goals, objectives, accommodations, and support services.

C. Myths & Misconceptions About Special Education

There is a lot of misinformation out there about special education. Let's clear up some of the biggest myths.

✗ **Myth #1:** Special Education is Only for Students with Severe Disabilities

> ✓ **Reality:** Many students in special education have mild disabilities like ADHD, dyslexia, or anxiety. You do not need a severe diagnosis for your child to qualify—just if their disability affects their ability to learn and they need specialized instruction.

✗ **Myth #2:** Special Education Lowers Academic Expectations

> ✓ **Reality:** Special education is about removing barriers, not lowering the bar. IDEA requires that students with disabilities make meaningful progress and be held to high, yet appropriate, standards.

✗ Myth #3: Special Education Is Only for Academic Issues, Not Behavioral Ones

> **✓ Reality:** Special education can address both academic and behavioral needs. If a student's behavior affects their learning, their IEP can include strategies for managing behavior and supporting social-emotional development.

✗ Myth #4: Special Education Stigmatizes Children

> **✓ Reality:** The real stigma comes from misinformation. Many students receive services discreetly and thrive with the right support.

✗ Myth #5: Parents Have No Say in Special Education Decisions

> **✓ Reality:** You are an equal, legally recognized partner in your child's education. You have the right to request evaluations, challenge decisions, and advocate for changes. The school does not get to call all the shots unilaterally.

✗ Myth #6: Special Education Services Are the Same for Every Child

> **✓ Reality:** Every child's needs are unique. Special education services are individualized through the IEP process to ensure each student gets the specific support they need for success.

✗ Myth #7: Teachers and Schools Always Know Best About My Child's Needs

> **✓ Reality:** You, as the parent, are the expert on your child. Your observations and input are crucial to understanding your child's strengths, challenges, and how to support them best.

✗ **Myth #8:** Once a Student Is Placed in Special Education, They cannot Move to a Regular Classroom

> ✓ **Reality:** Many students in special education are in the regular education classroom. Those who are not can ultimately transition to a general education setting with the right support. Inclusion is the goal, whenever possible and meaningful, and students who require intensive support may progress to less restrictive environments over time.

✗ **Myth #9:** My Child Will Be Stuck in Special Education Forever

> ✓ **Reality:** Special education services are there when needed—and can evolve or end as your child grows stronger. It is not a trap; it is a tool for growth. If a child makes meaningful progress and no longer needs support, their IEP can be modified or discontinued. Services are adjusted as needs change, and eligibility under IDEA is not indefinite. It typically ends when a student graduates with a regular high school diploma, is determined through evaluation to no longer qualify, or reaches age 22. Special education is never truly "forever"—it is there to support growth, not define limits.

✗ **Myth #10:** My Child Will Get All the Support They Need Once They Are in Special Education

> ✓ **Reality:** It is essential to stay actively involved and monitor your child's progress. Support services should be regularly reviewed and adjusted to ensure that your child is consistently making progress toward their educational goals.

Final Thoughts: Knowledge Is Power

Understanding the fundamentals—what special education is, who qualifies, and how it works—gives you something the system is not always quick to offer: leverage. You do not need to know every statute or master every acronym. But you do need to know that special education is not optional. It is a legal obligation.

Key Takeaways:

✓ **Special education is a right under federal law,** not something schools offer at their discretion.

✓ **FAPE and LRE ensure that students receive meaningful instruction** in inclusive settings with the supports they need.

✓ **The IEP is an individualized plan,** not a standard menu of services. Every child's program must be tailored to their unique needs.

✓ **Parents are full, legally protected members of the team.** Your insights, questions, and concerns must be considered in all decisions.

✓ **Understanding key terms and laws is essential.** You cannot advocate effectively if you do not speak the language of the system.

✓ **Do not fall for the myths.** Misinformation can derail your advocacy—stay grounded in facts.

✓ **Special education evolves.** Services change as your child grows—and that is a good thing.

➡ **Pro Parent Move:** If something feels unclear, ask for it in writing. When you put questions on the record, you change the power dynamic.

Closing Thought

You are not just learning the system—you are learning how to lead within it. Every term you decode, every law you understand, and every myth you unlearn moves you one step closer to effective advocacy. The more you know, the harder it is for anyone to push you—or your child—aside.

Knowledge is power—but documentation is leverage.

When in doubt, ask for everything in writing. Keep a record of every decision, every question, and every concern. When you document, you protect your child—and yourself.

You are just getting started. And you've got this!

CHAPTER 2:
Funding For Special Education

Funding is not just important—it is essential. Without adequate resources, special education services cannot exist. Supports, therapies, accommodations, and staffing all require funding—and when that funding falls short, it is students who pay the price.

Yet the funding system is often confusing, inconsistent, and deeply under-resourced. Many parents and educators struggle to understand where the money comes from, how it is allocated, and how to hold districts accountable for using it properly.

To be painfully clear: schools cannot deny special education services due to a lack of funding. If a service is written into an Individualized Education Program (IEP), the school must provide it. Budget limitations are not a valid excuse under the law.

This chapter breaks down the complex world of special education funding, explains where financial assistance may be available, and equips you to advocate for equitable resource allocation—because understanding the money is essential to protecting your child's rights.

✦ Note On The Current Federal Climate

As I write this, the U.S. Department of Education is facing potential defunding and restructuring efforts, at best—and complete dismantling, at worst. These changes could drastically reduce federal oversight and enforcement of special education protections. While IDEA currently remains federal law, implementation and accountability may increasingly fall to states and local districts. That makes understanding funding sources, asking critical questions, and monitoring spending more important than ever.

A. Overview Of Funding Sources

Special education funding is a patchwork—federal, state, local, private grants, and nonprofit aid. Unfortunately, although the Individuals with Disabilities Education Act (IDEA) provides federal funding, it does not fully cover the cost of services, forcing states and districts to fill in the gaps.

✱ Pro Parent Tip: Just because a school receives funding for special education does not mean the money is being spent wisely. Schools are legally required to disclose how they allocate special education funds—and reviewing this can reveal whether money is reaching students or getting lost in administrative costs.

Federal Funding Sources

IDEA Part B Grants – The most significant source of federal special education funding. It covers:

- Evaluations

- Related services (speech therapy, occupational therapy, counseling)

- Teacher and paraprofessional salaries

- Assistive technology

However, states must match part of these funds—if your district is underfunding special education, check how much state funding is actually being contributed.

Section 504 of the Rehabilitation Act – While it does not provide direct funding, it requires schools to provide reasonable accommodations for students with disabilities.

Title I Funds – Schools with high percentages of low-income students can use Title I funds to support students with disabilities in reading and math interventions.

Medicaid Reimbursement for Schools – Some schools bill Medicaid for therapy and medical services provided to eligible students—but many districts underutilize this funding source.

✱ **Pro Parent Tip:** If your child is enrolled in Medicaid, ask if the school is billing Medicaid for services. While parents do not receive direct payment, schools can use Medicaid funds to expand therapy, equipment, and support services that directly benefit eligible students.

State & Local Funding

- **State Special Education Grants** – Most states supplement federal IDEA funds with their own education grants. However, funding levels vary widely.

- **Local School District Budgets** – Public schools receive funding through local property taxes, state education funds, and federal allocations. The amount allocated for special education depends on the district's priorities.

- **Early Intervention (IDEA Part C)** – Provides funding for services to support children from birth to age three who have developmental delays or disabilities. Early intervention aims to address challenges early and build a solid foundation for future learning.

✱ **Pro Parent Tip:** Some states have a reputation for underfunding special education. Research your state's IDEA funding per student—if your state ranks low, advocacy is even more critical.

Private & Nonprofit Funding

- **Nonprofit Grants** – Organizations like The Arc, Easterseals, and United Cerebral Palsy provide financial aid for medical and educational needs.

- **Private Insurance** – Some services, such as therapy or specialized equipment, may be covered through private health insurance.

- **Community-Based Organizations** – Many local disability advocacy groups help families access financial assistance for assistive technology, tutoring, and therapy.

✱ **Pro Parent Tip:** Follow the Money. If a school claims a service is "not available" or suggests they "can't afford" it, that is not an acceptable reason under IDEA. Schools must legally provide the services written into your child's IEP—regardless of cost or staffing challenges. Ask for documentation: "Can you show me how special education funds are currently allocated—and how that aligns with student needs?" You are not just asking for proof—they must explain how funding decisions are made. If the money does not reach students, that conversation is for the school board.

B. Applying For Financial Assistance

Applying for financial support can feel overwhelming, but with persistence and strong documentation, families can access various funding sources—including grants, waivers, and school-based programs.

Step 1: Identify Available Funding Sources

Federal & State Programs

Explore Medicaid waivers that provide funding for services such as therapy, in-home behavioral support, and assistive devices. Waiver availability and criteria vary by state, so research programs specific to your location.

Some states also offer direct financial assistance to families of children with disabilities.

→ **For example:**

- In **New York**, families may benefit from state-supported grants for adaptive technology or intensive tutoring.

- In **Texas**, new legislation is creating Education Savings Accounts (ESAs) that may be available to students with disabilities.

- In **California**, Regional Centers may cover costs for services that fall outside of school responsibilities.

These programs evolve regularly—so it is important to verify what is current in your state.

Nonprofit & Private Grants

Numerous nonprofit organizations provide grants for educational and therapeutic needs. These may include:

- The National Autism Association
- The Christopher & Dana Reeve Foundation
- The UnitedHealthcare Children's Foundation
- Local community foundations and disability-specific organizations

These grants may cover items such as adaptive equipment, communication devices, therapies, or specialized camps.

School-Based Programs

Some schools partner with outside agencies or nonprofits to fund services such as assistive technology, social skills training, or counseling. Others may use discretionary funds to cover costs not directly tied to the IEP.

✳ **Pro Parent Tip:** Even if your school does not publicize financial aid options, ask if they partner with outside funding agencies or have access to discretionary special education funds.

What to Google

To uncover relevant opportunities in your area, search:

- "Special education family grants [your state]"
- "Medicaid waiver for children with disabilities [your state]"
- "Assistive technology funding [your region or state department of education]"
- "Nonprofit disability grants [name of condition or need]"
- "Education advocate funding support [Parent Training Information Center in your state]"

Step 2: Prepare Your Application

Most applications—whether public or private—require documentation such as:

- IEP or 504 Plan
- Medical or psychological evaluations
- Proof of income (for need-based programs)

Even if the issue is medical rather than IEP-related, when requesting assistance for school-related support, make sure to frame the request in terms of educational impact and outcomes. Funders and decision-makers are more likely to respond when they see how the support directly affects the student's ability to access, participate in, or benefit from their education.

→ **For example:**

✗ "My child needs a speech device."

> ✓ "This device will allow my child to meet their IEP communication goals and participate in classroom discussions."

Also consider contacting your Parent Training and Information Center (PTI). PTIs can help with writing applications, identifying funding options, and appealing denials.

Step 3: Follow Up & Appeal if Necessary

If an application is denied:

- **Request a written explanation**—Knowing why an application was denied will help you improve future submissions.

- **Submit additional documentation**—Teacher letters, updated evaluations, and data from progress reports can strengthen your case.

- **Seek support from advocacy groups**—Many disability rights organizations offer free or low-cost help with navigating funding disputes.

✱ **Pro Parent Tip:** A denial is not the end. Many programs accept reapplications, especially when new documentation is provided or deadlines reset annually.

C. Understanding The Budgeting Process

Even when funding is secured, how it is spent matters. Parents and educators must ensure funding is used effectively and not misallocated.

How Schools Allocate Special Education Funds

- **Staffing** – The most sizable portion of special education budgets goes to teachers, therapists, and paraprofessionals.

- **Assistive Technology** – Includes devices such as communication boards, tablets, and adaptive software.

- **Transportation Costs** – Many students need specialized transportation, including wheelchair-accessible buses.

- **Professional Development** – Training teachers on inclusion, assistive technology, and behavior interventions.

⚡ Common Budgeting Challenges in Special Education

- **Underfunding** – IDEA only covers a fraction of the actual special education costs.

- **Unequal Resource Distribution** – Rural and low-income schools often struggle to provide adequate services.

- **Legal Disputes Over Funding** – Parents sometimes file due process complaints when schools fail to provide required services.

Monitoring The Budget: What Parents Can Do

- Attend School Board Meetings – Demand transparency in special education budgeting.

- Request Expenditure Reports – Public schools are required to disclose how special education funds are spent.

- Join Parent Advocacy Groups – Strength in numbers helps push for reforms and accountability.

Final Thoughts: Securing & Advocating For Special Education Funding

Funding for special education is notoriously under-resourced—but that does not give schools the right to deny services. When families understand where funding comes from, how it should be used, and how to ask the right questions, they can help ensure the system works for their child—and advocate for accountability when it does not.

You may not be able to rewrite federal budgets, but you can change the conversation in your district. Follow the money. Demand accountability. Make sure every dollar works for your child—and for every child who needs it.

Key Takeaways:

✓ **Funding cannot be used as an excuse**. If a service is listed in the IEP, the school must provide it—regardless of cost or convenience.

✓ **Federal, state, and private grants help fill gaps**—but families often have to go looking for them. Knowing what is available can make a real difference.

✓ **Strong documentation matters**. Whether applying for grants, Medicaid waivers, or challenging a service denial, maintaining clear records and submitting written requests strengthens your case.

✓ **Follow the money**. Ask how your school's special education budget is spent— and whether those dollars reach students, not just administrators.

✓ **Transparency leads to accountability**. Budget oversight is not just for auditors. Parents have a right to ask how special education dollars are being used—and to expect answers.

➡ **Pro Parent Move:** If you are told a service is "not available" or "not in the budget," ask for written justification and review how your district allocates special education funds. The law is clear: students' needs come first.

When it comes to special education, money is not just math—it is mission.

CHAPTER 3:
Identifying Your Child's Needs

The moment you realize your child is struggling is the moment everything changes. You are no longer just a parent—you become an advocate. Trusting your instincts, asking the right questions, and understanding how to act are the first steps toward securing the support your child deserves.

Recognizing that something is wrong is one thing; knowing what to do about it is another. Whether your child struggles with reading, following directions, managing emotions, or making friends, parents are often the first to notice that something is not quite right. Acting on those concerns is critical, and early action can make all the difference.

This chapter will break down how to recognize the signs that your child may need support, explain how disabilities are categorized under special education law, and guide you through the evaluation process. By the end of this chapter, you will feel more confident, informed, and prepared to take the next steps toward advocating for your child's educational needs.

A. Signs Your Child May Need Support

Every child struggles at some point—whether it is a bad test grade, difficulty making friends, or trouble sitting still. But when challenges are persistent, severe, and impact daily life, they may indicate a deeper issue.

Common Signs That Your Child May Need Support

Some children breeze through school, while others face daily struggles that do not seem to improve with time or effort. If your child consistently experiences any of the following, it may be time to take a closer look:

◇ **Academic Struggles** – Your child has difficulty keeping up with reading, writing, or math, even when they try their best. Despite repeated instruction, tutoring, or extra help, they continue to fall behind.

◇ **Behavioral Challenges** – Frequent outbursts, emotional meltdowns, or trouble following rules in the classroom or at home. They may act out impulsively, struggle with self-control, or get into frequent conflicts.

◇ **Social Difficulties** – They have trouble making or keeping friends, avoid group activities, misinterpret social cues, or experience anxiety in social situations.

◇ **Lack Of Focus Or Organization** – Losing assignments, forgetting instructions, failing to complete tasks, or getting distracted easily. They may struggle to start and finish assignments independently.

◇ **Sensory Sensitivities** – Overreaction to lights, sounds, textures, or crowds that make learning environments overwhelming. They may be extremely bothered by loud noises, uncomfortable with certain fabrics, or distracted by background sounds that others ignore.

While all children experience temporary struggles, a consistent pattern of difficulties may signal the need for further evaluation—whether academic, behavioral, or emotional.

✶ Pro Parent Tip: Schools Must Identify Students—Even Without A Parent Request: Under the federal Child Find mandate, schools are legally required to identify, locate, and evaluate all children who may have disabilities—whether or not parents formally request it. If school staff suspect that a disability may be affecting a student's learning, they must act. Parents should not have to "prove" the need for an evaluation. If you sense hesitation from the school, remind them of their Child Find obligations under IDEA.

When Observation Should Lead To Action

If several of the signs above apply to your child—and your concerns are ongoing—it may be time to take the next step. Even if you are not sure whether special education is the answer, there are clear moments when observation is not enough and action is required.

Here are key moments that should prompt you to act:

- The school acknowledges problems but has not taken meaningful steps.
- You are being told your child will "grow out of it," but no support has been offered.
- Your child is being disciplined frequently without improvement.
- You feel like your concerns are dismissed, delayed, or minimized.
- Your gut tells you something is not right—and you have seen these struggles for more than a few months.

✱ Pro Parent Tip: You do not need a formal diagnosis to request help. You need documented concerns—and the courage to ask questions. If several of these situations feel familiar, it is time to move forward.

When To Request An Evaluation

If you suspect that your child's challenges go beyond typical struggles, it may be time to request an evaluation. Schools are legally required to evaluate students if a suspected disability is affecting their ability to learn. This process can (and should) be initiated by parents when concerns persist despite interventions, accommodations, or extra help from teachers.

If your child's struggles significantly impact their academic progress, social interactions, or emotional well-being, requesting an evaluation is the first step toward identifying their needs and securing appropriate support.

10 Signs It May Be Time To Request An Evaluation

If you are seeing any of the following, it may be time to formally request a special education evaluation for your child:

1. Your child is significantly below grade level in reading, writing, or math.
2. Teachers report consistent inattention, impulsiveness, or hyperactivity that disrupts learning.
3. Your child has difficulty following instructions or remembering multistep directions.
4. They struggle to make or keep friends or show signs of social withdrawal.
5. Your child has been suspended or disciplined repeatedly without improvement in behavior.
6. There are frequent meltdowns, shutdowns, or emotional outbursts at school.
7. They seem overwhelmed by noise, light, crowds, or physical touch.
8. You suspect your child has a disability, even if no formal diagnosis exists.
9. School staff mention your child's struggles, but have not offered solutions.
10. You feel, in your gut, that something is not right—and your concerns are not being heard.

✱ **Pro Parent Tip:** You do not need to wait for the school to suggest testing. You have the legal right to request an evaluation at any time.

Key Steps For Parents

▶ **Document your concerns**—Keep track of struggles, behavioral patterns, and examples of schoolwork. If you hear comments from teachers about academic or social challenges, write them down.

▶ **Request a formal evaluation in writing**—Schools must respond to evaluation requests within legally mandated timelines. Submit your request via email or certified letter to ensure a paper trail.

▶ **Collaborate with educators**—Work with teachers, school counselors, and psychologists to ensure a thorough assessment. But remember—you do not need teacher approval to request an evaluation.

✦ **Early intervention is key!** The sooner a child receives support, the better the long-term outcomes in school and beyond.

Common Roadblocks To Getting An Evaluation (And How To Overcome Them)

If your child is struggling in school and you suspect they need special education services, the first step is to request an evaluation. But some schools delay, discourage, or deny evaluations—often with misleading excuses. When schools hesitate to evaluate or provide services, it is often due to misunderstandings or systemic barriers—not bad intentions. Here is how to decode common pushbacks and respond with confidence.

What the School Says	What They Might Mean	Your Response
"Your child is too smart for special education."	They may not fully understand that special education services are based on educational impact, not IQ.	"Intelligence is not the issue—my child's disability affects their ability to learn. Under IDEA, eligibility is based

What the School Says	What They Might Mean	Your Response
		on educational impact, not IQ."
"Let's wait and see if they catch up."	They may believe the challenges are temporary or hope that additional time will resolve them naturally.	"Early intervention is critical. IDEA requires schools to evaluate promptly when a disability is suspected."
"We already provide informal supports—no need for an IEP."	They may feel that current accommodations are sufficient and want to avoid the legal structure of an IEP.	"Accommodations are not the same as specialized instruction. I am formally requesting a full evaluation under IDEA."
"We do not see enough evidence that an evaluation is necessary."	They may not have gathered enough data or are interpreting existing data differently than you.	"I'd like to see the data used to make that decision. If my child is struggling, that is evidence that an evaluation is needed."
"Your child is just lazy/disruptive/needs to try harder."	They may be viewing behavior as a choice rather than a possible symptom of an underlying need.	"Let's focus on the why behind the behavior. I'd like a Functional Behavioral Assessment (FBA) to determine if this is disability related."

◉ *Top 5 School Excuses—and How to Respond*

✶ Pro Parent Tip: Always ask for denials in writing. Schools must legally provide Prior Written Notice (PWN) explaining their decision. If they refuse, that is a red flag.

How To Request An Evaluation

◉ **When in doubt, put it in writing!** Schools must legally evaluate a child if a disability is suspected, but only if parents formally request it.

✎ *Sample Email/Letter*

> *Subject: Request for Special Education Evaluation*
>
> *Dear [**Special Education Coordinator**],*
>
> *I am formally requesting a comprehensive special education evaluation for my child, [**Child's Name**], who is in [**Grade**] at [**School Name**]. I suspect that my child may have a disability that is impacting their ability to learn, specifically in the areas of [reading, writing, math, attention, social skills, etc.].*
>
> *Under the Individuals with Disabilities Education Act (IDEA), I understand that my child has the right to a free, appropriate public education (FAPE) and an evaluation to determine if they qualify for special education services. I am requesting that this evaluation include assessments in the following areas:*
>
> - *Cognitive [**this measures intellectual abilities and problem-solving skills**]*
>
> - *Achievement [**this measures academic achievement – reading, writing, and math skills—and compares them to grade-level expectations**]*

- *[List additional specific concerns: reading comprehension, literacy, fine motor skills, executive functioning, speech and language, attention, sensory processing, etc.]*

I request that the school provide me with the necessary consent forms and a timeline for the evaluation process. I also request Prior Written Notice (PWN) if the school refuses to evaluate my child, as required under IDEA.

Please confirm receipt of this request as soon as possible. I look forward to working with the school to support my child's learning needs.

Sincerely,
[Your Name]
[Your Contact Information]

⚡ **Important:** Once you sign the consent forms, the school has 60 days (or less if your state's timeline is shorter) to complete the evaluation and hold an IEP meeting to discuss it.

B. Differences Between Disabilities

No two disabilities look the same. Some are obvious, while others are more subtle and may go unnoticed for years. Understanding how disabilities are categorized under the Individuals with Disabilities Education Act (IDEA) can help parents advocate for the right services and ensure their child's needs are fully addressed.

How Disability Categories Impact Special Education Eligibility

A diagnosis alone does not automatically qualify a child for special education. Under the IDEA, a student must meet two criteria:

1. The child has one or more of the 13 disability categories recognized under IDEA,

AND

2. The disability significantly affects their ability to learn, requiring specialized instruction.

▶ **Why This Matters:** A child may have a disability but still not qualify for an IEP if the school determines that they can succeed with general education accommodations (like a 504 Plan) rather than specialized instruction. If the school denies services, parents should request data supporting that decision and advocate for further evaluation if needed.

13 Disability Categories At A Glance

Under IDEA, students qualify for special education if they have one of the 13 disabilities below, which affects their ability to learn, and they require specialized instruction. But what does that actually mean? Here is a breakdown of the 13 disability categories, with real-world examples:

Disability Category	What It Means	Examples
Autism (ASD)	A developmental disability affecting communication and social interaction.	A child who struggles with social cues, needs structured routines, or has sensory sensitivities.
Deaf-Blindness	A combination of hearing and vision loss that severely impacts communication and mobility.	A student who uses a combination of sign language, braille, and assistive technology to learn.

Disability Category	What It Means	Examples
Deafness	A hearing impairment so severe that it affects language development.	A child who uses American Sign Language (ASL) or cochlear implants to access education.
Emotional Disturbance (ED)	Severe emotional or behavioral challenges that affect learning.	A student with extreme anxiety, depression, or mood disorders that interfere with school participation.
Hearing Impairment	A hearing loss that affects educational performance but is not classified as deafness.	A child who can hear with hearing aids but struggles in noisy classrooms.
Intellectual Disability (ID)	Below-average cognitive ability that impacts learning and daily functioning.	A student with Down syndrome or another intellectual disability needing modified instruction.
Multiple Disabilities	A combination of two or more disabilities that require intensive support.	A student with cerebral palsy and vision impairment who needs physical therapy and braille instruction.

Disability Category	What It Means	Examples
Orthopedic Impairment	Physical disabilities affect movement, coordination, or mobility.	A student with spina bifida who uses a wheelchair and needs accommodations for accessibility.
Other Health Impairment (OHI)	Chronic or acute health conditions that limit strength, energy, or alertness.	A child with ADHD, epilepsy, or chronic illness needs classroom modifications.
Specific Learning Disability (SLD)	A neurological disorder that affects reading, writing, or math skills.	A student with dyslexia, dysgraphia, or dyscalculia who struggles with academic tasks.
Speech or Language Impairment	Difficulties with articulation, fluency, or expressive/receptive language.	A child with a stutter, delayed speech, or difficulty understanding instructions.
Traumatic Brain Injury (TBI)	Brain injury affects cognitive, behavioral, or physical abilities.	A student recovering from a concussion who has memory and attention difficulties.
Visual Impairment (Including Blindness)	Partial or complete vision loss that affects learning.	A student who uses large-print materials, braille, or screen readers.

13 Disability Categories under the IDEA

✦ **Special Note for Younger Children (Ages 3–9):** In addition to the 13 disability categories, IDEA allows schools to use the eligibility label "Developmental Delay" for young children. This category covers significant delays in areas like communication, motor skills, learning, or social-emotional development—without requiring a specific medical diagnosis. If your child is between the ages of three and nine and struggling, ask whether "Developmental Delay" could open the door to early support.

Understanding Overlapping Disabilities

Many children have co-occurring disabilities, meaning they qualify under more than one category. Some examples include:

- A child with ADHD (OHI) may also struggle with dyslexia (SLD).

- A student with autism (ASD) may need speech therapy (SLI) for communication challenges.

- A child with cerebral palsy (Orthopedic Impairment) may also have learning challenges (SLD).

✱ **Pro Parent Tip:** In most states, schools can only designate one primary disability category, but this does not mean other disabilities should be ignored. The primary designation reflects the most significant impact at that time, but the IEP must address all disabilities affecting your child's education. Parents should advocate to ensure all their child's needs are considered and supported.

Why Disability Categories Matter

- A diagnosis alone does not guarantee special education services; eligibility depends on whether the disability affects learning and requires specialized instruction.

- Schools often focus on one "primary disability," but all areas of need must be addressed.

- If your child is denied services, request documentation that shows how they determined the disability does not affect their educational performance.

➡ **Pro Parent Move:** Do not let disability categories limit your child's support. Focus on documenting needs and pushing for services based on real challenges, not just labels.

C. Effective Evaluations

Once a referral is made, the evaluation process begins. The goal is to understand the child's strengths, challenges, and learning needs through a comprehensive assessment.

Understanding The Evaluation Process

A formal special education evaluation is more than just a test—it is a multi-step process that gathers data from multiple sources to determine a child's needs.

Step 1: Parent or School Referral—A parent, teacher, or school team can request an evaluation. Parents should always submit requests in writing to ensure legal timelines begin.

Step 2: Review of Existing Data—The school will hold an IEP meeting to review grades, classroom observations, and previous interventions (if applicable) to determine which areas need to be assessed.

Step 3: Formal Assessments—You must sign consent for all the assessments to be done. Then the specialists conduct standardized tests, observations, and interviews to evaluate multiple areas of development. They will write reports that should include all the results and recommendations.

Step 4: IEP Meeting to Review Results—Within 60 days of signing consent for the evaluations, the school must complete the evaluations and corresponding reports, and hold an IEP meeting to go over the data and determine eligibility for services. In some states it is only 45 day so check you state to know your timelines.

➡ **Pro Parent Move:** *Insist on a Comprehensive Evaluation.* Under IDEA, schools must assess all areas related to a suspected disability—not just academics. This includes cognitive functioning, communication, social-emotional development, behavior, physical skills, and adaptive behavior. If your child struggles in multiple areas, ensure the evaluation is broad enough to capture the full picture. You have the right to request testing in any area where you see concerns.

Common Categories Of Evaluations

A comprehensive evaluation should assess all suspected areas of need, not just academic struggles. If a school only tests for one issue when broader concerns exist, parents should push for additional assessments.

- **Cognitive Testing** – Measures intellectual abilities and problem-solving skills.

- **Academic Achievement Testing** – Identifies reading, writing, and math strengths and weaknesses.

- **Speech & Language Evaluations** – Assesses communication abilities, comprehension, and social language skills.

- **Behavioral & Social-Emotional Assessments** – Evaluates attention, emotional regulation, and peer interactions.

- **Occupational & Physical Therapy Assessments** – Determines motor skill and sensory needs.

➥ **Pro Parent Move:** If the school refuses to evaluate a specific area of concern, request Prior Written Notice (PWN) in writing explaining their decision.

For a more thorough description of evaluations and what they cover, see ***APPENDIX 1: Understanding What Evaluations Cover.***

What About RTI? A Pre-Referral Process, Not A Roadblock

Before moving forward with evaluations, many schools suggest Response to Intervention (RTI)—a process that can either support or stall, depending on how it is used. So, what does it actually involve?

RTI is a general education support system for any students who are struggling (and do not have an IEP). It provides targeted interventions (like small-group instruction, skill-building, or behavioral supports) and tracks how well those interventions work over time. The goal is to address academic or behavioral concerns early, without immediately labeling a student as needing special education.

At its best, RTI is a proactive, data-driven framework that helps schools identify which students just need a boost—and which may need formal evaluation for special education. At its worst, it becomes a bureaucratic delay, where schools ask parents to "wait and see" while the child continues to struggle.

➤ **Bottom line:** RTI is not a substitute for special education. It can be useful, but it should never be used to delay an evaluation if there is reason to suspect a disability. If you are told RTI must happen before your child can be evaluated, that is just plain wrong—and you have the right to request an evaluation at any time.

Let's break it down further.

What RTI Is Supposed To Do

RTI is an educational framework that uses a multi-tiered system of support to identify students who need help and give them interventions early—before special education is considered.

Think of it like triage in an academic emergency room:

◇ **Tier 1:** Everyone receives high-quality, differentiated instruction.

◇ **Tier 2:** Students who are not making progress in Tier 1 receive small-group support targeted to specific skills.

◇ **Tier 3:** If a student still struggles, they receive more intensive, individualized help—often involving specialists or one-on-one support.

Throughout this process, the school should collect data, monitor progress, and tweak supports as needed. This is called data-driven decision-making, and in theory, it helps schools quickly identify what works and what does not.

What RTI Is Not Allowed To Do

RTI is not a substitute for an evaluation. It is not a holding pattern. And it definitely does not put your legal rights under IDEA on pause.

➥ **Pro Parent Move:** If the school says, "Let's wait and see how they do in RTI," say, "Great—please go ahead with RTI. But I am formally requesting a special education evaluation today." Put that request in writing to start the legal timeline.

By law, the RTI process cannot be used to delay or deny an evaluation. If you suspect your child has a disability and needs services, you have the right to request an evaluation at any time, regardless of where they are in the RTI process.

The Fine Print: What You Should Watch For

Here is what can go wrong:

- **Vague timelines:** "Let's give it a few more weeks" becomes months of lost progress.
- **No parent involvement:** RTI decisions are often made without clear communication to families.
- **Missing documentation:** Interventions are happening (or not), but no one is tracking progress in a way that you can see or verify. No path forward: The child is not improving, but the school keeps trying new strategies instead of referring them for evaluation.

✷ Pro Parent Tip: Ask for documentation of RTI interventions—what is being done, how often, and what data are being collected. If they cannot provide that, it is a red flag.

Can RTI Lead To Special Education?

Yes—but it is not automatic.

If a student does not respond to Tier 3 interventions and there is evidence that their difficulties extend beyond what general education can address, the school should initiate a referral for special education. But again, you do not have to wait for them to reach that conclusion.

If your instinct says something deeper is going on—trust it.

➤ Bottom Line

RTI can be helpful. It can catch children early. It can provide targeted support. But it is not a gatekeeper. It is not a legal barrier. And it should never, ever be used to keep you from getting the evaluation your child needs.

✓ RTI = early support, not a replacement for special education.

✓ You can request an evaluation any time—regardless of what tier your child is in.

✓ Document everything. Ask questions. And if needed, push back—politely, persistently, and in writing.

What Happens After The Evaluation?

Once assessments are completed, the school team will:

- Hold an IEP meeting to review the data and determine if your child is eligible for special education services.

- Develop an Individualized Education Program (IEP) if your child qualifies.

- Discuss accommodations and supports tailored to your child's needs.

* Pro Parent Tip: If you disagree with the school's findings, you have the right to request an Independent Educational Evaluation (IEE) at the school's expense (See next section).

What If You Disagree With The School's Evaluation?

Technically, an Independent Educational Evaluation (IEE) is any private evaluation conducted by a qualified professional who is not employed by the school district. Parents always have the option to obtain their own IEE at their own expense.

However, most people refer to an IEE as the independent evaluation that the school district is expected to pay for. Sounds too good to be true? That is because it often is. Let's break down how the IEE process actually works.

✦ **Important:** You are only entitled to a publicly funded IEE if you disagree with the school's evaluation—so be sure to use that exact language in your request.

When Should You Request An IEE?

➡ **The school's evaluation was too limited** – The school only tested for one suspected issue (e.g., reading difficulties) but did not assess for other concerns (e.g., ADHD, executive functioning, or emotional needs).

➡ **The evaluation results do not match what you see at home** – If the school determines your child does not qualify for services, but they still struggle significantly, an outside evaluation may provide a more accurate picture.

➡ **The testing was rushed or incomplete** – Some evaluations lack depth or fail to assess all areas of concern.

➡ **You suspect bias or procedural errors** – If the school minimized your child's struggles or failed to follow IDEA's evaluation requirements, an IEE can provide a more objective perspective.

➡ **Pro Parent Move:** If you feel the evaluation was inadequate, ask for a detailed explanation of the school's findings. If their conclusions do not align with your child's daily struggles, it may be time to request an IEE. You are not required to explain why you disagree, but having clear reasons can strengthen your argument. If you choose to share, focus on specific concerns—such as missing assessments, inaccurate conclusions, or data that does not reflect your child's challenges.

How The IEE Request Works

➡ **Make the Request in Writing or at an IEP Meeting** – Submit a formal written request stating that you disagree with the school's evaluation and are requesting an IEE at the school's expense. If you request the IEE at an IEP meeting, the school does not need to respond immediately, but must respond within a reasonable timeframe under the law.

→ **The School Must Respond Without Undue Delay** – Some states have defined specific timelines for what constitutes "undue delay," so it is important to check your state's statutes or consult a local attorney or advocate. Once your request is received, the school must either:

➤ Approve the IEE request and provide their criteria for IEEs (which cannot be overly restrictive) along with a list of independent evaluators (which is not an exclusive list),

OR

➤ Deny the request and file for due process to prove that their evaluation was appropriate.

If your school grants the IEE,

1. **You Choose the Evaluator** – The district may provide a list of approved providers, but you are not required to choose from their list. You can select any qualified professional as long as they meet reasonable district criteria. The district must provide its criteria for IEE, and they may not be unreasonably restrictive.

2. **The IEE is Conducted** – The independent evaluator assesses your child and provides a detailed report with recommendations.

3. **The District Holds an IEP Meeting to Review and "Consider" the Results** – The school must hold an IEP meeting to review and "consider" the results of the IEE. While they are not required to accept every recommendation, they must discuss them and provide reasons for any decisions made.

What Happens if the District Says No to the IEE?

✦ **Important:** If the school denies your request, they must initiate a due process hearing to defend their original evaluation. If they fail to file for due process, they are legally required to approve the IEE.

Check with a local special education attorney or advocate for guidance. If several weeks pass with no response and no due process hearing is filed, a State Complaint could compel the district to provide the IEE.

As you will learn in later chapters, you can attend a resolution session or mediation with your district. Often, these IEE disputes are resolved by agreeing on a mutually acceptable evaluator.

✦ **But beware**—make sure the evaluator is known for conducting thorough assessments and providing detailed, actionable recommendations. Your local special education attorneys or advocates can likely provide you with trusted names.

✱ **Pro Parent Tip:** If your district files for due process (or threatens to) and efforts to resolve the issue are not successful, you can withdraw your request for an IEE. This renders the due process hearing moot, and the hearing officer will dismiss the matter. However, this may be a good time to consult with a special education attorney or advocate, as you could be reaching a crossroads with your school.

Using An IEE In The IEP Process

Once the IEE report is completed, parents can:

- Request an IEP meeting to review the results and discuss necessary changes.

- Use the findings to advocate for additional services, accommodations, or different eligibility criteria.

- Challenge the school's initial evaluation with data from an independent expert.

➥ **Pro Parent Move:** Schools must consider the results of an IEE, but they are not required to follow every recommendation. Come to the IEP meeting prepared to explain why the recommendations are necessary and how they will support your child's learning.

Why IEEs Matter

- An IEE is a parent's legal right if they disagree with a school evaluation.

- The school must either approve the request or file for due process.

- Independent evaluations can provide deeper insights into a child's needs.

- Parents should use IEE findings to strengthen their advocacy in IEP meetings.

◉ **When in Doubt:** If something feels off about your child's school evaluation, trust your gut! A second opinion can be the key to unlocking the right supports for your child.

Final Thoughts: The Power Of Effective Assessments

The evaluation process is more than just a set of tests—it is the foundation for understanding how a child learns, where they struggle, and what supports will help them succeed. A thorough, well-conducted assessment ensures that services and accommodations are not just guesses—they are tailored to the child's actual needs.

However, not all evaluations are created equal. If assessments miss key areas, feel rushed, or do not align with what you see at home, parents must step in and ask the right questions. A strong evaluation leads to strong support—and that support can change everything.

Key Takeaways:

✓ **Early intervention leads to better outcomes.** The sooner challenges are identified, the sooner children can receive the support they need. Delays in evaluation can lead to missed opportunities for growth.

✓ **Disabilities vary—there is no one-size-fits-all.** Every child's learning profile is unique. A diagnosis is not a label that limits potential—it is a tool that helps determine the right path forward.

✓ **Comprehensive assessments are essential.** Rushed or incomplete evaluations can lead to incorrect placements, inadequate supports, or misdiagnoses. If the school's findings do not align with what you see at home, request more information, push for additional assessments, or seek an Independent Educational Evaluation (IEE).

◉ When In Doubt

☑ **Trust your instincts.** No one knows your child better than you. If something feels off, do not ignore it.

☑ **Ask questions.** Evaluations can be overwhelming, but you have the right to ask for explanations, clarity, and additional assessments if needed.

☑ **Advocate with confidence.** If you believe your child's needs are not being fully addressed, push for additional support, seek outside opinions, and ensure their educational plan is built for success.

★ *The goal is not just to assess—it is to empower.* A strong evaluation opens doors to the right services, accommodations, and interventions. When parents stay informed and engaged, they ensure their child's education is built on real needs, not assumptions.

CHAPTER 4:
The IEP Process

Navigating the Individualized Education Program (IEP) process can feel like preparing for a marathon you did not sign up for—but this document is the backbone of your child's special education journey. It determines what support they receive, how their progress is measured, and, ultimately, whether they get the education they deserve.

This chapter will break down the IEP process step by step, explain common challenges, and equip you with advocacy strategies so you can confidently navigate meetings, push for the right services, and hold the school accountable.

A. Understanding The IEP

The IEP is not just paperwork—it is a legally binding document that serves as a roadmap for your child's education. If special education were a contract, these would be the terms and conditions the school must follow.

Every student who qualifies for special education services under the Individuals with Disabilities Education Act (IDEA) is entitled to an IEP. The goal? To provide individualized instruction, accommodations, and support so the student can access and benefit from their education—just like their peers.

An IEP is not just a list of services—it is a comprehensive plan designed to meet your child's unique needs. Here is what is included:

Present Levels Of Academic Achievement And Functional Performance (PLAAFP)

The PLAAFP section is the foundation of your child's IEP. It tells the story of where your child is right now—academically, socially, emotionally, and functionally. It is not fluff. It is not filler. It is the evidence-based snapshot that drives every goal, service, and placement decision that follows.

A strong PLAAFP should be:

- **Detailed** – No vague language like "making progress" or "doing well." It should describe what your child can and cannot do with real-life context.

- **Data-Driven** – This means current evaluations, classroom data, informal assessments, observations, and input from parents and providers.

- **Individualized** – It must reflect your child—not a generic description or cut-and-paste from another student's plan.

- **Balanced** – It should highlight both strengths and challenges. What motivates your child? What supports are working? Where are the barriers?

A vague PLAAFP leads to vague goals. A strong PLAAFP keeps the team focused and accountable.

✱ **Pro Parent Tip:** If the PLAAFP feels generic, outdated, or light on data—ask questions. Request the specific assessments or observations on which it is based. You have the right to ensure your child's IEP starts from a clear and accurate picture.

Measurable Annual Goals & Objectives

The goals section of the IEP is not optional. It is the engine that drives progress—and it must be built with precision. These goals define what your child is working toward over the year. The short-term objectives are the roadmap for getting there.

There is no filler language. This is not educational fluff. The goals and objectives are the legal and instructional contract that the school agrees to follow. If they are weak, vague, or copied and pasted from last year's plan, the IEP will stall out—because there is nothing specific to measure or deliver on.

Goals & Objectives Must Be SMART

Every annual goal and short-term objective in your child's IEP should follow the SMART framework:

- **Specific** – It should state exactly what your child will work on.

- **Measurable** – You should understand exactly how success will be tracked and measured.

- **Achievable** – Ensure the objective is both ambitious and realistic based on current skills.

- **Relevant** – The goal should directly address your child's unique educational needs and support meaningful progress—not just reflect general curriculum benchmarks.

- **Time-bound** – There must be a defined deadline or clear schedule for meeting the goal, ensuring accountability, and allowing you to measure growth effectively.

If you see vague language like "Student will improve reading comprehension" or "Student will be more independent," that is a red flag. There is no skill defined. No metric. No deadline. No way to tell if your child is making progress— or if the school is doing its job.

How Progress Will Be Measured

A goal is only as strong as its progress monitoring. The law requires schools to track and report on your child's IEP goals. That does not mean vague report card comments like "making progress" or "working toward goal." Every IEP should specify:

- **How** will progress be measured—test data? classroom observations? performance on assignments?

- **How often** will progress be reviewed—monthly? quarterly?

- **Who** will collect and report the data—teacher? therapist? aide?

You are not being difficult by asking these questions. You are doing your job as a parent and team member.

✽ **Pro Parent Tip:** If there is no baseline data—no mention of where your child is starting from—ask the team to add it. You cannot measure growth without knowing where the journey began. A goal that says "will increase reading fluency by 30 words per minute" means nothing if the IEP does not tell you their current reading rate.

The following examples are drawn from real IEPs I have encountered (with identifying details removed), to show the difference between vague language and truly meaningful goals.

Sample Goals And Objectives

Some IEP goals and objectives sound great on paper but fall apart under real scrutiny. That is why SMART goals are not just a recommendation; they are non-negotiable. A strong goal does more than look official. It gives your child a clear target, gives the team a plan to follow, and gives you a tool to hold everyone accountable. Below are real-world examples that show what weak goals look like—and how to transform them into something meaningful.

✗ **Weak Goal:** "[Student] will improve math skills."

Why it is weak: There is no specific skill, no measurable outcome, no way to track progress, and no time limit. "Improve" could mean anything—and usually does.

> ✓ **SMART Goal:** "By June 2025, [Student] will solve two-step word problems involving addition, subtraction, multiplication, and division with 80% accuracy across three consecutive trials."

>> ➤ **Why it works:** This goal names a specific task, covers content areas, defines success with a data point (80% accuracy), and sets a clear timeline. No ambiguity. No guessing.

✗ **Weak Objective:** "[Student] will practice problem-solving strategies with teacher support."

Why it is weak: "Practice" is vague. What strategies? What does success look like? And how much teacher support are we talking about—constant prompting or occasional help?

> ✓ **SMART Objective:** "By the end of Q2, [Student] will use visual aids (e.g., number lines, bar models) to break down two-step word problems in 4 out of 5 trials."

>> ➤ **Why it works:** This objective shows how the student will work on the skill, what tools will be used, how often it must occur, and when it should happen.

➡ **Pro Parent Move:** If goals or objectives sound generic, outdated, or suspiciously similar to last year's IEP, ask the team:

- What exact skill will my child be working on?
- How will progress be measured?

- What happens if progress stalls?

Push for clarity. Push for specificity. These are not just goals on paper—they are the blueprint for your child's growth. If you cannot picture what your child will do to meet the goal, it is not specific enough. If the school cannot describe how they will measure it, it is not measurable. Keep asking until the answers are clear.

✗ "85% Safe" Is Not Safe. One of my all-time favorite terrible objectives read: "Student will independently pause and look both ways before crossing the street 85% of the time."

Let me translate: "We hope they don't get hit by a car the other 15% of the time."

- When writing goals for safety, the bar is not "almost good enough." It is "safe enough that a lapse does not put the student at risk."

  ✓ That means embedding supports, prompts, and real-world practice until the skill is consistently reliable—not just statistically average.

▶ *Questions To Ask At The IEP Meeting*

Use these questions to assess whether the team has done their homework—or just plugged in standard language:

- What skill is this goal addressing?
- How did you decide on this goal—what data did you use?
- What is my child's current performance in this area?
- How will progress be tracked and reported?
- What specific services or instruction will be used to help my child meet this goal?
- What is the backup plan if the goal is not met mid-year?

These questions do not just open conversation—they close loopholes. They make it harder for anyone on the team to gloss over vague language or rely on assumptions.

If you walk away from the IEP meeting and you are still wondering what your child is supposed to be working on—or how anyone will know if they are making progress—the goals are not done yet. Keep going. You have the right to ask for revisions until they reflect your child's real needs, real skills, and real future.

Accommodations And Modifications

Accommodations and modifications are key tools the IEP team uses to support a student's access to learning. They may sound similar, but they serve very different purposes—and the distinction matters.

Accommodations do not change what your child is expected to learn. They change how your child learns or demonstrates knowledge. These supports help students access the general education curriculum alongside their peers.

> → **Examples include** extra time on tests, preferential seating, speech-to-text technology, frequent breaks, or reduced distractions.

Modifications change the learning expectations. These adjustments are made when a student needs the material to be adapted so they can participate. Modifications may reduce the level of difficulty or change what is being taught.

> → **Examples include** shortened assignments, alternative reading materials, simplified grading standards, or functional goals replacing academic ones.

These supports are usually written into the IEP under Supplementary Aids and Services, and their impact on curriculum, instruction, and assessment should be discussed thoroughly with the team.

✪ *Want more? Accommodations and modifications are covered in detail in* <u>**Chapter 7:**</u> <u>**Accommodations, Modifications, & Related Services**</u>, *including how to request them, how they show up in real IEPs, and what to watch out for.*

Related Services

Related services are not bonus features—they are often essential to a student's ability to access and benefit from their education. These services support the child's progress toward IEP goals and help meet unique needs that go beyond academics.

Under IDEA, related services may include:

- Speech-language therapy
- Occupational therapy
- Physical therapy
- Behavioral supports or counseling
- Social skills training
- Transportation (when needed to access the program)

The IEP team determines which related services are needed by reviewing evaluation data and discussing how your child's challenges impact learning and participation. If a child needs these services to benefit from special education, the district is required by law to provide them.

✪ *Looking for more information? Related services are covered in depth in* <u>**Chapter 7:**</u> <u>**Accommodations, Modifications, & Related Services**</u>—*what they are, how to request them, and what to do if they are not being delivered appropriately.*

B. Steps to Develop An IEP

The IEP process is a team effort involving parents, educators, and specialists. Here is how it unfolds:

Step 1: Referral And Evaluation

Who can request an evaluation?

Parents, teachers, or medical professionals. You do not need teacher permission to request an evaluation.

What happens next?

The school must obtain written parental consent before administering the test. A comprehensive evaluation follows, covering cognitive testing, academic achievement, and any other areas of concern, such as speech and language skills, sensory issues, and behavioral observations.

✱ **Pro Parent Tip:** If the school drags its feet, send a formal evaluation request in writing—this starts the legal timeline for their response.

Step 2: Eligibility Determination

After testing, the IEP team (which includes you!) reviews the evaluation results to determine whether your child qualifies for services.

⭐ Does My Child Qualify For An IEP?

Step 1: Does your child have a diagnosed or suspected disability?

- **Yes** → Go to Step 2

- **No** → Your child may not qualify under IDEA. Consider a 504 Plan instead.

Step 2: Does the disability significantly impact their education (remember, more than just academics) or ability to learn in a general education setting?

- **Yes** → Go to Step 3

- **No** → A 504 Plan may be a better fit.

Step 3: Does your child need specialized instruction (not just accommodations) to make progress?

- **Yes** → Your child qualifies for an IEP under IDEA.

- **No** → A 504 Plan may be a better fit.

Common Roadblock: Some schools say, "Your child has a disability, but they are not struggling enough *academically* to need an IEP," or my favorite, "Their grades are too high for special education." That is not how IDEA works! First, under IDEA, education is defined as more than academics. It includes social, emotional, and behavioral needs. Furthermore, multiple data sources should be used to identify needs; grades alone do not determine eligibility. If your child needs specialized instruction, they qualify. Period.

✱ Pro Parent Tip: If you disagree with the school's evaluation or feel it does not fully capture your child's needs, you can request an Independent Educational Evaluation (IEE). Please refer back to ***Chapter 3: Identifying your Child's Needs*** for detailed instructions on how to request an IEE and what it entails.

Step 3: The IEP Meeting

The IEP meeting is where the evaluations are planned and reviewed, eligibility is discussed, and recommendations made. This is your chance to ask questions, request changes, and ensure the plan is truly individualized. Once finalized, the IEP is legally binding, and if services are recommended, they should start shortly thereafter.

▶ *Who is at the table?*

Before we discuss how the IEP is developed, we must discuss who is developing it. There are many different scenarios that could require different teams but as a rule, the IEP is comprised of the following:

- ➤ **Parents & Guardians** – Your voice matters most. You are the expert on your child.

    ✱ **Pro Parent Tip:** You are not just an observer in the IEP development process; you are a full participant. You have the right to request changes or even ask for more time to review and negotiate the plan. Remember, this is your child's education, and your input must be taken seriously.

- ➤ **General & Special Education Teachers** – If your child spends any time at all in the regular education environment, then there must be a general education teacher there, someone who can speak to the general education curriculums. Since you are at the IEP table, your child obviously received special education services so the special education teacher must be there as well. Both teachers can provide insight into classroom expectations, strategies, and how goals and objectives are being addressed.

- ➤ **School Psychologists & Therapists** – If there are evaluations to review, there must be someone qualified to review the evaluation and recommendations and answer questions. If there is a speech and language evaluation and no speech and language pathologist, reconvene when they can be there to discuss the evaluation. Similarly, if your child is receiving any related services, those service providers should be there to discuss their components and recommend services.

➤ **The Student (if appropriate)** – Under the Individuals with Disabilities Education Act (IDEA), schools **must invite students to their IEP meetings by age 16** if the meeting includes transition planning. Some states require this as early as age 14. Regardless of age, however, early participation builds confidence, teaches self-advocacy, and ensures the IEP reflects the student's own goals—not just the adults' priorities.

There are different perspectives on whether students should attend their IEP meetings. Some believe children should only participate when they are old enough to fully understand the process, while others argue that it is never too early to learn self-advocacy. I will not take a stance on that debate, but I will say this: If you anticipate conflict among the adults, it is best to limit your child's exposure to that tension.

➤ **For younger students or in tense meetings,** consider having the student attend for the first 10–15 minutes to share how they feel about school, what is working for them, and what they would like to see happen. After that, they can return to class while the adults handle the logistics and disagreements.

For older students, participation is key. They should be involved in setting their own goals and learning to advocate for their needs, especially as they move toward high school and transition planning.

✱ **Pro Parent Tip:** Whether your child actively participates or observes, hearing adults discuss their education (positively and productively) can help them feel empowered and involved in their learning journey.

➤ **Parent-Invited Participants** – Parents have the right to bring individuals of their choosing to IEP meetings. These participants are there to support, advocate, and help parents navigate the process. Common parent-invited participants include:

   ○ **Advocates:** Experts in special education who help ensure the child's rights are protected and the parent's voice is heard. Think of them as your educational GPS when the road gets bumpy.

   ○ **Attorneys:** Legal professionals who can advise and represent parents—especially helpful during disputes or when big decisions are on the table. **Heads up: If you are bringing an attorney, you must let the school know in advance.**

   ○ **Private Providers & Evaluators:** These are the professionals who work with your child outside of school—speech therapists, occupational therapists, psychologists, neuropsychologists, or developmental pediatricians. Their input can add valuable context, especially when the school's view feels too narrow.

   ○ **Family Members or Friends:** Trusted individuals who offer emotional support, help with notetaking, or provide insights based on their relationship with the child.

✶ **Pro Parent Tip:** If you plan to bring someone to the IEP meeting—especially a professional—give the school a heads-up. It is not just polite; it helps the meeting run more smoothly and avoids unnecessary drama when everyone is prepared.

➤ **Translators & Interpreters** – Schools are legally required to provide interpreters or translated materials for families who speak a language other than English. This ensures that parents can fully understand and participate in the IEP process.

○   **Parents** also have the right to bring a trusted interpreter of their own (such as a family member or community liaison), but this does not relieve the school of its obligation to provide accurate, accessible language support.

Clear communication is essential. If you are not understanding the documents or the conversation, speak up. Ask for a translation. Ask for clarification. The IEP process is confusing enough in English—language should not be another barrier.

⚡ *When the Room Feels Like a Firing Squad*

Sometimes schools bring 8, 10, even 12 staff members to an IEP meeting—and you are sitting there alone with a notepad and a stomachache. You are not imagining the imbalance. It happens. And no, it is not okay. But you are not powerless. What You Can Do:

- **Bring someone with you:** An advocate, friend, therapist, or spouse—someone on your side.

- **Ask for an agenda in advance:** So you are not blindsided by surprises or new team members.

- **Request introductions at the start:** "Can each person quickly share their name and role?"

- **Record the meeting,** if allowed in your state. (Always check recording laws ahead of time.)

- **Pause the meeting if needed:** Say, "This feels overwhelming. Can we slow things down or speak one at a time?"

➡ **Pro Parent Move:** If the school brings a huge team, say., "If the district feels this many staff members are necessary, I'd like to bring an advocate to help me participate fully." That changes the tone fast—and shifts the balance back toward equity.

Team Consensus

It is important that the IEP team works together and reaches a consensus about your child's plan. The goal is for all team members to agree on the proposed goals, services, and placement. If there is significant disagreement or the team is not on the same page, ask for a follow-up meeting to resolve the conflict or bring in a third-party mediator to help guide the discussion.

✱ **Pro Parent Tip:** Schools often prepare a *draft* IEP before the meeting—and that is fine. In fact, it is better than walking into a room full of unprepared staff. But that draft is exactly that: a draft. You are not there to rubber-stamp it. Read it carefully beforehand so you know what to question, clarify, or flat-out push back on. The team cannot present it as final or refuse to make changes—you are a vital part of the decision-making process, not just a signature.

Step 4: IEP Development

This is where the IEP stops being theory and becomes a real plan.

Once the team is gathered and evaluations have confirmed eligibility, the next step is designing the actual IEP—the document that determines whether your child gets what they need or just what the district is offering. Do not let the team rush past this. Goals and services are the foundation of the entire document, and everything else—placement, related services, accommodations—should be based on them. Not the other way around.

✱ **Pro Parent Tip:** You are not just an observer in the IEP development process; you are a full participant. If something feels off during the meeting or you don't agree with a proposed goal or service, you have the right to request changes or even ask for more time to review and negotiate the plan. Remember, this is your child's education, and your input must be taken seriously.

▶ *Goals and objectives*

As mentioned earlier, you should ideally receive draft goals and objectives before the IEP meeting. Sometimes parents meet with team members in advance to review and refine these drafts—an excellent strategy that ensures the goals get the focused attention they deserve.

If you have not had time to review the draft in advance, you have every right to ask for more time. Do not let the team rush you. Say clearly, "I would like time to review this section and follow up. Who should I contact if I have questions or request changes?"

And yes, it bears repeating—make sure every goal and objective is SMART. If it is not Specific, Measurable, Achievable, Relevant, and Time-bound, it is not ready.

Once your child's goals are in place, the IEP must clearly outline how the team will help your child reach them. That means instruction, supports, and services tied directly to each goal—not just a list of what the district happens to offer.

If the services in the IEP cannot reasonably deliver the goals, the plan is not just weak—it is legally out of compliance.

For older students, one of the most critical types of goals is tied to life after high school. That brings us to the next essential part of IEP development: transition planning.

▶ Transition Planning (for students 14 and older)

Under the IDEA, transition planning is required to begin by age 16. However, many states begin the process earlier—often at age 14. If your child is 14 or older, their IEP should include a transition plan that helps prepare them for life after high school.

This plan must address postsecondary goals, such as attending college, pursuing vocational training, securing employment, or achieving independent living, and outline the services, supports, and activities needed to move toward those goals.

A strong transition plan should:

- Be based on age-appropriate assessments.
- Reflect your child's interests, strengths, and preferences.
- Include clear, actionable steps for developing independence and real-world readiness.

Transition planning is not a future conversation—it is a present-tense responsibility. This section of the IEP should grow and evolve as your child matures, gaining more clarity each year.

📖 *More on this in* <u>*Chapter 8: Transition Planning*</u>*, where we dig into what transition planning really looks like, how to make sure your child's voice is central, and how to make those plans meaningful—not just mandatory.*

▶ Instructional and Related Services: The Delivery System

Every goal must be supported by services—**who will teach the skill, where, how often, and with what methods.**

Services should not be listed generically. You are entitled to specificity:

- **What** is the instructional method or support?
- **Who** will provide it? (Special ed teacher, therapist, specialist?)

- **How often**, for **how long**, and **where** will it take place?

Service minutes and delivery details are where accountability lives. Each service must list:

- **Frequency** (e.g., 3x/week)
- **Duration** (e.g., 30 minutes/session)
- **Location** (e.g., general ed, resource room, separate setting)

Vague language gives the school room to minimize delivery. Do not let that slide. If the plan says, "counseling provided weekly," ask, "Is that 10 minutes? 60? Individual or group?" Get clarity in writing.

⚡ "As needed" is unacceptable. "Weekly" without duration is a dodge. If a goal matters, then the service must be clearly defined and trackable.

➡ **Pro Parent Move:** Ask, "Which service is connected to this goal?" Make them tie every service back to a specific need.

Everything Must Connect

Goals without services are useless. Services without goals are unfocused. Accommodations that do not match needs are performative. Placement that cannot deliver any of the above is illegal.

The IEP is only as strong as its internal logic.

➡ **Pro Parent Move:** Before the team finalizes anything, say, "Let's make sure every goal has a direct service tied to it, and that the setting we're discussing can actually deliver everything we've written in this plan."

If the team cannot walk you through those connections, they are not ready to finalize the IEP.

▶ Accommodations and Modifications

Once the IEP team has agreed on goals and services, the next question is: What needs to be in place to help your child access instruction and succeed?

That is where accommodations and modifications come in.

You will dive deep into these tools in *Chapter 7: Accommodations, Modifications, & Related Services*—but here is what you need to know right now, during IEP development:

- **Accommodations** support *how* your child learns and shows what they know.
- **Modifications** change *what* your child is expected to learn.

These supports should not be treated as afterthoughts or filler. They are essential, especially if your child's disability impacts executive functioning, behavior, attention, reading, or output.

Every accommodation and modification must be connected to a documented need in the IEP. If the IEP team is hesitant to include them, ask, "What's the plan for supporting this area of need during instruction?"

➡ **Pro Parent Moves:**

- If an accommodation is vague (like "frequent breaks"), ask, "What does frequent mean—every 10 minutes? Twice per class?"
- If a modification is proposed, ask whether it changes the diploma path or affects credit.
- Always confirm how these supports will be communicated to all teachers—general ed, specials, substitute staff, everyone.

▶ *Behavioral and Social-Emotional Support*

If your child struggles with behavior, executive functioning, anxiety, or emotional regulation, the IEP must include support for those needs.

This might include:

- A Behavioral Intervention Plan (BIP)
- Counseling sessions
- Sensory breaks
- Check-in/check-out systems
- Structured support for transitions

These are not "extras." They are **core services** for students whose challenges affect behavior, focus, or emotional regulation.

If behavior impacts learning, it must be addressed—**directly, proactively, and in writing**.

If behavior is interfering with access to education, the school district is legally obligated to provide appropriate behavioral supports under IDEA. **This is not a judgment call. It is a compliance issue.**

▶ *Placement Decisions*

Decisions about where the IEP will be implemented—whether general education, resource room, special class, therapeutic day school, or residential facility—must be based on your child's *individual goals and needs*. This is not just best practice—it is federal law under IDEA's least restrictive environment (LRE) requirement. **Not what the school has available. Not staffing issues. Not what is convenient**. The IEP team is legally required to determine placement only *after* services and supports are identified. The setting must be able to deliver the IEP— not the other way around.

➡ **Pro Parent Move:** If the school recommends a placement *before* writing goals or identifying services, that is a red flag. Politely push back, *"Let's finalize services first—then determine the setting that meets those needs."* That is how the law is supposed to work.

Sometimes the IEP team will determine a student requires a separate school. This happens when the school cannot provide the services or supports needed.

Sometimes, the team may determine that your child's needs cannot be met in the public school setting, even with all available supports. This is not a failure— it is a sign that your child needs a higher level of care and structure.

An outside placement—such as a therapeutic day school or residential program—might be considered when:

- Your child is **not making progress** despite appropriate services and accommodations.
- The public school is **unable or unwilling to implement the IEP** as written.
- Your child's behavior, mental health needs, or learning profile requires **specialized staff or programming** that does not exist in the district.
- **Safety becomes a concern**—either for your child or others—and cannot be addressed through supports in the current setting.
- Your child has been **suspended, isolated, or sent home repeatedly** instead of being served.
- The school environment is so overwhelming that your child **shuts down, melts down, or refuses to attend**.

This is not a placement of last resort. It is a placement of **right fit**—based on data, documented need, and your child's right to meaningful access to education.

* **Pro Parent Tip**: If the school resists considering an outside placement, ask, "What evidence do we have that this current setting is working—and what is the plan if it continues not to?"

You are not asking them to give up on your child. You are asking them to **get serious about what success actually requires**.

The IEP Is A Living Document

The IEP is not set in stone. It is designed to evolve as your child's needs change. If something is not working, you have the right to request a review and make revisions at any time. Your child's needs may shift, and the IEP should reflect that. Make sure that you remain proactive in requesting updates if you notice your child is not making the expected progress.

➡ **Pro Parent Move:** If you disagree with the finalized IEP and the team moves forward without your consent (in states that allow it), you can request Prior Written Notice (PWN). PWN is a written explanation from the school that outlines the team's decisions and the reasons behind them. This forces the school to document their reasoning, which will be helpful if further disagreements arise.

Step 5: Implementation & Progress Monitoring

Once the IEP is in place:

✓ The school must provide all agreed-upon services.

✓ Student progress should be monitored through regular data collection and parent-teacher meetings.

✓ The IEP is reviewed at least annually, with a full reevaluation every three years (or sooner if necessary).

IEP Timelines To Know:

- **Initial Evaluation:** From the time you sign consent for your child's initial evaluation, your school has 60 days to conduct the evaluations, write reports, and hold a PPT to discuss the results. Some states have shorter timelines so check your state regulations.

- **Annual Review:** Once your child is found eligible for special education, the IEP must be formally reviewed and updated at least once a year.

- **Interim Reviews:** You can request an IEP review any time your child is not making expected progress.

- **Emergency Reviews:** You have the right to request an IEP meeting at any time if urgent needs arise (e.g., sudden regressions, safety concerns, behavioral escalations).

- **Reevaluation:** Every child must be reevaluated at least once every three years (unless the parent and district agree it is unnecessary—which is a rarity).

✱ Pro Parent Tip: If you notice your child is not making progress, request an IEP review meeting as soon as possible—do not wait until the annual review.

C. What To Do When It Breaks Down

The IEP process is supposed to be collaborative—but the reality is, it is not always so rosy, and parents often face roadblocks. Here is how to handle them:

Common IEP Process Challenges

1. Disputes Over Eligibility

→ The school says your child does not qualify for an IEP.

> ✓ **Solution:** Request an Independent Educational Evaluation (IEE)—if they agree, the school must pay for an outside expert (of your choosing) to assess your child.

2. Vague Or Weak Goals

→ Your child's IEP says, "Improve reading skills."

> ✓ **Solution:** Demand SMART goals, like "Increase reading fluency to 90% accuracy by June 2025."

3. Lack Of Services Or Accommodations

→ The school is not providing the supports listed in the IEP.

> ✓ **Solution:** Document everything. Request a meeting and ask for written justification if services are missing. Then ask compensatory services– these are meant to bring the student back to where they would have been had they received the services in the first place.

4. Communication Breakdowns

→ You feel like you are being ignored, dismissed, or misled.

> ✓ **Solution:** Keep a written record of all communication. Follow up every conversation with an email summarizing what was discussed.

Advocacy With Impact: What Helps, What Hurts

When frustration builds and communication breaks down, it is easy to lash out—but doing so can backfire. Advocacy is not just about being right; it is about being effective. Here is what to avoid—and what to do instead.

⚡ Here's What Not To Do (And What To Do Instead)

Before you hit send or vent your frustration—pause. The way you show up in advocacy can either open doors or slam them shut. Here is what to avoid if you want to protect your child's relationships and outcomes.

✗ **Do not take out your frustrations on the general education teacher.**

> ✓ **Instead:** Remember—nine times out of ten, the real barrier is not the person in the classroom. Teachers often have no control over what services are approved, how supports are delivered, or even whether they have seen your child's IEP (yes, really). They are juggling large caseloads and conflicting directives. If you come in hot, they are far less likely to engage openly. I am not saying they will ignore your child—but if they think every interaction with you might get them written up, they are going to keep their distance.

✗ **Do not write anything in an email that you would not say face-to-face.**

> ✓ **Instead:** Keep your communication clear, respectful, and grounded. Emails get saved. They get forwarded. They land in the inboxes of people you did not intend. If you would not say it to someone's face, do not put it in writing. And if you would not want it shared with the paraeducator, the art teacher, the principal—or the superintendent—then do not email it to the general education teacher either. These things always find their way back.

✗ Do not go over the teacher's head without trying to work it out first.

> **✓ Instead:** Even if you suspect the teacher's hands are tied, always start by giving them a chance to respond. Not only is it respectful—it gives them a heads-up and helps maintain trust. If you need to escalate, let them know, *"I appreciate your time. I think the next step is to speak with [case manager / administrator] to explore more options. I just wanted to keep you in the loop."* That one sentence preserves relationships, shows transparency, and makes you look reasonable even when you are frustrated.

✗ Do not tell your child that school staff are incompetent, don't care, or "out to get them."

> **✓ Instead:** Keep adult frustrations between adults. Children process things differently. If your child is already anxious or struggling, hearing from you that the people around them cannot be trusted only adds fuel to the fire. You do not have to sugarcoat things, but you also should not dump your distrust onto a child who needs to feel safe at school. Let your advocacy happen in meetings and emails—not at the dinner table.

Your words will shape how your child is treated—by the team and by the system. Lead with clarity, protect your credibility, and never let your justifiable frustration cost your child a better outcome.

I wish I could say I have always followed this advice as a parent—or even as a professional. But I cannot. This work is personal, emotional, and overwhelming, and sometimes... you will lose it. That does not make you a bad advocate—it makes you human. The key is what you do next: regroup, reframe, follow up in writing. You can always come back to the table stronger.

Let that one bad moment be the exception—not your whole strategy.

✱ **Pro Parent Tip:** Assume most people are trying their best within a broken system. When you lead with calm and clarity—even when you are frustrated—you give people fewer excuses to avoid doing the right thing.

When To Stop Arguing (Seek Help Or Let It Go?)

Navigating the special education process often requires persistence, patience, and strategic advocacy. However, there comes a point when arguing with the school is not just exhausting—it is ineffective. When productive discussions turn into endless back-and-forths or the school refuses to provide legally required services, it may be time to escalate and seek outside help.

✱ **Pro Parent Tip: Know Your Right To Prior Written Notice (PWN)**—If the school refuses an evaluation, denies services, or proposes changes you disagree with, you have the right to request Prior Written Notice (PWN). PWN requires schools to document their reasoning and data behind the decision, providing a written record of any refusals or proposals. This is critical because it protects your right to challenge those decisions in the future. Always request PWN in writing to ensure you have the official documentation to support your case and make it easier to challenge mistakes later.

⚡ Signs It Is Time For Outside Support:

- The school repeatedly denies reasonable requests without justification.

- Meetings go in circles, rehashing the same issues without resolution.

- The school ignores written concerns or fails to document parent input in meeting notes.

- You suspect legal rights under IDEA, Section 504, or the ADA are being violated.

- The school refuses to evaluate or dismisses expert recommendations without providing an explanation.

When the system is not working as it should, knowing when to shift gears and pursue formal dispute resolution can make all the difference. Understanding these processes helps you choose the best path forward when collaboration fails.

Mediation: A Collaborative Approach

Mediation is a voluntary process where a neutral third party helps parents and schools reach a mutually acceptable solution. It works best when both sides are willing to engage and explore compromises to resolve disagreements.

If successful, mediation results in a legally binding agreement outlining next steps—so it is highly advisable to consult an attorney before mediation or at least before signing anything.

When to Request Mediation:

- You have hit a standstill, but the school seems open to discussion.

- Disagreements are based on differences in interpretation, not outright denial of services.

- You want to preserve a positive relationship with the school while resolving disputes.

- A mutually agreed-upon evaluation could help clarify the issues.

★ **Key Benefit:** Mediation is often faster and less adversarial than due process hearings, keeping the focus on finding solutions rather than engaging in legal battles.

State Complaints: Holding Schools Accountable

If a school violates special education laws, parents can file a state complaint with their state's Department of Education. The state investigates the complaint and issues a written decision.

When to File a State Complaint:

- The school has **failed to implement the IEP** (e.g., not providing services, ignoring accommodations).
- The district has **violated procedural safeguards** (e.g., failing to provide Prior Written Notice or refusing an evaluation without explanation).
- The issue involves a **clear IDEA violation**, not just a difference in opinion about what's best for the child.

⭐ **Key Benefit:** State complaints are based on legal compliance—if the district is in violation, the state can order corrective action.

Due Process: The Legal Route

Due process is a formal legal hearing where both sides present evidence before an impartial hearing officer. This option is complex and legally binding, making it *highly advisable* to have an attorney represent you.

When to File for Due Process:

- The school **denied eligibility** or services, and other resolution efforts have failed.
- There is a **fundamental disagreement** about what the child needs.
- The school is **refusing necessary placement** or supports despite clear evidence.

Key Considerations: Due process can be lengthy, expensive, and adversarial, but it may be necessary for serious violations affecting your child's education.

Choosing The Right Path

- Start with communication—sometimes issues can be resolved at the IEP table.

- Mediation works well when both sides are open to problem-solving.

- State complaints hold schools accountable for legal violations.

- Due process is the last resort for major disputes requiring a legal ruling.

➡ **Pro Parent Move:** No matter which route you take, document everything. A strong paper trail strengthens your case at any stage of the dispute resolution process.

Hiring A Non-Attorney Special Education Advocate

When navigating the maze of special education, sometimes you need a knowledgeable ally by your side. Non-attorney special education advocates should be trained in the IDEA, Section 504, and best practices in special education. They can help you understand evaluations, participate in IEP meetings, and support your efforts to ensure your child's needs are clearly communicated and effectively addressed.

✦ *Important Note On Non-Attorney Advocates*

Advocacy is not a regulated profession, meaning anyone can call themselves an advocate regardless of their training or experience. This makes it especially important to vet your advocate's background before relying on their guidance.

➤ **Look For Professional Training** – One of the most reputable advocacy programs is the **Special Education Advocacy Training** (SEAT) provided by the **Council of Parent Attorneys and Advocates** (COPAA). This program not only offers rigorous training but also includes a voluntary Code of Ethics, which adds a level of accountability.

⚡ Be Cautious – Some advocates are parents who have been through the process themselves. While experience can be valuable, if their only training is their own experience, it does not always equate to expertise.

➤ Bottom Line: Even with excellent training programs available, advocacy remains an unregulated field. Do your research and ensure your advocate has the knowledge, skills, and ethical approach needed to support your child effectively.

When to Hire an Advocate:

- You need help understanding complex evaluations and assessments.

- The IEP process can feel overwhelming, and you need someone to help you organize your approach.

- The school is responsive, but you are struggling to advocate effectively.

- You want a stronger ally in meetings to keep the conversation focused on your child's needs.

✱ Pro Parent Tip: Think of an advocate as a translator and strategist—someone who understands the system and knows how to keep the conversation moving in the right direction.

Calling An Attorney: When Legal Help Becomes Necessary

Sometimes, even the best advocacy efforts are not enough. If the school outright refuses to comply with IDEA, denies services, or violates your child's legal rights, it may be time to bring in an attorney.

When To Call An Attorney:

- The school refuses to provide services outlined in the IEP or fails to implement accommodations.

- Your child's rights under IDEA, Section 504, or the ADA have been violated.

- The school has denied evaluations or misrepresented eligibility for services.

- You are considering enrolling your child in a private special education school without the district's approval and want them to pay for it.

- You are considering mediation. You often have to sign a settlement agreement, a legal document, so it is definitely a good idea to have it reviewed by an attorney.

- You are considering a due process hearing—a legal proceeding that can significantly impact your child's education. While parents (and in many states, advocates) are legally allowed to represent themselves, I strongly discourage going in without an attorney.

- Communication with the school has completely broken down, and further discussions seem futile.

- You arrive at any meeting, and the school district has brought an attorney. Shut that down immediately and call someone!

➥ **Pro Parent Move:** If you are considering due process, consult with a special education attorney first to assess whether it is the right strategy and how it could impact both your child and the broader special education community.

⚡ *Special Situations That Require Extra Caution*

Some situations in special education law have special rules or higher risks attached. If you are navigating any of these, consulting an attorney early is critical to protecting your rights.

◇ **Unilateral Private School Placements**: If you plan to remove your child from public school and place them in a private special education setting while seeking reimbursement from the district, this is known as a unilateral placement under IDEA. **Be aware:** this process comes with strict requirements—including **advance written notice** and proof that the public school failed to offer a Free Appropriate Public Education (FAPE). Failing to follow these steps can permanently forfeit your right to reimbursement.

⚡ **Do not pursue the unilateral placement path without consulting a special education attorney.** This is one of the most complex and high-stakes areas of special education law—so make sure you do it right!

✪ *See* **Chapter 6: Navigating The School System** *for a detailed breakdown of your placement options, including private, unilateral, and homeschool pathways.*

◇ **Signing Settlement Agreements**: In mediation or settlement negotiations, schools often require you to sign a legally binding agreement. Because these agreements waive certain rights, they should always be reviewed by an attorney to ensure you understand the full consequences.

▶ **Keep in mind:** The school has legal counsel on staff—professionals trained to defend the district's decisions. If you go into mediation or a due process hearing without a special education attorney, you are already behind. This is not the time for a generalist or someone who dabbles. Special education law is dense, procedural, and full of traps for the unprepared. You need an attorney who knows the system, the strategies, and how to hold the district accountable—because they will absolutely show up ready to do the same.

✱ **Pro Parent Tip:** Most special education attorneys offer a free consultation or low-cost case review. If you are unsure whether you need legal help, an initial conversation can help clarify your next steps.

◇ **Due process should be a last resort—not a weapon.** Filing for a hearing out of frustration or to make life difficult for the district can backfire. Bad cases create bad case law, and that weakens protections for everyone. Using due process strategically—to bring a district to the table in good faith through mediation or a resolution session—can be a smart move. But pushing forward to a full hearing out of anger or without preparation? That is a gamble, and one that could set a precedent in all the wrong ways. Every decision in due process becomes part of the legal landscape. If your case is not solid, it might not just hurt your child—it could hurt the next family too.

Formal Legal Actions

If informal resolution efforts fail, legal action may be the only way to ensure compliance.

State Complaints

If a school violates IDEA, parents can file a formal complaint with their state's Department of Education. The state must investigate and issue a ruling, which may require corrective action, training, or compensatory services.

OCR Complaints

When the issue involves discrimination—especially under Section 504 or the Americans with Disabilities Act—parents can file a complaint with the U.S. Department of Education's Office for Civil Rights (OCR). OCR investigates claims of unequal treatment, access barriers, and retaliation. While it does not award services or money, an OCR finding can result in binding corrective action and serious accountability.

Due Process Hearings

A due process hearing is a formal legal proceeding similar to a trial. Both sides present evidence before an impartial hearing officer.

What To Expect In Due Process

1. Filing The Complaint

You begin by submitting a due process complaint—a formal legal document, not just a letter of concern. It must detail the school's violations and what remedies you are seeking. It sets the boundaries of the case, and vague or poorly written complaints can get tossed before they even get off the ground.

2. The Resolution Session

Within 15 days of filing a due process complaint, the school district must offer a **resolution session**. This meeting is **mandatory** unless both parties agree in writing to waive it or choose mediation instead. The purpose is to give everyone one last opportunity to resolve the dispute informally before moving toward a full hearing.

The setting is intentionally designed to be less formal than a due process hearing. Sometimes it is just the director of special education and the parents; other times, it can feel more like a full IEP team meeting. There are no strict rules about who attends—**except one:**

➔ **The school district may not bring an attorney unless the parent brings one.**

This safeguard exists to prevent the school from having an unfair power advantage if the parents are unrepresented.

The tone of the session may feel more casual and **it is not a confidential meeting,** so parents and advocates should still proceed with caution. That said, if the session leads to a written settlement agreement, confidentiality usually applies to the terms of that document— not the discussion itself, unless explicitly stated.

3. Pre-Hearing Prep

This phase involves heavy lifting: gathering evidence, preparing witness testimony, organizing exhibits, and exchanging materials under strict legal timelines—think depositions, subpoenas, and procedural wrangling—not casual prep. This is where having legal counsel matters most.

4. The Hearing

This is a full-on legal proceeding. Both sides present evidence, question witnesses, and make legal arguments in front of a hearing officer. It is formal, adversarial, and bound by rules. You cannot simply tell your story and hope for sympathy—you need a clear legal theory and facts to back it up.

5. Post-Hearing Brief

After the hearing wraps, both parties are typically required to submit a post-hearing brief. This written argument summarizes the evidence and legal points made during the hearing. It is the last word before the decision—and it can carry serious weight. A strong brief ties everything together and shows the hearing officer exactly why your side should prevail.

6. The Decision

After reviewing the evidence, testimony, and legal arguments—including the post-hearing briefs—the hearing officer (HO) will issue a written decision. The decision addresses each issue raised in the complaint and may rule in your favor on some, all, or none of the claims. If the HO finds a violation, they may order specific remedies, such as compensatory education, changes to the IEP, or reimbursement. However, the remedies may not match exactly what you asked for—they can be more, less, or entirely different. Either party has the right to appeal the decision, which can extend the litigation and increase the emotional and financial toll, including potential attorney's fees.

⚡ **Warning:** Due process is not just hard—it is litigation. Districts will show up with lawyers, experts, and well-prepared teams. Parents who show up without representation are at a severe disadvantage. If you are going to a hearing, hire a special education attorney who is familiar with the system. This is not the place for trial and error.

Making The Right Call: Choosing The Best Path Forward

There is no single "right" way to resolve disputes, but knowing your options can help you make informed decisions.

✓ **Start with collaboration:** When possible, work with the school to resolve concerns.

✓ **Bring in an advocate:** If discussions become overwhelming, an advocate can help strengthen your voice.

✓ **Consider legal action:** If the school refuses to comply with the IDEA, an attorney can help protect your child's rights.

The goal is not to win a battle—it is to get your child the support they need to thrive. Sometimes, that means strategic persistence. Other times, it means bringing in reinforcements. Knowing when to pivot can make all the difference.

Maybe, When To Let It Go

Advocacy is essential, but not every battle is worth fighting. There are times when stepping back—or finding an alternative solution—may be the most strategic choice. Knowing when to push and when to pivot can save time, energy, frustration, and $, allowing you to focus on high-impact issues that truly affect your child's education.

Not every disagreement with the school needs to become a full-scale battle. Here are situations where letting it go—or shifting your approach—might make sense:

The Issue Is Annoying, But Not Impacting Your Child's Learning

→ **Example:** The school will not change your child's IEP meeting time to accommodate your schedule. Frustrating? Yes. Worth escalating? Probably not.

You Can Easily Provide It Privately

→ **Example:** The school is offering 30 minutes less speech therapy per week than you feel is appropriate.

★ **Reality check:** While you should not let the school off the hook, if it is a minor gap that you can supplement privately, it may not be the time to start a war.

The School Offers An Alternative That Still Meets The Need

→ **Example:** You requested pull-out math intervention, but the school proposes in-class small-group support instead. If the alternative is still research-based and effective, fighting for the original request might not be the best use of your energy.

It Is A Matter Of Preference, Not Necessity

→ **Example:** You prefer a specific reading program, but the school offers a different research-based one. If both are effective, insisting on one over the other might not be worth the battle.

The Outcome Will Not Change, No Matter How Hard You Push

- Advocacy is about strategy, not just persistence. There are times when pushing forward makes sense—and times when stepping back to reassess your approach is the smarter move.

  → **Example:** You have exhausted all available advocacy strategies, presented clear data and legal backing, and the district has made it clear they will not budge. In these situations, continuing the same approach may not be productive.

Instead of giving up or going nuclear, consider:

- **Shifting tactics** – Would mediation, legal action, or outside advocacy be more effective?

- **Gathering more data** – Could additional assessments, expert opinions, or external evaluations strengthen your case?

- **Timing your next move** – Sometimes, districts resist changes in one school year but become more flexible the next.

- **Deciding if the fight is worth it** – Not every battle has to be fought immediately. Some issues resolve on their own over time, while others require a more comprehensive strategic plan.

→ **Pro Parent Move:** Persistence is powerful—but strategic persistence is even more effective. Know when to push forward, when to pivot, and when to plan your next move to capitalize on a better opportunity. Before escalating, ask yourself:

- Will this issue affect my child's ability to access their education?

- Am I fighting for their needs or my preferences?

- Is there a way to meet in the middle and still achieve the goal?

When It Is Your Problem, Not Theirs

There is a difference between what the school is legally responsible for and what is a parental challenge. Schools are required to provide a Free Appropriate Public Education (FAPE)—but that does not mean they are responsible for every difficulty a family faces.

➡ **Example:** Homework help when you work late—Your child needs help with homework, but your work evenings and cannot provide it.

★ **Reality check:** This is a parental challenge, not necessarily the school's obligation.

✓ **Solution:** Ask about after-school tutoring, peer mentoring, or modified homework assignments that fit within the IEP.

➡ **Example:** You do not have the patience to implement the behavior plan – The school provides a structured behavior program, but at home, you struggle to maintain consistency.

★ **Reality check:** A lack of consistency at home can undermine school progress, but that does not mean it is all the school's responsibility.

✓ **Solution:** Instead of arguing over additional school services, consider requesting parent training as a related service in the IEP. Schools can provide behavior coaching, modeling, or direct training to help parents effectively implement strategies.

➡ **Pro Parent Move:** Recognizing that not every issue is the school's fault allows you to focus on solutions instead of frustrations.

When To Pick Your Battles Strategically

Instead of fighting every issue, focus your energy on high-impact battles:

✓ When the school denies essential services that impact your child's ability to learn.

✓ When your child's safety, access, or rights under IDEA or Section 504 are at risk.

✓ When the school is breaking the law (e.g., refusing evaluations, ignoring IEP requirements).

➡ **Pro Parent Move:** Save your energy for battles that truly affect your child's education—because those fights ARE worth it.

Final Thoughts: Taking Charge Of The Process

The IEP process is more than a series of meetings and forms—it is the foundation of your child's educational journey. It can feel overwhelming, emotionally charged, and at times, downright unfair. But when you understand how the process works—and where your power lies—you can step into those meetings with more clarity, more confidence, and a whole lot more control.

You are not a guest at the table—you are a required member of the team. Your insight, your questions, and your persistence shape the supports your child receives. And when things do not go as planned (because let's be real—they sometimes don't), you are not stuck. You have options, tools, and the right to demand better.

Strategic advocacy means choosing your moments. It means asking for data, documenting decisions, and knowing when to bring in help. You do not have to fight every fight. Just the ones that matter most.

Key Takeaways:

✓ **The IEP is a legally binding document**—if it is written in the plan, it must be provided.

✓ **Parents are equal members of the IEP team**. Do not let the school minimize your role.

✓ **IEP goals must be specific and measurable.** Push for SMART goals, not vague statements.

✓ **Progress should be tracked and shared regularly**—do not wait for annual reviews.

✓ **Document everything**—requests, concerns, and follow-ups. Paper trails protect your child.

✓ **If services are not being delivered, ask for compensatory services.**

✓ **You have options when conflicts arise**—you can request a meeting, escalate the issue, or seek help.

✓ **Not every issue needs to become a battle**—but the important ones are always worth it.

➡ **Pro Parent Move:** If something feels off in a meeting, you do not have to sign anything on the spot. You have the right to take it home, review it, and come back with questions.

Closing Thoughts

You did not sign up to be an expert in special education law—but here you are, stepping up, speaking out, and shaping the future for your child. Every form you fill out, every question you ask, every meeting you attend—it all matters.

The system may be complex, but your voice cuts through the noise. Keep using it. You are not just participating in the process—you are owning it.

CHAPTER 5:
Building A Support Team

Navigating special education is not something you have to do alone—you deserve a dedicated team behind you. The right support system can mean the difference between fighting every battle alone and having a group of knowledgeable allies who help advocate for your child's needs.

A solid support team includes professionals, educators, advocates, and—most importantly—you, the parent. But simply having a team in place is not enough—you also need to understand your role and how to advocate effectively.

A. The Role Of Parents As Advocates

You are not just a participant in the IEP process—you are an equal partner in shaping your child's education. Schools are required under the Individuals with Disabilities Education Act (IDEA) to include you in all major educational decisions. However, being included and being heard are not always the same thing.

✱ **Pro Parent Tip:** Preparing Before You Need It—Advocacy begins before issues arise. The earlier you start learning about your child's rights, the better equipped you will be to address challenges when they come. A proactive approach includes understanding the law, attending IEP meetings regularly, and keeping track of your child's progress over time. Your early involvement ensures that you are not just reacting to problems as they come, but anticipating and addressing them before they become significant hurdles.

Action Plan:

1. **Read up on IDEA** and familiarize yourself with the key terms such as IEP, FAPE, Section 504, and related services.

2. **Attend parent training sessions** or workshops on special education.

3. **Monitor your child's progress regularly**, not just during IEP meetings. Use informal check-ins and progress reports to stay ahead of issues.

4. **Reach out to other parents** in support groups or online forums for insights into the process and advice on staying proactive.

Your role? Be informed, proactive, and persistent.

Your Legal Rights As A Parent Under IDEA

Under IDEA, you have the right to:

◇ **Participate** in all IEP meetings – Schools cannot make major decisions without your input.

◇ **Receive** written notice before any changes are made to your child's services.

◇ **Request** an Independent Educational Evaluation (IEE) if you disagree with the school's assessment—at the school's expense.

◇ **Challenge** decisions through mediation or due process hearings if your child is not receiving appropriate services.

✱ **Pro Parent Tip:** Schools sometimes "forget" to tell parents about these rights. If the school resists your requests, remind them that IDEA is a federal law—not a suggestion.

Why These Rights Matter

Understanding these rights is empowering. When you request an Independent Educational Evaluation (IEE), for example, it signals to the school that you are informed about your rights and prepared to challenge the school's findings if necessary. Similarly, knowing that you can challenge decisions through mediation or due process hearings can help you advocate for your child without feeling powerless. Being aware of these rights from the start prevents the school from overstepping or misinterpreting their obligations under the law.

Being An Effective Advocate For Your Child

☑ **Stay Informed** – Learn about IDEA, IEPs, 504 Plans, and your child's rights. The more you know, the harder you are to dismiss.

✷ **Pro Parent Tip:** Schools sometimes test the waters to see how much you do or do not know. The more confident and informed you are, the less likely they are to cut corners.

☑ **Document Everything** – Keep copies of evaluations, emails, meeting notes, and progress reports. If it is not in writing, it didn't happen.

☑ **Build Positive Relationships** – Approach educators as partners, not adversaries, at least at first. A good working relationship can help solve problems before they escalate.

☑ **Ask Questions** – If something is unclear, ask for a written explanation. Schools must justify their decisions.

☑ **Build Emotional Resilience** – Advocating for your child's needs can be emotionally draining, especially if there are setbacks or resistance. Building a support network outside of the IEP team—whether it is a therapist, a close friend, or a parent group—can help you maintain emotional resilience. This support system gives you the strength to stay focused on the goal: your child's success. Take care of yourself so you can advocate effectively.

✳ **Pro Parent Tips:**

1. **Practice mindfulness**—spending a few minutes each day focusing on your breath can help calm your mind during stressful moments.

2. **Reach out to support groups**—join parent networks and forums where other parents share their experiences and strategies. Emotional support from others who have walked the same path is invaluable.

3. **Seek professional counseling**—a therapist who specializes in parental stress or special education can help you navigate the emotional challenges of advocacy.

☑ **Know When to Seek Help** – If your child is not getting the support they need, an advocate or attorney can help negotiate services and hold the school accountable.

✳ **Pro Parent Tip:** When selecting an advocate, be diligent. Look for advocates who are specifically trained in special education law and are familiar with IDEA and Section 504. Red flags include advocates who cannot provide clear references or do not have documented experience with special education disputes. Make sure the advocate understands your state's regulations and has worked successfully with schools in the past. An experienced advocate will know how to leverage the law to get the services your child needs.

B. Who Should Be On Your Team?

Special education is not a solo journey—having a strong, knowledgeable team in place makes all the difference. Each team member plays a key role in implementing and advocating for your child's Individualized Education Program (IEP).

But simply having people in these roles is not enough—you need to ensure they are truly part of your team. A good team is one that works collaboratively, communicates openly, and prioritizes your child's needs. While disagreements may occur, the goal should always be to find solutions, not create division.

A strong team does not mean an "us vs. them" dynamic. Schools and parents should be partners, not adversaries. However, if you consistently feel like you are fighting alone, it may be time to reevaluate who is truly supporting your child's needs.

Key Members Of The Support Team

■ **Parents & Caregivers** – You are your child's first and most important advocate. No one knows them better than you. Your insights into their strengths, challenges, and daily experiences provide crucial context that schools simply cannot see. But you should not be on an island by yourself.

> **✱ Pro Parent Tip:** If you ever feel that your concerns are not being taken seriously during an IEP meeting, consider bringing an advocate, private provider, or other professional. Schools tend to take outside professionals more seriously, which can help move discussions forward in a productive way.

■ **General Education Teachers** – Play a key role in implementing IEP accommodations inside the classroom. They provide insight into how your child functions in a typical school setting, help with inclusion strategies, and communicate academic progress.

■ **Special Education Teachers** – Serve as the bridge between the IEP and daily learning. They develop specialized instruction, modify lessons, and ensure that IEP accommodations are actually being implemented as written.

■ **School Psychologists & Counselors** – Assess cognitive, emotional, and behavioral development. They help identify learning disabilities, ADHD, anxiety, and other support needs, making recommendations for appropriate interventions.

- **Speech, Occupational, & Physical Therapists** – Work on specific skill areas:

  - Speech therapists focus on communication, articulation, and social language skills.

  - Occupational therapists support fine motor skills, sensory processing, and executive functioning.

  - Physical therapists help with mobility, posture, and gross motor coordination.

- **Medical & Mental Health Professionals** – If your child has a medical or mental health condition that impacts their education, it is essential to include relevant professionals in your child's support team. A mental health professional—such as a therapist, counselor, or psychologist—can provide essential insights for creating an effective IEP. For instance, if your child experiences anxiety, ADHD, or depression, these professionals can offer recommendations for strategies to reduce anxiety during testing or classroom adjustments that support mental health.

- **Paraprofessionals & Classroom Aides** – These individuals are often the most consistent source of hands-on support for your child in the classroom. Their role is crucial for implementing IEP accommodations, especially when your child requires more personalized help. In some districts, paraprofessionals may be allowed to attend IEP meetings and provide additional insights into your child's day-to-day learning experiences. Ensure their responsibilities are clearly outlined in the IEP and request that they attend meetings where appropriate to ensure continuity and consistency of support.

  ➡ **Pro Parent Move:** Ask the school district to include your child's assigned paraprofessional in the IEP meetings if possible. Their direct knowledge of your child's classroom experience will offer valuable input and strengthen your case for accommodations.

■ **IEP Case Managers & District Representatives** – Oversee IEP compliance, track progress, and act as a liaison between parents and the school district.

■ **External Experts (Advocates, Therapists, and Attorneys)** – Special education advocacy can sometimes be complex, and it is important to know when to seek expert help. A special education advocate can be an invaluable resource when you feel stuck in the process, especially when it comes to navigating IEP meetings, ensuring accommodations are implemented, and negotiating services. If the situation escalates or legal rights are violated, an attorney specializing in special education law can protect your child's rights.

➡ **Pro Parent Move:** When selecting an advocate or attorney, look for individuals who are familiar with IDEA and Section 504, and who understand your state's specific regulations. Ask for references and past case experiences to ensure they are well-suited for your child's needs.

■ **Community Support Groups & Parent Networks** – You are not alone in this journey. Other parents who have navigated the special education process can offer invaluable emotional support, advice, and strategies. Local and national organizations, such as the **Council of Parent Attorneys and Advocates** (COPAA) or **Parent Training and Information Centers** (PTIs), often provide resources for parents in need. These organizations are discussed in more detail in *Chapter 18: Staying Informed*.

✶ **Pro Parent Tip:** Seek out parent support groups in your community or online forums where you can ask questions, share experiences, and learn from others who have gone through similar challenges. These groups can help you stay informed and encouraged as you advocate for your child.

★ **Reality Check:** As helpful as shared experiences can be, remember to take them with a grain of salt. No two children, families, or school districts are the same—

and outcomes can vary wildly, even in similar situations. I have seen schools treat nearly identical cases in radically different ways for reasons that made no sense to the families involved. What worked for one parent may not work for you. That does not mean anyone is wrong; it just means you are working within a messy, inconsistent system. You also may not know the full story behind someone else's experience—and they may not know yours. Use what resonates, leave what does not, and trust your judgment.

Why Building A Strong Team Matters

The right team can mean the difference between constantly battling the system and having strong, knowledgeable allies on your side.

- Know who is on your child's team and what their role is.

- Communicate regularly—a good team works best when everyone is informed.

Bring in professionals when necessary—sometimes, having an expert in the room makes all the difference.

➡ **Pro Parent Move:** If you ever feel like you are fighting alone, that is a sign your team is not strong enough yet. The more support you have, the more effectively you can advocate for your child's needs.

C. Communication Strategies With Educators

Communication is everything. Parents and educators do not always see eye to eye, but a strong, professional, and proactive approach can make all the difference. Good communication not only helps resolve issues—it also reveals when collaboration is not happening. If conversations feel one-sided or dismissive, it may signal that adjustments need to be made in how you communicate or with whom you are communicating.

Strategies For Effective Communication

▶ Establish Regular Check-Ins

Frequent updates via email, phone calls, or quick meetings can help prevent small issues from becoming big problems. A simple, "How is my child adjusting to their accommodations?" keeps communication open and shows that you value the educator's perspective. However, manage expectations—teachers often juggle many responsibilities, so responses may not always be immediate. Setting a realistic timeline for follow-ups can help maintain communication without frustration.

▶ Document Everything

Keep records of all communication, IEP meeting notes, and progress reports. Educators work with multiple students and may not always recall every detail, so having documentation benefits both parents and school staff. If a service is not being provided, written documentation gives you leverage to hold the school accountable and ensures clarity on expectations. However, be mindful that changes often take time—even when everyone is on the same page, implementation may not happen overnight.

✳ Pro Parent Tip: Bring in External Experts When Needed – If you feel that the school is not understanding the full scope of your child's needs, consider inviting an expert—such as a behavioral therapist, occupational therapist, or psychologist—to attend an IEP meeting. This third-party input can be especially helpful when the school dismisses your concerns or if you need expert validation for specific accommodations. Schools often give more weight to outside professionals, and having them present can add a layer of credibility to your concerns.

▶ *Handle Disagreements Constructively*

When faced with conflict, it is crucial to approach the situation as a collaborative problem-solving opportunity rather than a confrontation. If an issue arises, such as a service not being delivered or a strategy not working, avoid making it an "us vs. them" situation. Instead, focus on working together to find a solution.

1. **State the issue clearly:** "I've noticed that this accommodation is not working as intended."

2. **Offer a potential solution:** "Can we discuss ways to adjust it to better support my child's learning needs?"

3. **Stay solution-focused:** Emphasize that both parties share the same goal—your child's success.

✗ **Instead of:** "This accommodation is not working, and I need it fixed right now."

✓ **Try:** "I have noticed that this accommodation is not having the intended effect. Can we work together to adjust it to better support my child's learning?"

This approach acknowledges that everyone—parents and educators—has the same goal: the success of the child. It also sets the tone for open collaboration.

▶ *Frame Disagreements As Opportunities For Growth*

When disagreements arise, focus on constructive feedback and solutions, rather than placing blame. For example, instead of saying "I have told you this strategy is not working," you can say, "We have observed that this approach is not yielding the expected results. Let's collaborate to find a solution that better supports my child." By focusing on improvement rather than fault, you foster a more cooperative atmosphere where all team members are encouraged to be part of the solution.

▶ Use Data To Support Your Concerns

Bring progress reports, classroom work samples, and evaluation results to meetings. While you see your child's struggles at home, teachers and school staff may see different behaviors in the classroom. Using objective data helps align perspectives and makes it harder for schools to overlook concerns. At the same time, manage expectations—some progress is incremental, and not every strategy will produce immediate results.

▶ Follow-Up After Meetings

After meetings, it is important to send a follow-up email summarizing the discussion and any next steps. This helps ensure everyone is on the same page and gives the school a written record of what was agreed upon. If your child is making progress, it is a good idea to acknowledge those improvements and thank the educators for their hard work. Conversely, if progress is not being made or accommodations are not working, sending a professional email requesting a meeting to reevaluate the situation can keep momentum moving forward.

* **Pro Parent Tip:** Regularly following up after meetings ensures that the agreed-upon plans are being implemented, and it reinforces that you are actively involved in your child's education.

▶ Frame Issues As Collaborative Problem-Solving

Teachers and administrators often want to help but may have limitations in resources, time, or training. Instead of framing concerns as demands, try inviting collaboration:

✗ **Instead of:** "This accommodation is not working."

> ✓ **Try:** "I have noticed my child is still struggling with this. How can we adjust it to better support them?"

This approach acknowledges that both parents and educators have a shared goal: the child's success. It also sets the expectation that solutions may require adjustments over time, rather than a quick fix.

▶ *Acknowledge Positive Contributions*

Educators work within a complex system with many demands, and while advocacy is crucial, recognizing their efforts builds goodwill. A simple, "I really appreciate the effort you have put into supporting my child," can help maintain a cooperative and solutions-focused relationship. It also sets a tone of mutual respect, making future advocacy conversations smoother.

▶ *Ensure Follow-Through On Advocacy*

Being informed and persistent is important, but it is also essential to ensure that any agreed-upon actions from IEP meetings are followed through. If the school agrees to a new strategy or service, follow up regularly to ensure its implementation. You might say, "I just wanted to check in to see how the new reading strategy is being applied in class and if we are seeing improvements." This not only helps keep the school accountable but also allows them to share progress and any concerns they may have.

▶ *Be Persistent But Professional*

If you feel your concerns are being ignored, request a formal meeting or mediation. Remember that school staff may not have bad intentions, but they may be overwhelmed or constrained by policies. Staying firm, factual, and focused on solutions—not emotions—helps keep the conversation productive.

At the same time, manage expectations: not every disagreement means the school is being negligent, and some resolutions require multiple steps before real change happens.

✱ Pro Parent Tip: If emails and conversations go nowhere, send a formal letter requesting an IEP review—schools are required to respond. Parents can request an IEP meeting at any time! Keeping the tone professional but direct reinforces that you are informed, engaged, and ready to work together toward a resolution.

▶ *Identify When Communication Is Not Working*

- If repeated attempts to collaborate are met with resistance, vague responses, or a lack of follow-through, take note.

- If a particular staff member is consistently dismissing your concerns, it may be time to escalate the issue to an administrator or bring in an advocate.

- Schools work best when everyone is on the same team—if that's not happening, you may need to reconsider who is actively supporting your child's needs.

➡ Pro Parent Move: If someone on the IEP team seems disengaged or dismissive, ask direct, solution-focused questions (e.g., "How can we work together to address this?"). If responses remain unhelpful, document your concerns and escalate them as needed.

- **Request a Meeting with an Administrator** – If a team member is not engaging constructively, ask to discuss the issue with the special education director or school principal.

- **Ask for Clarification on Roles & Responsibilities** – Sometimes, simply asking "Who is responsible for ensuring this is implemented?" can shift accountability and encourage follow-through.

- **Bring an Advocate or Outside Professional** – A third-party perspective can reinforce concerns and help facilitate more productive discussions.

- **Use the IEP Process to Address Issues** – If a staff member is not implementing accommodations or services properly, request an IEP review meeting to document the issue and develop a corrective plan.

✦ If the situation persists, consider filing a formal complaint or requesting mediation to ensure your child's needs are met.

▶ *Mediation: A Collaborative Approach*

If you need to escalate the issue, mediation may be the next step. Mediation is a neutral, non-confrontational process where a third-party mediator helps both parties reach an agreement. It is less formal and allows both the parent and school to come to a mutually agreeable solution with guidance from a mediator.

➡ **Pro Parent Move:** Before entering mediation, consult with an advocate or attorney to ensure you are fully prepared. They can help you understand the process, gather supporting evidence, and guide you through how to effectively communicate your child's needs.

▶ *Due Process Hearings: Legal Proceedings To Protect Your Child's Rights*

If mediation fails, you may need to proceed to a due process hearing. A due process hearing is a formal legal proceeding where both parties present evidence before an impartial hearing officer. It is a more structured and adversarial process, so it is important to be prepared.

➡ **Pro Parent Move:** Before entering a due process hearing, it is crucial to consult with an attorney who focuses on special education law. They can help you prepare for the hearing by gathering all necessary documents, understanding the legal framework, and providing the best strategy to present your case.

▶ *Be Persistent But Professional*

Effective advocacy is about consistency. If your child is not receiving services as specified in the IEP or if you encounter resistance from the school, remain professional, persistent, and focused on solutions. Sometimes the follow-up is just as important as the initial request. Keep a paper trail and document every follow-up. This shows the school that you are committed to your child's success, and it can help hold them accountable for any missteps.

Final Thoughts: Navigating The Labyrinth Together

Special education advocacy can often feel like a labyrinth—twisting paths, hidden doors, and the occasional Minotaur in a meeting. But one of the most powerful tools you have in this process is not just knowledge—it is people. The right team can turn a confusing, overwhelming system into one that actually works for your child.

That said, a team is not defined by job titles or attendance at meetings. A true support team is made up of individuals who collaborate, communicate, and center your child's needs—not their own convenience. If that is not happening, it is not a sign to give up. It is a signal to reevaluate, redirect, and reinforce your efforts with the right people.

Key Takeaways:

✓ **You are an equal partner in your child's education**—your insights and input must be taken seriously.

✓ **A strong support team** includes both school staff and external professionals who prioritize your child's success.

✓ **Effective advocacy requires knowledge**, preparation, and persistence—not perfection.

✓ **Good communication is proactive**, respectful, and documented. If it is not working, try changing the strategy or the team.

✓ **You do not need to tolerate dismissiveness or delay**. If collaboration fails, escalate appropriately and bring in reinforcements.

✓ **Relationships matter, but results matter more**. A positive tone is helpful—but it should not come at the cost of progress.

➡ **Pro Parent Move:** If a team member consistently dismisses concerns or delays action, do not just "hope it improves." Address the issue directly, document your efforts, and take steps to protect your child's access to support.

Closing Thoughts

You do not need to be everything for everyone—you just need to be unwavering for your child. The most effective advocates are not the loudest or most confrontational. They are the ones who build strong teams, ask the right questions, and refuse to back down when the stakes are high.

When you surround yourself with the right people, advocacy becomes more than a burden—it becomes a shared mission. And your child deserves nothing less.

CHAPTER 6:
Navigating The School System

Navigating special education is like learning a new language while simultaneously playing a never-ending game of chess—except the rules keep changing, and sometimes, no one tells you.

The good news? You do not have to play blindly. Understanding your rights, the school district's responsibilities, and how to handle conflicts will help you advocate strategically and ensure your child gets the support they need.

This chapter will break down your legal rights, what schools are required to provide, and how to handle conflicts when things do not go as planned.

A. Understanding Your Rights As A Parent

The law is on your side—but only if you know how to use it. Schools are required to provide an explanation of your rights, but that does not mean they will make them easy to understand. And, unfortunately, some may even downplay or "misinterpret" them. The more informed you are, the harder it is for the system to dismiss your concerns. Knowledge is power—use it.

Knowing your rights helps you ask better questions, push back when needed, and ensure that decisions are being made based on what is legally required, not just what is convenient for the school.

Key Rights Under IDEA

The Individuals with Disabilities Education Act (IDEA) guarantees several legal protections for students with disabilities and their families. Understanding these rights ensures that parents can advocate effectively and hold schools accountable.

The Right To A Free Appropriate Public Education (FAPE)

Your child is entitled to educational services tailored to their unique needs—at no cost to you.

- Your child has the right to an education that is appropriate to their unique needs—not just access to a general program. This includes special education services, related therapies, behavioral supports, and transition planning.

- FAPE must be provided at no cost to you, even if services are expensive or inconvenient for the school. Schools cannot deny services simply because they are expensive, inconvenient, or unavailable.

- FAPE includes more than academics—it also covers behavioral, social, and emotional supports components as needed.

- If the school cannot meet your child's needs, they may be required to fund additional services, private services, or even out-of-district placements.

The Right To Parental Participation

Parents are equal members of their child's IEP team and have the right to meaningfully participate in all decisions.

- You have the right to attend all IEP meetings, provide input, and challenge decisions. You are a legally required member of your child's IEP team—not an optional attendee.

- You have the right to participate in all decisions related to evaluations, eligibility, services, and placement. Schools must consider your input—this is a legal obligation, not just a courtesy.

- Meetings must be scheduled at a mutually agreed-upon time, and schools must attempt to include you—even if they are in a hurry. On the other hand, demanding an IEP meeting only be held outside of school hours is also not reasonable.

The Right To Request Evaluations

If you suspect your child has a disability, you have the right to request a formal evaluation at no cost.

- You do not have to wait for the school to suggest it—parents can initiate the evaluation process at any time.

- You are not required to wait for RTI (Response to Intervention) to play out—see *Chapter 3: Identifying your Child's Needs* for more on RTI.

- If you disagree with the school's evaluation, you can request an Independent Educational Evaluation (IEE) at public expense.

The Right To Prior Written Notice (PWN)

Schools must provide you with written notice before making any changes to your child's IEP, placement, or services. This is called Prior Written Notice (PWN)—and it is not optional. PWN must include a clear explanation of:

- What is being proposed (or refused);

- Why the decision was made; and

- What data was considered in making the decision?

These decisions are typically discussed during an IEP meeting, but nothing can be changed until you receive the PWN. Even if you have already had the meeting, written notice must still be provided before the school can act.

If the school denies your request, the PWN must include specific data and rationale—not just a blanket "no." It should also explain what alternatives were considered and why they were rejected.

➡ **Pro Parent Move:** If a decision is made verbally, follow up in writing: "Please send a Prior Written Notice documenting the team's decision, the data used, and the options that were considered."

The Right To Disagree (And Be Heard)

If you disagree with any decision, you can pursue multiple dispute resolution options:

- **Mediation** – A neutral third party helps parents and schools negotiate a resolution. It is voluntary but can be effective when communication has broken down.

- **Due Process Hearings** – A formal legal proceeding where both sides present evidence before an impartial hearing officer. This is typically used for major disagreements involving FAPE or placement.

- **State Complaints** – If a school violates special education law (e.g., fails to implement the IEP), you can file a complaint with your state's Department of Education. The state must investigate and issue a written decision.

- **OCR Complaint** – If the issue involves discrimination (e.g., denial of services based on disability), you can file a complaint with the Office for Civil Rights (OCR). This is especially helpful if your child is protected under Section 504 and not receiving equal access to education.

➥ **Pro Parent Move:** You do not have to pick just one option. For example, you can file a state complaint and request mediation at the same time—depending on the issues. The key is choosing the tool that best fits the problem.

If the school uses vague or confusing language—and avoids giving a clear yes or no—ask for clarification. These questions help cut through the fog:

- "Can you provide that in writing?"

- "What data supports that decision?"

- "What alternatives were considered, and why were they rejected?"

↯ Knowing your rights ensures that decisions are based on law—not school convenience.

When To Push, And When To Pause

You are not required to accept any service, placement, or decision that you do not agree with. But you also do not have to fight every battle.

Ask yourself:

- Is this a preference or a legal issue?

- Is this a short-term challenge or a long-term pattern?

- Can this be resolved through collaboration, or do I need to escalate?

◉ **When in doubt, write it down.** When they deny something, ask for it in writing. When they promise something, ask for a timeline. Paper trails are power.

B. What Districts Are Responsible For

School districts must follow IDEA and ensure students receive services—but how they interpret the law varies wildly.

✱ **Pro Parent Tip:** Not all districts are created equal. Some are collaborative and proactive. Others? Experts in delay, deflection, and doing the absolute minimum. So how can you tell the difference? Watch how they respond when you ask questions, request evaluations, or push for services. A district working in good faith will engage, explain, and follow timelines. A district playing defense will stall, confuse, or overwhelm you with jargon. Pay attention early—because their patterns speak louder than their promises.

Conducting Evaluations & Determining Eligibility

Schools are legally required under IDEA to identify, locate, and evaluate all students suspected of having a disability (this is known as "Child Find"). When a parent or school suspects a disability, they must conduct a **comprehensive evaluation**—not a narrow snapshot.

Evaluations must:

- Be timely, individualized, and free of bias

- Use multiple data sources: testing, teacher reports, observations, and parent input

- Cover all suspected areas of need, including academics, communication, behavior, sensory, and emotional functioning

✦ **Common Pitfall:** Some schools will deny eligibility because the student has high grades or is "doing fine academically." This is legally flawed. IDEA defines education broadly—including social, emotional, and behavioral functioning. If your child needs **specialized instruction** to make progress, they qualify.

➡ **Pro Parent Move:** If the school's evaluation feels off, incomplete, or does not match what you see at home—request an **Independent Educational Evaluation (IEE)** at the district's expense. You are legally entitled to one if you disagree with their evaluation.

→ **Use checklists (Appendices II & III)** and your state's timeline laws to stay on track. And remember: the goal is not just eligibility—it is an accurate understanding of your child's needs so the right services can follow.

Providing Special Education & Related Services

Schools are required to develop and implement an Individualized Education Program (IEP) tailored to each child's unique needs. The IEP must include special education and related services that are necessary for the student to access a Free Appropriate Public Education (FAPE). These can include:

Specialized Instruction

Tailored academic support based on the student's learning profile. This instruction is often delivered in small groups or one-on-one and focuses on helping the student meet IEP goals.

Related Services

Such as speech therapy, occupational therapy, physical therapy, or counseling, provided when needed to support access to the curriculum and overall educational success.

Accommodations and Modifications

Changes to how a student learns (accommodations) or what they are expected to learn (modifications). Accommodations level the playing field—like extended time, preferential seating, or assistive technology—while modifications adjust expectations, such as reducing the number of homework problems or using simplified texts.

Behavioral Supports

For students who need help with emotional regulation, executive functioning, or behavior management in the school setting. Supports might include behavior intervention plans (BIPs), check-in/check-out systems, or access to a quiet space to de-escalate.

✱ **Pro Parent Tip:** Not every IEP includes every related service—services must be based on your child's individual needs, not a checklist. If you believe a service is needed, request that it be assessed and considered.

Ensuring Placement In The Least Restrictive Environment (LRE)

Under the IDEA, students with disabilities have the right to be educated in the Least Restrictive Environment (LRE)—meaning they should be placed with their nondisabled peers as much as possible while still receiving the necessary support to succeed. What This Means:

- General education should be the default. Schools must exhaust all possible supports (such as co-teaching, in-class accommodations, or pull-out services) before considering a more restrictive setting.

- Separate classrooms and restrictive settings require clear justification. If the school proposes a self-contained class or alternative placement, they must show why the general education setting would not work even with supports in place.

- Placement decisions must be individualized. Schools cannot automatically place a student in a restrictive setting just because they have a specific disability or because it is the school's usual practice.

➡ **Pro Parent Move:** If the school suggests a more restrictive placement, ask:

- "What additional supports have been tried in the general education setting?"

- "What data supports the need for this change?"

- "Can we try additional interventions before considering a more restrictive setting?"

Funding And Resource Allocation

Schools cannot deny or reduce services based on budget constraints—if a service is in the IEP, they must provide it. Lack of funding is not an excuse to deny a child the support they are legally entitled to under FAPE (Free Appropriate Public Education). What This Means:

- **Schools must prioritize student needs over budget limitations.** If an IEP team determines that a student needs a service, accommodation, or assistive technology, the school is legally obligated to provide it—regardless of cost.

- **"We don't offer that here" is not an acceptable answer.** If a school lacks a required service (such as speech therapy, behavior interventionists, or specialized instruction), they must contract with an outside provider or find another solution.

- **Parents have the right to challenge resource-based denials.** If a school refuses to provide services due to funding, parents can request Prior Written Notice (PWN), file a state complaint, or escalate through due process.

➡ **Pro Parent Move:** If a school denies services due to budget concerns, ask:

- "Can you provide written documentation explaining why this service is not being provided?"

- "What alternatives has the district explored to ensure my child receives the support they need?"

- "What steps are being taken to address this lack of resources?"

What You Can Do: Look Into Past Disputes

If your district has a history of denying services, you are not alone. Many parents before you have likely faced similar battles—and some may have already challenged these denials in due process hearings. How to Use This to Your Advantage:

- **Research past due process cases in your state.** Some states maintain public records of special education disputes, which can provide insight into how your district handles service denials.

- **Connect with advocacy groups or parent networks.** Local special education groups often track trends in school districts and may have strategies or legal resources to help.

- **Leverage legal precedent.** If a past ruling forced your district to provide certain services, you could use that information in your advocacy.

➡ **Pro Parent Move:** If the district denies a service, check if a similar case has been ruled on in your state—having a legal precedent to reference can strengthen your position.

C. How To Handle Conflicts With Schools

Even with the best intentions, conflicts happen. Schools may refuse services, delay evaluations, or underplay your child's needs. Knowing how to advocate and escalate disputes effectively can make all the difference.

When Things Go Off Track

Even with the best intentions, conflicts between families and schools happen. Services get denied, evaluations are delayed, or needs are underestimated. When that happens, here is a clear, strategic path for getting things back on track—with the right balance of diplomacy and pressure.

1. Start Informally—But Be Strategic

- Begin with a conversation with your child's teacher or case manager.
- If needed, request an IEP meeting to formally discuss concerns.
- Keep communication professional and solution focused.
- Always document the interaction—send a follow-up email summarizing what was discussed.

✱ **Pro Parent Tip:** If the school says, "We'll look into it," ask, "By when?" Then follow up in writing. Ambiguity is not your friend.

2. Elevate the Concern

- If the issue is not resolved, escalate to the school principal or special education director.

- Put concerns in writing—email beats hallway conversation every time.
- Ask for a timeline and follow up persistently.

✳ **Pro Parent Tip:** Be polite, but firm. The squeaky wheel moves the IEP.

3. Ask for a Prior Written Notice (PWN)

- If the school denies a request (e.g., service, support, evaluation), formally request a Prior Written Notice.
- This legally required document must explain what the school is refusing, why, and what data they used to decide.

✳ **Pro Parent Tip:** Asking for PWN signals you know your rights—and schools take that seriously.

4. Try Mediation

- If conversations are going nowhere, request IDEA mediation—a free, voluntary process with a neutral facilitator.
- You can try mediation before or instead of filing a complaint or due process hearing.
- Any agreement reached in mediation is legally binding.

✳ **Pro Parent Tip:** Many districts are more flexible in mediation than they are in meetings. It is often where real movement happens.

5. File a Complaint or Request a Hearing

- **State Complaint:** Report violations of IDEA to your state education agency.
- **Due Process Hearing:** A legal proceeding where both parties present evidence before an administrative law judge.

- **OCR Complaint:** If discrimination is involved, consider filing with the Office for Civil Rights.

* Pro Parent Tip: Some schools do not start listening until you lawyer up. Sad but true.

Understanding Your District's Track Record

- Some districts have a reputation for fighting families. Do your homework.
- Many states have public databases of past due process decisions—see how your district handles disputes.
- This helps you prepare strategically and anticipate the school's likely moves.

* Advocacy Tips for Navigating Conflict

- Stay calm, firm, and relentlessly focused on your child's needs.
- Put everything in writing—verbal promises mean nothing.
- Ask for data to justify decisions. If the school says "no," ask for it in writing.
- Know your rights, your options, and your thresholds. You do not have to accept "no" as the final answer.

* Pro Parent Tip: The school may not always be right—but they are hoping you do not know that.

⚡ When Public School Is Not Working:
Exploring Private Placement, Unilateral Placement, and Homeschooling

There may come a point where you realize the public school system is not going to meet your child's needs—at least not in a way that is timely or appropriate. In those moments, you might consider removing your child and finding an alternative. That is your right as a parent. You may always choose to privately educate your child. But depending on the path you take, the legal and financial implications can be quite different.

Let's break down your options.

◇ *Private Placement (Parent-Paid)*

You always have the right to remove your child from public school and place them in a private school. You do not need the district's permission, and you do not need to file anything formal (though you usually need to inform the school). This is true whether your child has a disability or not.

If you go this route, you assume full financial responsibility. The school district does not pay for tuition, and it has no legal obligation to provide services once your child is enrolled in a private setting.

Some families choose this path simply because they want something different or better for their child. That is entirely valid—but you should understand that you are voluntarily walking away from public supports.

◆ Unilateral Placement (Parent Pays First, Seeks Reimbursement)

This is where things get legally complex—and financially risky.

If your child is eligible for special education and the school has failed to offer a Free Appropriate Public Education (FAPE), you may have the right under the IDEA to remove your child from public school, place them in a private setting, and seek reimbursement from the district. This is called a **unilateral placement**.

> ✦ **Note:** The private school does not have to be a special education school, but it must meet your child's special education needs.

Here is the key: **you must follow very specific legal procedures to preserve your right to reimbursement**. That includes:

- **Providing written notice** to the school district—typically at least **10 business days before** you withdraw your child.
- **Demonstrating that the district's proposed placement or IEP was inappropriate.** This is not about your opinion—or even what seems like compelling evidence to you. It is about what an attorney can prove to a hearing officer under IDEA standards. That is why having an attorney involved from the very beginning is non-negotiable.
- **Proving that the private school is appropriate** for your child's needs. Again, this is not about how well your child is doing. It is about what the courts have previously found acceptable and what can be documented and defended in a hearing.
- **Participating in the IEP process in good faith.** Even if you plan to reject the school's proposal, you still need to engage, collaborate, and exhaust reasonable options.

If you miss **any one of these steps**, you may not be entitled to reimbursement—even if the public school failed miserably and your child is now thriving in the private school.

✦ **Important**: Reimbursement is **never automatic**. The school district can—and often will—challenge your unilateral placement in a due process hearing. You will need to prove both the school's failure and the private school's appropriateness. Most cases settle, with the district covering part of the cost and the parents covering the rest. **You should never assume you will get full reimbursement—or reimbursement at all.**

✦ **Do not do this on your own.** If you are considering a unilateral placement, you need a special education attorney guiding you from day one. Mistakes—even small ones—can cost you tens of thousands of dollars and permanently shut the door on reimbursement.

◇ Homeschooling or Home-Based Programs

Homeschooling is a fundamentally different path. Once you officially withdraw your child to homeschool, the public school district is generally **no longer obligated** to provide special education—or any other—services. At that point, **you are fully responsible** for your child's education.

Each state has different laws about homeschooling. Some require you to:

- File an intent to homeschool.
- Submit a curriculum plan.
- Provide annual assessments or portfolios.

You must follow your state's rules—but beyond that, the district is typically out of the picture.

◆ What About Home-Based "Placements"?

That said, some families consider **home-based educational programs** as a workaround when they cannot afford a private special education school. These families piece together a program using private services—tutors, therapists, online curricula—with the hope of later seeking reimbursement from the district.

This is a **high-risk legal maneuver**.

> ⚡ **Do not attempt this without legal counsel.**
> If your goal is to preserve your legal rights or pursue reimbursement, you will need **precise legal guidance** from start to finish.

You can construct your own unilateral placement—but it must:

- **Meet IDEA standards**
- **Document how it addresses your child's specific special education needs**
- **Be implemented alongside all required procedural safeguards**

If your goal is simply to homeschool, that is your right—and you do not need the district's involvement.

But if your goal is to eventually ask the district to pay for what you are doing, you must treat it like any other legal placement. That means consulting an attorney, documenting everything, and being prepared to defend the appropriateness of your program in a hearing.

➤ Bottom Line

You have options. But each comes with trade-offs. If you are pulling your child out of public school for any reason tied to unmet special education needs, assume you are walking into a legal and financial decision. That is not a reason to avoid it—it is a reason to plan it carefully and with the right team beside you.

Final Thoughts: Holding The System Accountable

Navigating the school system can feel like trying to decode a secret language with shifting rules—and foggy transparency. But once you understand your rights, the school's responsibilities, and how to respond when things go sideways, you stop playing defense and start leading the conversation.

The law is your shield. Your voice is your power. The more informed you are, the harder it becomes for anyone to sideline your child's needs or sidestep their legal obligations. You do not need to know every acronym or memorize every regulation—you just need to ask sharp questions, document everything, and advocate from a place of clarity.

Conflict does not mean you have failed. It just means you are advocating in a system that often resists change. So, when things get hard—and they will—do not doubt yourself. Step back, get support, and return smarter and stronger.

Key Takeaways:

✓ **Your rights under IDEA are legally protected**—know them and use them.

✓ **FAPE means access to meaningful education**, not just presence in a classroom.

✓ **The school cannot deny services due to cost** or convenience.

✓ **Always follow up in writing**—paper trails matter.

✓ **If the school says no, ask for Prior Written Notice (PWN).**

✓ **You have multiple paths to resolve conflict:** mediation, complaints, due process.

✓ **The smartest advocacy is strategic.** Not every fight needs to escalate.

✓ **Do not go it alone**—advocates, attorneys, and parent groups can shift the power dynamic.

◉ **When in doubt, ask yourself:** Is this decision based on what is best for my child—or what is easiest for the school?

Closing Thoughts

You did not choose this path, but now that you are on it, you get to walk it with power. Taking charge does not mean knowing everything—it means showing up, staying curious, and refusing to be silenced. The system may be slow to change, but parents like you are the reason it does change.

Keep going. You are not just navigating the process—you are reshaping it.

CHAPTER 7:
Accommodations, Modifications, & Related Services

Navigating school can feel like running an obstacle course for students with disabilities—but accommodations, modifications, and related services exist to remove unnecessary barriers. These supports do not change what a student is expected to learn, but they adjust how they access information, demonstrate knowledge, or engage in the learning process, and remove unnecessary barriers to provide access to a meaningful education.

These supports help students learn, participate, and make progress—without watering down expectations unnecessarily or pushing unrealistic goals. This chapter will walk you through what each type of support means, how they differ, how to request them, and how to ensure they are implemented effectively.

A. Types Of Accommodations

Accommodations are designed to level the playing field—not lower expectations. They ensure students with disabilities have the same opportunity to learn as their peers by modifying how information is delivered or how a student responds, while still maintaining academic rigor. Accommodations fall into five key categories:

1. Presentation Accommodations (How Information Is Provided)

These accommodations change the way material is presented so students can process and understand it more effectively.

- **Audiobooks or Text-to-Speech Software** – Helps students with dyslexia or reading difficulties access content.

- **Visual Schedules and Graphic Organizers** – Beneficial for students who need structure, including those with ADHD or autism.

- **Large Print or Braille Materials** – Supports students with visual impairments.

- **Closed Captioning or ASL Interpreters** – Helps students with hearing impairments access classroom discussions and videos.

2. Response Accommodations (How Students Show What They Know)

Some students struggle with traditional ways of demonstrating knowledge, so these accommodations allow for alternative methods of response.

- **Speech-to-Text Software** – Supports students who struggle with writing or fine motor skills.

- **Use of a Calculator or Multiplication Charts** – Helps students with dyscalculia or math processing issues.

- **Alternative Response Formats** – Allows students to give verbal responses instead of written answers or use multiple-choice instead of essay responses.

- **Typing Instead of Handwriting** – Useful for students with dysgraphia or motor skill difficulties.

3. Setting Accommodations (Where And How Learning Occurs)

For some students, the learning environment itself creates challenges. These accommodations modify where or how instruction happens.

- **Quiet Testing Locations** – Helps students with attention issues, anxiety, or sensory sensitivities focus.

- **Flexible Seating Options** – May include standing desks, wobble stools, sensory cushions, tactile strips, or discreet fidget alternatives like textured pencil grips.

- **Noise-Canceling Headphones** – Reduces distractions for students sensitive to auditory input.

- **Small Group Instruction or One-on-One Support** – Provides a lower-stimulation environment for students who struggle in large classroom settings.

4. Timing & Scheduling Accommodations (Adjustments To Time Constraints)

Some students need extra time to process information or frequent breaks to maintain focus.

- **Extended Time on Tests & Assignments** – Supports students who need more time to process, organize, or physically write answers.

- **Frequent Breaks** – Helps students with ADHD, anxiety, or executive functioning challenges maintain focus.

- **Chunking Assignments into Smaller Steps** – Reduces overwhelm for students who struggle with planning and organization.

- **Testing Over Multiple Days** – Prevents fatigue and cognitive overload, particularly for students with processing disorders or anxiety.

5. Assistive Technology Accommodations (Tools & Devices That Support Learning)

Technology can bridge gaps for students with physical, language, or cognitive challenges.

- **Communication Devices** – Supports nonverbal students or those with speech impairments.

- **Speech-Generating Apps** – Helps students with language disorders express themselves.

- **Eye-Gaze or Switch-Access Tools** – Assists students with mobility impairments in interacting with digital content.

- **Voice Recognition Software** – Helps students who struggle with writing or fine motor skills.

Beyond The Basics: Additional Accommodations That Matter

Some accommodations extend beyond the classroom and into related services that impact a student's ability to learn.

- **Transportation Accommodations** – Includes wheelchair-accessible buses and behavioral support during transit.

- **School Health Services** – Supports students with medical conditions like diabetes or seizures.

- **Rehabilitation Counseling** – Prepares older students for employment, independent living, or vocational training.

B. Understanding Modifications

Changing the Task—Not Just the Tools

Modifications change what the student is expected to learn. They are more intensive than accommodations and may adjust curriculum standards, assignment complexity, or grading expectations.

While modifications are sometimes necessary, they can impact diploma options, standardized testing, and long-term academic goals—so they should be discussed carefully.

➜ Example: When a Modification Might Be Appropriate

Scenario: A 10th-grade student with a cognitive disability is reading at a 3rd-grade level. The class is assigned Of Mice and Men.

Modification: The student reads a simplified adaptation of the novel and completes a basic comprehension worksheet instead of a literary analysis essay.

Why it fits: The goal is access to content—not mastery of complex literary analysis. If the team agrees this aligns with the student's IEP goals and long-term plan, it is a valid modification.

Caution: This should be clearly documented in the IEP and reviewed annually. The team should regularly assess whether the student can move back toward grade-level expectations.

Common Modifications Include:

- Different homework problems at the student's level
- Alternate grading scales (pass/fail)
- Simplified reading materials
- Alternate assignments (e.g., poster instead of essay)

✳ Pro Parent Tip: If modifications are proposed, ask:

- Will this impact graduation or college readiness?
- Can accommodations meet the need instead?
- Is this being offered out of necessity—or convenience?

✦ Impact Of Modifications On Graduation

Some modifications—especially those that lower academic expectations—can disqualify students from earning a standard diploma. Instead, students may be placed on an "alternate assessment track," limiting options for college or competitive employment later.

✳ Pro Parent Tip: Always ask -

- "Will this modification affect graduation requirements?"

- "Can we document that this is a temporary support rather than a permanent change to expectations?"

Document the answers. Push for accommodations first whenever possible before agreeing to significant modifications.

C. Related Services—The Backbone Of Support

Related services are not perks—they are essential supports that allow your child to access and benefit from their education. Under IDEA, related services are provided when necessary to help a student meet their IEP goals. Think of them as the gears that keep the IEP running—quietly working behind the scenes to remove barriers and build confidence.

Common Related Services You Should Know

Speech Therapy

Supports speaking clearly, understanding language, and social communication.

Ask:

→ "Will therapy target both academics and social skills?"
→ "How will progress beyond testing be measured?"

Occupational Therapy (OT)

Builds fine motor skills, sensory regulation, and everyday independence.

Ask:

→ "Will strategies be used inside the classroom too?"
→ "Are teachers and aides trained to reinforce OT techniques?"

Physical Therapy (PT)

Improves balance, posture, strength, and safe movement around school.

Ask:

→ "Will skills be tied to real school activities (e.g., playground, stairs)?"
→ "Is progress tracked in both therapy and school settings?"

Counseling Services

Teaches coping, emotional regulation, and resilience for school success.

Ask:

→ "Will counseling focus on proactive skills, not just reacting to problems?"
→ "How are strategies reinforced across classrooms?"

Social Skills Instruction

Provides direct teaching of friendship skills, peer interaction, and group behavior.

Ask:

→ "Will skills be explicitly taught, not just supervised?"
→ "Will practice happen during real school activities?"
Behavior Intervention Services

Real-time support to build coping, regulation, and problem-solving—not just reacting after problems.

Ask:

→ "Will my child get in-the-moment coaching?"
→ "How will success be tracked beyond discipline data?"

Parent Counseling and Training

Equips parents with tools to reinforce IEP goals at home.

Ask:

→ "Will strategies be modeled, not just explained?"
→ "Can we customize strategies for home life?"

Transportation Services

Provides safe, accessible transportation with necessary supports.

Ask:

→ "What safety supports will be in place?"
→ "Are bus staff trained on my child's needs?"

Beyond The Basics

IDEA allows for a range of lesser known but powerful supports:

- **Assistive Technology Services** – Tools like speech-to-text software or communication devices.

- **Interpreting Services** – Support for students who are deaf or hard of hearing.

- **Rehabilitation Counseling** – Prepares students for independent living or employment.

- **Recreation Therapy** – Uses structured play to build social and physical skills.

- **School Health Services** – Supports medical needs, such as medication, seizure plans, or diabetes management.

➡ **Pro Parent Move:** If your child needs help beyond academics, ask, "What related services are available to address social, emotional, or behavioral goals?"

Advocacy Tips For Related Services

★ **Demand Specificity:** The IEP must clearly state the type, frequency, duration, location, and provider for every service. For example, "OT, 30 minutes/week in a 1:1 setting outside the classroom."

★ **Question Exclusions:** If something was discussed but left out, ask for an explanation—and request it in writing. For example, "Given my child's sensory needs, why isn't OT part of the support plan?"

★ **Think Outside the Box:** Related services extend beyond just speech or OT. Consider behavior support, family training, assistive tech, or counseling.

★ **Push for Integration:** Ask how related services will align with academic goals—not pull your child away from learning.

★ **Monitor Implementation:** A service written into the IEP does not help if it is not delivered. Check logs, ask questions, and track consistency.

▶ *Propose A Trial Period*

If the team hesitates to approve a new support, propose a time-limited trial:

➡ **Example:** "Let's implement this accommodation for 6 weeks and then review the data together." This keeps momentum moving without locking the school (or your child) into something long-term before evidence shows if it is helping.

➡ **Pro Parent Move:** Put the trial terms in the IEP—timeline, how success will be measured, and next steps after the trial.

Related services are lifelines, not luxuries. They remove obstacles, foster independence, and help your child thrive—not just academically, but emotionally, socially, and physically.

Stay informed. Ask questions. Advocate for what your child needs—and follow up to ensure it is delivered.

Accommodation Or Related Service? Understanding The Overlap

Some supports—like assistive technology, counseling, or transportation—can fall under either accommodations or related services, depending on how and why they are provided.

If it is just a classroom adjustment, it may be an accommodation.

If a specialist delivers it to support progress on IEP goals, it is likely a related service.

* Pro Parent Tip: If you are not sure which category something falls into, ask, "Is this an accommodation provided by the teacher, or a related service that requires support from a specialist?"

▶ Common Pitfalls To Watch For

Even with a strong IEP, implementation can fall short. Watch for these red flags:

- Accommodations listed in the IEP are not being used consistently in the classroom.

- Related services are scheduled "as needed" without specific time or frequency (this weakens accountability).

- Schools are substituting one support for another without team discussion (e.g., giving extra homework help instead of providing reading intervention).

- "One-size-fits-all" accommodations that are not tailored to your child's needs.

➡ **Pro Parent Move:** If you spot these issues, request a written clarification or an immediate IEP review meeting. Specificity protects your child.

Final Thoughts: The Right Supports At The Right Time

Accommodations, modifications, and related services are not favors or extras—they are essential tools that give your child access to learning. The goal is not to lower expectations or over-accommodate, but to ensure your child can fully engage with the curriculum, demonstrate what they know, and make meaningful progress.

Each Support Plays A Different Role:

- **Accommodations** level the playing field without changing what your child is expected to learn.

- **Modifications** adjust the expectations themselves, which may be necessary but should be used thoughtfully and with clear long-term goals in mind.

- **Related services** provide the foundational supports—such as speech, OT, counseling, and more—that make learning possible in the first place.

The right combination of supports can open doors your child did not even know were closed.

Your job is not to be an expert in every service. Your job is to be the person who keeps asking the right questions, notices when something is off, and keeps showing up until the plan actually works.

Key Takeaways:

✓ **Support must match need.** Accommodations and services should be tailored—not generic. If the support does not reflect your child's specific profile, it will likely not be effective.

✓ **Document everything.** If it is not written in the IEP or 504 Plan, it is not guaranteed. Get it in writing.

✓ **Ask the category question.** If you are unsure whether something should be an accommodation, modification, or related service, ask: "Is this a classroom support, or does it require a specialist?"

✓ **Review and adjust regularly.** The support that worked last year might not work this year. Your child's needs will evolve—so should their plan.

✓ **Push for integration.** Related services and accommodations should not be siloed. Ask how supports align with academic goals and classroom instruction.

✓ **Know the impact of modifications.** Be clear on how they affect academic tracks, diploma eligibility, and long-term goals. Do not accept them automatically—understand the tradeoffs.

✓ **Monitor delivery.** Services and supports listed in an IEP are legal obligations—but they only matter if they are actually provided. Check logs, follow up, and speak up when something falls through.

➥ **Pro Parent Move:** Do not wait for someone else to notice that a support is not working. You are often the first— and sometimes the only one—connecting the dots.

Speak up early, document everything, and remember—you are not asking for special treatment. You are asking for access. And your child is entitled to that.

CHAPTER 8:
Transition Planning

Planning, Pathways, And Lifelong Supports

Transition is not a finish line—it is the beginning of the rest of your child's life.

The shift from the structured world of special education to the open-ended maze of adulthood can feel overwhelming. After years of navigating IEPs, 504 Plans, support services, and familiar school environments, many parents find themselves asking: What happens next?

The good news? With early planning, a strong support network, and continued advocacy, students with disabilities can build fulfilling, independent lives.

The reality? This transition does not happen overnight—and it does not come with the same built-in protections you have relied on. Once the school bus stops coming, families often face a patchwork of adult services, long waitlists, and fewer legal safeguards.

That is why long-term planning is essential.

Transition planning is not just about what comes next—it is about equipping students with the skills, resources, and confidence to step into adulthood with purpose. Whether their future includes college, vocational training, employment, or independent living, a well-developed transition plan ensures they have the guidance and support they need.

This chapter will show you how to build that roadmap—from transition assessments to life skills, from postsecondary goals to lifelong support networks. Because a strong IEP is just the beginning.

A. Importance Of Early Planning

Transition planning is a federally mandated part of the IEP process—but you should not wait until the last minute. Under IDEA (Individuals with Disabilities Education Act), transition services must begin no later than age 16. However, some state laws mandate starting by age 14, giving students more time to develop skills, explore career options, and prepare for adulthood.

That said, you can begin even earlier if it makes sense for your child. The earlier the planning begins, the more opportunities your child has to build independence gradually, at their own pace.

The most effective transition plans are not written for students; they are built with students. Even before formal transition planning starts, students should be encouraged to dream, explore, and speak up about their goals.

The Framework of Transition Planning

A transition plan is not just a box to check—it is a personalized roadmap that should reflect a student's goals, strengths, and challenges while identifying the support they need to succeed.

Here is how the plan should take shape:

◇ *Post-Secondary Education Goals*

If a student is considering college, vocational training, or a certification program, the plan should focus on academic preparation, self-advocacy, and understanding available disability support services.

◇ Employment Goals

The plan should help students identify their interests and strengths, explore how they align with potential careers, and build the skills needed to find and keep a job. This includes learning how to search for employment, complete job applications, participate in interviews, and understand workplace expectations.

◇ Independent Living Goals

Students with deficits in daily living skills—regardless of where they plan to live—should receive instruction and support in areas like money management, personal care, transportation, healthcare, and self-advocacy. The goal is to build as much independence as possible, whether a student lives alone, with family, or in a supported environment.

Under IDEA §300.320(b), every student with an IEP must have measurable postsecondary goals based on age-appropriate transition assessments in the following areas:

- **Education or Training** – This includes college, vocational school, job training programs, adult education, or apprenticeships.

- **Employment** – This must be addressed separately from education. It is not enough to say "go to college and get a job"—each area must have its own goal.

- **Independent Living (when appropriate)** – Required only when a student's needs indicate it is necessary, but essential when relevant.

✱ **Pro Parent Tip:** If your child's IEP does not include measurable postsecondary goals for education or training and employment—and independent living skills, if needed—request an IEP meeting. Transition planning is not optional under federal law. It must be individualized, goal-driven, and based on your child's needs.

The Role Of The IEP In Transition Planning

A strong transition plan must be embedded into the IEP—and it should be highly individualized, not a generic, one-size-fits-all statement.

→ **Student Involvement:** Transition planning should be student-driven. What do they want for their future? What careers interest them? Their voice matters.

→ **Parent Collaboration:** Parents bring critical insight into their child's strengths, needs, and long-term goals. Your input helps shape both assessments and services. Do not wait to be asked—share your perspective early and often.

→ **Measurable Postsecondary Goals:** These must be clear, specific, and address all relevant areas—education or training, employment, and independent living (when appropriate).

→ **Required Services and Supports:** This may include job training, assistive technology, self-advocacy instruction, transportation planning, or any accommodation that helps a student move toward their goals.

→ **Summary of Performance (SOP):** Before graduation, the IEP team must provide a summary of the student's academic and functional performance, including recommendations for postsecondary education, work, and daily life.

✱ **Pro Parent Tip:** If transition planning has not been mentioned in your child's IEP meetings by age 16 (or earlier in some states), bring it up. It is not optional— federal law requires it. You have every right to ask, "What are we doing to help my child prepare for life after high school?"

B. Steps For Successful Transitions

A strong transition plan is not created overnight—it requires ongoing assessment, goal setting, skill-building, and collaboration with both school and community resources.

The steps that follow will walk you through the practical side of transition planning: how to evaluate your child's strengths, set meaningful goals, and build the skills needed for life after high school. Later in this chapter, we will also cover the adult systems, services, and legal tools that support this work long-term.

Step 1: Conduct Ongoing Assessments

Transition planning isn't guesswork—it is guided by meaningful, ongoing assessments. Under IDEA, schools are required to use both formal and informal evaluations to build a comprehensive picture of a student's strengths, preferences, and support needs. These assessments help ensure the plan is tailored to the student's goals—not based on assumptions or outdated information.

Key areas to assess include:

- **Strengths** – Academic and vocational talents, social skills, and problem-solving abilities

- **Preferences** – Interests, hobbies, and career aspirations

- **Support Needs** – Identifying areas where accommodations or services are necessary

If your child's school is not conducting formal transition assessments, request one in writing—it is required under IDEA.

Formal Assessments

Formal assessments are standardized tools that provide objective, quantifiable data. These results guide the IEP team in setting postsecondary goals and identifying services needed to achieve them. Examples include:

- **Adaptive Behavior Assessments:** Evaluate self-care, communication, and social functioning (e.g., Vineland, SIB-R).

- **Vocational Aptitude Tests:** Identify job-specific strengths and areas for growth (e.g., ASVAB, OASIS-III).

- **Achievement & Intelligence Tests:** Measure academic proficiency and cognitive ability (e.g., WISC-V, Woodcock-Johnson).

- **Interest Inventories & Work Values:** Help align transition plans with career preferences (e.g., Strong Interest Inventory, WRIOT-R).

- **Personality & Career Maturity Inventories:** Assess employability traits and career readiness (e.g., 16PF, Career Maturity Inventory).

✱ Pro Parent Tip: If your child's school has not conducted a formal transition evaluation, request one in writing. It is not optional—it is required by federal law.

Informal Assessments

Informal assessments help capture the student's lived experience and day-to-day skills. These tools are just as important for shaping realistic, student-centered goals. Common approaches include:

- **Student Interviews & Questionnaires:** Help identify preferences, strengths, and concerns directly from the student and family.

- **Direct Observation:** Evaluates how students perform tasks in real settings (e.g., work experience, classroom routines).

- **Situational/Environmental Analysis:** Compares job or activity environments with the student's skill set to identify needed supports or accommodations.

- **Curriculum-Based Assessments (CBAs):** Collect performance data through classroom tasks, portfolios, or functional skill checklists.

These tools reveal not just what your child can do—but what motivates them, what supports they truly need, and where they are most likely to thrive.

What Transition Assessments Should Cover

A well-rounded transition evaluation should explore:

- Academic and Functional Skills
- Vocational Abilities and Interests
- Social and Emotional Development
- Daily Living Skills
- Learning Styles and Career Preferences

Together, formal and informal assessments provide a roadmap for setting measurable postsecondary goals in education, employment, and, when appropriate, independent living. The team can then align services and supports to help your child achieve them.

◉ Step 2: Set SMART Goals (That Actually Teach Something)

As with all the other goals and objectives in your child's IEP, transition goals should be Specific, Measurable, Achievable, Relevant, and Time-Bound (SMART). Transition goals are often written like a to-do list:

✗ "The student will explore colleges."

✗ "The student will complete a work interest inventory."

That is not skill-building. That is assigning homework.

True SMART goals should help students develop the skills, independence, and confidence they will need in adulthood—not just check off boxes someone else hands them.

What SMART Really Means In Transition Planning

	Meaning	In Practice: Transition Example
S	Specific	What exact skill is being developed?
M	Measurable	Can you clearly track progress?
A	Achievable	Is it realistic and based on the student's current level?
R	Relevant	Does it help with postsecondary success?
T	Time-bound	Is there a clear deadline or review date?

Smart Goals and Objectives are Critical to Progress

↔ *The Key Shift: From "Tasks" To "Teach"*

Transition services are meant to prepare your child for life after high school—not just keep them busy during it. If the IEP goals sound like errands, it is time to speak up. Ask the team:

- "What skill is my child actually learning here?"

- "How will we know they have mastered it?"

- "What support will they need to build this skill independently?"

Step 3: Explore Career & Education Pathways

Whether your child is considering college, a training program, or jumping straight into the workforce, this step is about helping them explore real-world options and build the skills they will need to succeed after high school.

For students pursuing higher education or training programs:

- Research colleges, universities, trade schools, and technical programs that offer disability accommodations and academic support.

- Visit campuses and meet with disability services coordinators to better understand how support works after high school.

- Explore certification programs and apprenticeships in fields like automotive repair, culinary arts, cosmetology, IT, or healthcare.

- Identify programs that offer hands-on learning, flexible schedules (day, evening, or hybrid), and strong transition support.

- Ask if the program partners with community agencies or support services that help students with disabilities succeed.

For students preparing to enter the workforce:

Set up job shadowing, internships, or volunteer opportunities to build real-world experience and explore interests. Begin connecting with your state's Vocational Rehabilitation (VR) agency to help with:

- Resume writing
- Interview practice
- Workplace readiness and job coaching

➡ **Pro Parent Move:** These experiences can (and should!) be written into your child's IEP. Ask the team how your student's transition goals align with real-world exploration.

Rewrite The "To-Do" List Into Skill-Building Goals

SAMPLE GOAL: Postsecondary Education

✗ **Not SMART:** "The student will research colleges."

> ✓ **Better SMART Goal:** "By May, the student will identify three colleges that offer disability services and compare their support options using a self-created checklist."

Sample Objectives:

1. By [date], the student will research and summarize two key differences between college disability services and high school IEPs in a written or oral format, with 80% accuracy as measured by a teacher-created rubric.
2. By [date], the student will draft a professional email to a college disability services office requesting information about available accommodations, including an appropriate greeting, request, and closing, with 3 out of 4 elements present.

3. By [date], the student will complete a comparison chart of disability support offerings at three post-secondary campuses using a provided template, identifying at least 2 support features per campus.
4. By the next IEP meeting, the student will present their research on college disability services to the IEP team using visual aids (slides, checklist, or handout), demonstrating clear organization and verbal explanation in at least 3 of 4 presentation components.

★ Now we are building skills in research, comparison, organization, and self-advocacy.

SAMPLE GOAL: Vocational

✗ **Not SMART Goal:** "The student will get a job."

> ✓ **Better SMART Goal:** "By the end of the school year, the student will participate in two work-based learning experiences and complete a mock interview, demonstrating appropriate workplace communication skills in 3 out of 4 observed scenarios."

Sample Objectives:

- By October 30, the student will use a career interest inventory to identify and list at least three job interests and discuss the results with a staff member.

- By December 15, the student will complete a job application (either paper or online) with 90% accuracy in the required fields, using a sample or real form and with staff support.

- By March 15, the student will participate in one job shadow or volunteer opportunity and complete a reflection worksheet identifying at least two workplace behaviors observed (e.g., punctuality, dress code, communication).

- By May 1, the student will demonstrate appropriate interview behavior (e.g., greeting, answering questions clearly, eye contact) in 3 out of 4 observed criteria during a mock interview, as measured by a teacher-created rubric.

⭐ Now we are building skills in communication, self-advocacy, organization, and real-world planning—not just completing a checklist, but preparing the student to navigate life after high school with confidence.

Step 4: Build Independent Living Skills

Academics and career planning are essential, but if a student cannot manage daily life tasks, they will struggle with independence.

- **Financial Management:** Budgeting, banking, and understanding credit.

- **Daily Life Tasks:** Cooking, cleaning, and personal hygiene.

- **Transportation Skills:** Using public transit, rideshare apps, or obtaining a driver's license.

If the school is not providing training in these areas, request an IEP meeting to add them.

SAMPLE GOAL: Independent Living Skills

✗ **Not SMART Goal:** "The student will learn how to manage money."

> ✓ **Better SMART Goal:** "By the end of the school year, the student will follow a 3-step budgeting process to plan for a $200 monthly allowance, demonstrating the ability to track expenses and adjust spending in 3 of 4 trials."

Sample Objectives:

1. By March 15, the student will categorize at least 10 common expenses as either "needs" or "wants" using sample budgets, with 90% accuracy on a teacher-provided checklist.
2. By April 1, the student will enter a provided list of income and expenses into a digital budgeting app or worksheet with adult support, completing all required fields with 100% accuracy in 2 out of 3 trials.
3. By April 15, the student will revise a sample monthly budget based on adult feedback, making at least two specific changes (e.g., reducing discretionary spending or reallocating funds) with support in two out of three attempts.
4. By May 1, the student will write or verbally share a reflection identifying one specific spending habit and one strategy for saving money each month, across 3 separate weeks, with adult prompting as needed.

★ These objectives build concrete budgeting skills and support executive functioning, all while staying tied to real-world independence.

The final (and arguably most important) step? Teaching your child how to advocate for themselves. Without strong self-advocacy, even the best academic or vocational plans can fall apart in adulthood.

Build Self-Advocacy Skills

One of the most critical (and often overlooked) parts of transition planning is helping students become their own advocates. As they move beyond high school, the ability to understand their needs, know their rights, and clearly communicate with others becomes essential—not just for school success, but for employment, healthcare, independent living, and daily decision-making.

In high school, parents and teachers often do much of the advocating. But once a student enters adulthood, they become responsible for self-advocacy—

whether that is requesting disability accommodations at a college, asking a boss for needed supports at work, or navigating adult healthcare systems.

Teaching self-advocacy is not about letting go of support—it is about empowering students to recognize when they need help, understand how to ask for it appropriately, and know their legal protections under laws like the ADA (Americans with Disabilities Act) and Section 504.

✦ *Core Self-Advocacy Skills To Build:*

- Understanding their disability and how it impacts learning or work.
- Knowing which accommodations they use and why they matter.
- Practicing how to explain their needs respectfully and clearly.
- Learning how to problem-solve when challenges arise.
- Understanding basic disability rights and protections after high school (especially under the ADA and Section 504).

✱ Pro Parent Tip: Ask the IEP team, "How are we building self-advocacy skills into transition services?" Self-advocacy should be taught, modeled, and practiced—not left to chance.

SAMPLE GOAL: *Self-Advocacy*

✗ **Not a Strong Goal:** "The student will understand their accommodations."

> ✓ **Better SMART Goal:** "By May, the student will explain their IEP accommodations to two new adults (e.g., college disability services coordinator, workplace supervisor) using a prepared script, across 2 out of 3 role-play simulations, as measured by teacher observation."

◇ *Sample Skill-Building Objectives:*

- **By February**, the student will list at least three personal accommodations and describe how each supports their learning needs, with 90% accuracy during a guided discussion.

- **By March**, the student will practice requesting accommodations during two mock interviews, demonstrating clear explanation of needs in 3 out of 4 critical areas (eye contact, specific request, reference to documentation, appropriate closure).

- **By April**, the student will identify one potential challenge in postsecondary environments (e.g., large lecture classes, timed assignments) and create a self-advocacy plan to address it.

★ **Why This Matters:** Students who can clearly and confidently communicate their needs are far more likely to succeed in college, the workplace, and beyond. Self-advocacy is not just a nice skill—it is a survival tool for adulthood.

➡ **Pro Parent Move:** Role-play real-world situations at home. Practice how your child would request disability services at a college, ask for schedule adjustments at a job, or explain their needs to a healthcare provider. Familiarity builds confidence.

C. Tools For Transition Readiness

Transitioning into adulthood still requires the classic foundations—practical tools, support systems, and hands-on experience—but in today's post-COVID world, what students need to succeed has evolved.

The pandemic did not just disrupt learning—it changed how we work, communicate, and access opportunities. That means transition planning must now include virtual skills, emotional resilience, and real-world flexibility, in addition to job training and independent living.

Traditional Tools That Still Matter

These are the tried-and-true supports that continue to provide critical readiness:

- **Vocational Aptitude Tests (e.g., ASVAB, O*NET Interest Profiler):** Help students identify career interests, preferences, and work styles.

- **Independent Living Centers:** Offer training in budgeting, time management, cooking, transportation, and navigating adult systems.

- **College Disability Resource Centers:** Provide support with accommodations, assistive tech, and self-advocacy in higher education.

- **Transition Fairs & Workshops:** Local and state agencies often host free events where students and families can connect with programs, job training, and adult service providers.

➡ **Pro Parent Move:** Ask your IEP team about incorporating these tools directly into the student's transition goals or services.

New Skills To Consider In A Post-COVID World

COVID-19 did not just pause life—it reshaped it. Students now need to master hybrid skills that prepare them for a workforce, classroom, and world that may be in-person or online at any given moment.

Here is what that means in practice:

Digital Literacy

- Using technology (computers, mobile devices, apps) to access information, complete tasks, and navigate daily life.
- Understanding digital etiquette, online safety, and privacy basics.

Virtual Communication & Collaboration

- Participating in video calls, using chat and email appropriately, and collaborating on shared documents in real time.
- Practicing clear, respectful communication—even when not face-to-face.

Remote Learning & Working

- Managing time, completing tasks independently, and asking for help in a virtual environment.
- Using organizational tools like calendars, timers, and digital checklists.

Emotional Resilience & Flexibility

- Adapting to sudden changes (schedule shifts, hybrid work, evolving expectations).
- Managing anxiety, stress, or disappointment with healthy coping strategies.
- Reframing setbacks as learning opportunities—what went wrong, what to try next.
- Recognizing when to pause, ask for help, or change tactics without giving up.
- Practicing self-regulation skills (e.g., deep breathing, journaling, physical movement).

Self-Advocacy & Social Awareness

- Speaking up when needs are not being met—whether in class, at work, or in health settings.
- Setting and respecting boundaries, especially in shared digital or physical spaces.
- Learning to recognize red flags—signs you are being taken advantage of, dismissed, or manipulated.
- Building support networks by identifying trusted adults, mentors, or allies.
- Navigating power dynamics with confidence—whether emailing a professor, managing a conflict with a peer, or negotiating accommodations.

Health & Safety Awareness

- Following personal hygiene and public safety protocols in shared environments (e.g., workplaces, dorms, public transit).
- Advocating for accommodations in health-related contexts (e.g., mask breaks, safe distancing).

✱ **Pro Parent Tip:** Postsecondary readiness now includes power cords, passwords, and personal resilience. Do not forget to help students practice self-advocacy in hybrid spaces—like emailing a professor about accommodations or asking a supervisor for remote work flexibility.

Incorporating These Into The Transition Plan

These skills are not just "nice to have"—they are essential. And they can (and should) be woven into IEP goals and objectives.

→ **Examples:**

- "By March, the student will participate in a mock Zoom interview, using appropriate virtual etiquette and verbal responses in 3 out of 4 trials."

- "By the end of the semester, the student will use a digital calendar to manage assignments and deadlines for two classes with 80% accuracy."

✱ **Pro Parent Tip:** Consider asking your IEP team, "How are we preparing my child for success in both in-person and virtual environments?"

A truly effective transition plan does not just prepare students for the world we used to have—it prepares them for the world that exists now. When we teach students how to adapt, communicate virtually, stay safe, and manage change, we are not just helping them graduate—we are helping them thrive.

⚡ Transition Planning Red Flags

If you spot any of these issues, it is time to speak up—and fast. Transition planning is too important to leave to chance.

◇ *Transition Planning Is Delayed Until Senior Year*

Transition planning should begin no later than age 16 (or earlier, depending on your state). If your child's IEP team waits until senior year to discuss postsecondary goals or services, critical time for building skills and exploring options has already been lost.

→ **Pro Parent Move:** Ask at every IEP meeting starting in middle school, "What are we doing now to prepare for life after high school?"

◇ Goals Are Vague ("Student will explore jobs")

Vague transition goals are a major red flag. "Explore" is not a skill. A strong transition plan must focus on teaching specific, measurable skills that prepare students for education, employment, and independent living—not just exposing them to ideas.

➡ **Pro Parent Move:** Insist on SMART goals (Specific, Measurable, Achievable, Relevant, Time-bound) that build independence, not just check boxes.

◇ No Formal Transition Assessment Is Conducted

Federal law requires that transition planning be based on age-appropriate, measurable assessments. If no formal evaluation has been completed—or if the team is relying only on casual teacher observations—the transition plan is on shaky ground.

➡ **Pro Parent Move:** If no assessment has been offered, request a formal transition evaluation in writing immediately.

◇ Independent Living Skills Are Ignored, Even When Needed

Independent living skills—like money management, cooking, self-care, and using public transportation—are critical for many students' futures. If your child struggles in these areas but the IEP does not address them, important opportunities for building real-world readiness are being missed.

➡ **Pro Parent Move:** Bring up specific life skills at IEP meetings and ask how they will be assessed, taught, and measured.

◉ **Want even more?** For a downloadable, detailed breakdown of life skills by domain and age, check out resources from The Autism Life Skills Lady, who offers visual tools, IEP-ready templates, and family-centered strategies to support independent living.

◇ *The Student Is Not Involved In Discussions About Their Future*

Transition planning must be student-centered. If your child is not attending meetings, being interviewed, or having a say in goal-setting, the plan is incomplete—and probably not meaningful.

➡ **Pro Parent Move:** Encourage your child to participate, even if only for part of the meeting, and ask the team how they are helping your student build self-advocacy skills.

Final Thoughts: Preparing For A Future that Works

Transition planning is not a formality—it is a launchpad. It is how we prepare students for a future where they can thrive, not just survive.

And in today's post-COVID, post-IEP world, that means more than choosing a college or landing a job. It means learning how to:

- Navigate hybrid environments (in-person and virtual).
- Build digital fluency and emotional resilience.
- Manage daily life with independence and confidence.
- Access support systems that extend beyond high school.
- Adapt to change and advocate for their needs in real time.

The most effective transition plans are:

- Student-driven
- Grounded in real-world skills
- Supported by both school teams and community resources
- Future-focused and flexible

Key Takeaways:

✓ **Start early**—by age 16 or 14 (depending on your state), or even sooner if possible.

✓ **Use formal and informal assessments** to tailor the plan to your child's strengths and support needs.

✓ **Set SMART goals** in academics, employment, and independent living that focus on skill-building—not just checking boxes.

✓ **Incorporate post-COVID readiness**—like virtual communication, digital organization, and emotional resilience.

✓ **Connect with adult services early**, such as Vocational Rehab, disability resource centers, or independent living programs.

✓ **Center your child's voice in every step**—and help them build the self-advocacy skills they will need long after graduation.

⚡ Transition is not "extra paperwork."

It is the bridge to adulthood.

It is the difference between surviving and thriving in adulthood.

With the right plan and support, your child can move into adulthood prepared, confident, and in charge of their own life.

This is their future—do not let anyone treat it like a checkbox.

CHAPTER 9:
Behavioral Challenges – Understanding And Addressing Behavior In Schools

Behavior is communication. When a child struggles with emotional regulation, executive function, or social interaction, their behavior is often a signal of an unmet need—not just a "bad attitude" or an attempt to be difficult. Whether they are acting out due to frustration, sensory overload, anxiety, or task avoidance, the key to addressing these behaviors is understanding what is driving them rather than just reacting to the surface-level behavior.

Unfortunately, many schools still default to punishment instead of support, missing the opportunity to actually help the child learn better coping strategies. The good news? There are legal protections, evidence-based strategies, and advocacy tools that can help parents ensure schools handle behavioral challenges appropriately.

This chapter will break down Functional Behavioral Assessments (FBAs), Behavioral Intervention Plans (BIPs), and your child's legal rights regarding restraint and seclusion, so you can advocate effectively for solutions that work.

A. Functional Behavioral Assessments (FBAs): Decoding Behavior

What Is An FBA?

A Functional Behavioral Assessment (FBA) is a structured process used by schools to identify why a student is exhibiting challenging behavior. Instead of just punishing the behavior, the goal is to figure out what is triggering it and how to replace it with a more appropriate response.

Schools cannot effectively address behaviors if they do not first understand what drives them. That is where an FBA comes in.

What An FBA Entails

A high-quality FBA is not a quick checklist or casual observation, and it should definitely not be something created by AI. It is a data-driven, multi-step process that includes:

◇ **Direct Observations:** A trained professional (usually a school psychologist or behavior specialist) observes the student in different settings (classroom, lunchroom, playground) to identify patterns.

◇ **Data Collection:** Behavior rating scales, teacher reports, and incident tracking are used to measure how often the behavior happens, how intense it is, and what circumstances surround it.

◇ **The ABC Model (Antecedent-Behavior-Consequence):**

➤ **Antecedent:** What happens right before the behavior? (e.g., teacher gives an assignment)
➤ **Behavior:** What is the student doing? (e.g., yelling, leaving their seat)
➤ **Consequence:** What happens after the behavior? (e.g., teacher removes the task, reinforcing avoidance)

◇ **Input from Key Team Members:** Parents, teachers, specialists, and sometimes even the student provide insight into behaviors observed at school and at home.

◇ **Hypothesis Development:** Based on all the gathered information, the team determines what function the behavior serves—is the student trying to escape a task? Seeking attention? Managing anxiety? Responding to sensory overload?

Who Should Conduct The FBA?

An FBA should be conducted by a Board Certified Behavior Analyst (BCBA) or another professional with specialized training in behavior analysis.

BCBAs are the gold standard.

A BCBA is a licensed, board-certified professional with:

- A master's or doctoral degree in behavior analysis or a related field

- Supervised fieldwork experience

- Extensive training in applied behavior analysis (ABA)

- Certification from the Behavior Analyst Certification Board (BACB)

Why is this important?

Because behavior is complex—and guessing will not help. BCBAs are trained to use data, research-based practices, and environmental analysis to:

- Accurately determine the function of a behavior.

- Design effective, individualized interventions.

- Monitor progress and adjust strategies based on tangible results.

✦ If the school provides a generic FBA with vague observations or no clear hypothesis, ask who conducted it. If it was not a BCBA or a similarly qualified professional, you have the right to request a more thorough evaluation.

✱ **Pro Parent Tip:** Ask directly, "Who conducted this FBA, and what is their training in behavior analysis?" and "Was a BCBA involved in the data collection and hypothesis development?"

When Are FBAs Required By Law?

Under IDEA, a school must conduct an FBA if a child with a disability is facing suspension or expulsion due to behavior that may be related to their disability. However, parents can also request (and schools should conduct) an FBA at any time if they believe their child's behaviors are interfering with learning.

How To Ensure A Quality FBA

Not all FBAs are created equal. Some schools rush through the process or rely on vague observations that do not actually lead to a helpful plan. To ensure the FBA is meaningful, parents should make sure:

- The observations take place in multiple settings (not just one classroom on a single day).

- The language used is specific and objective, not vague or judgmental ("The student threw a pencil" instead of "The student was being disruptive").

- The FBA actually leads to a plan for intervention, rather than being used to justify disciplinary action.

If the school refuses to conduct an FBA, request one in writing and escalate if necessary.

➜ *Real-Life Example: Turning Behavior Data Into A Plan*

FBA Finding: Student yells out during math to avoid challenging assignments.

BIP Action Steps:

➜ *Preventive Strategy: Break math assignments into smaller steps.*

➜ **Replacement Behavior:** *Student is taught to request a "help" card instead of yelling.*

➜ **Reinforcement:** *Praise and extra break time for using the "help" card appropriately.*

Once the FBA identifies why the behavior is happening, the next step is turning that information into a practical, student-centered action plan: the Behavioral Intervention Plan (BIP).

B. Behavioral Intervention Plans (BIPs): The Roadmap To Solutions

What Is A BIP?

Once an FBA identifies why behavior is occurring, the next step is to develop a Behavioral Intervention Plan (BIP)—a customized plan designed to reduce challenging behaviors and teach positive alternatives. This last part is an important piece. BIPs are not just about reducing bad behavior, but also about providing appropriate replacement behaviors to help students meet their needs productively.

If a student has a BIP, it should be part of a student's IEP or 504 Plan, which ensures it is legally binding and that the school is required to follow it.

Key Elements Of An Effective BIP

A strong BIP includes:

◇ *Preventive Strategies: Avoiding the Triggers*

- Modifying the classroom environment to reduce sensory overload.
- Providing structured transitions to prevent anxiety-driven behaviors.

- Offering alternative work formats (e.g., oral responses instead of written tests).

◇ *Teaching Replacement Behaviors*

- If a student acts out to avoid challenging work, they might be taught to request a break instead.
- If a child yells for attention, they might be taught to raise their hand.

◇ *Reinforcement Strategies*

- Token systems, praise, and privilege-based rewards reinforce positive behavior.
- Natural consequences (e.g., completing missed assignments) ensure accountability.

◇ *Consistent Consequences*

- The BIP should outline clear, predictable responses when challenging behavior occurs.

◇ *Progress Monitoring*

- Schools must track data regularly to determine whether the plan is working.
- Adjustments should be made if the plan does not produce positive results.

⚡ Common Issues With BIPs & How To Address Them

➤ **The BIP is too generic.** If the plan is vague or full of generic strategies that do not work for your child, request specific, individualized supports.

➤ **The school fails to implement the BIP consistently.** Request regular progress updates with data and schedule meetings to discuss any concerns.

➤ **The school refuses to conduct an FBA or BIP.** Submit a formal written request and escalate if needed. If an FBA is warranted, refusal could be a violation of IDEA.

Behavior Intervention Services: More Than Just A Behavior Plan

Writing a Behavior Intervention Plan (BIP) is a key step—but behavior support should not end at paperwork. Real progress happens when students receive direct, real-time services to help them build coping skills, self-regulation strategies, and social-emotional resilience during the school day—not just reactively after problems arise.

Behavior Intervention Services might include:

● **In-Class Behavior Coaching:** A trained staff member models coping strategies, prompts self-regulation, and provides immediate feedback during real classroom situations.

● **Self-Regulation Training:** Direct instruction in techniques like mindfulness, emotional check-ins, and recognizing early signs of frustration before behaviors escalate.

● **Social and Emotional Learning (SEL) Support:** Teaching skills like conflict resolution, emotional labeling, peer interaction, and perspective-taking.

- **Crisis Prevention and De-Escalation:** Staff trained to recognize early warning signs and intervene with calming strategies before a situation becomes disruptive.

- **Behavior Data Collection and Analysis:** Regular, detailed tracking of behaviors—not just office referrals—to identify patterns and drive adjustments to the plan.

➡ **Pro Parent Move:** If the school offers a BIP without any direct services, ask:

> → "Who will provide real-time behavior support during the day?"
> → "Will my child receive direct instruction in coping or regulation skills?"
> → "What ongoing data collection will be used to adjust the plan?"

✦ **Key Reminder:** A BIP without behavior intervention services is like trying to learn a new language without ever hearing it spoken. As strong as a BIP may be, students also need hands-on support, just like anyone learning a new skill needs coaching, not just a plan on paper.

C. Restraint And Seclusion: Protecting Your Child's Rights

What Are Restraint And Seclusion?

These are crisis interventions sometimes used in schools when a student is perceived to pose an immediate danger to themselves or others. They are serious, high-risk practices—and they are not "just part of school discipline."

Used improperly, they can cause trauma, injury, and a serious breakdown in trust between students and adults.

⚡ Restraint

Restraint means physically restricting a student's movement—either with a physical hold or, in rare and often prohibited cases, mechanical devices.

Restraint should only be used to prevent imminent serious harm, and never: as punishment, for noncompliance, or because someone skipped their morning coffee!

There is a difference between guiding a student by the arm and full-on immobilizing them. If it is not something you would do in a workplace setting, chances are it is not appropriate in a classroom either.

Seclusion

Seclusion involves isolating a student in a room or space where they are not free to leave. The door might be locked, blocked, or monitored by an adult. The key distinction? It is not voluntary.

This is not the same as a student taking a break in a sensory space. If the space is locked, empty, or used as a threat, it is not support—it's isolation. Let's call it what it is.

⚡ When (If Ever) Are These Allowed?

Both restraint and seclusion should only be used:

- As a last resort
- Where there is imminent danger
- If everything else has failed

Many states now require schools to report each incident to parents and document the event in detail. Some even prohibit certain practices entirely.

✻ Pro Parent Tip: Ask your school,

➤ "What is your district's policy on restraint and seclusion?"

➤ "How are staff trained to handle crisis situations without using these interventions?"

➤ "What positive behavior supports are in place to prevent escalation?"

If your child has experienced restraint or seclusion, you have the right to request:

- A written incident report
- A debriefing meeting
- A behavioral support plan that emphasizes prevention, not punishment

What To Ask Your School

- What de-escalation strategies are used?

- Are staff trained in trauma-informed behavior intervention?

- Does my child's IEP or BIP include a sensory break plan?

◉ *Prevention is the goal: The focus should always be on teaching self-regulation — not enforcing compliance through control*

Restraint vs Seclusion vs Break Space

Here is how to tell the difference—and why it matters:

Term	What It Is	What It's Not	Key Concerns
Restraint	Physically holding or restricting a student to prevent harm	A hug, hand-holding for guidance, or prompting a movement	Can be traumatic or cause injury; should be a last resort

Term	What It Is	What It's Not	Key Concerns
Seclusion	Forcibly isolating a student in a room they cannot leave	A voluntary break or sensory room the student chooses to enter and exit freely	Often illegal or restricted; can escalate fear or distress
Break Space	A calm area a student voluntarily uses to self-regulate or take a sensory break	Forced removal from class, or isolation used as punishment	Should be student-driven and built into a behavior plan

Understanding Restraint, Seclusion, and Break Spaces in Schools

Legal Protections Against Restraint And Seclusion

Under IDEA and Section 504, restraint and seclusion are not permitted as routine behavioral interventions. They are considered last-resort emergency actions, not classroom management tools.

Schools must:

- Notify parents on the same day a restraint or seclusion occurs.
- Provide a detailed written incident report, including.
- What led to the incident?
- Who was involved?
- What de-escalation strategies were attempted first.
- How long did the intervention last?
- What supports will be used to prevent recurrence?

➡ **Pro Parent Move:** Always ask for this report in writing. Keep a copy. And do not let vague descriptions slide—"student became escalated" is not a sufficient explanation. You need clarity to protect your child and improve supports. Ask for specifics: What exactly happened? What was tried first?—and make sure you receive them in writing.

Safer Alternatives To Restraint And Seclusion

Instead of high-risk interventions, schools should be investing in tools that actually work. That means:

Crisis Prevention Training

Staff should be trained in de-escalation, relationship-building, and sensory regulation strategies. Crisis situations require calm, trained responses—schools cannot afford to improvise. Students are safest when staff are equipped with proven tools, not left to figure it out on the fly.

Sensory & Regulation Spaces

A break space should feel like a yoga studio, not a storage closet. Students should choose to go, know how to use it, and be able to leave when ready.

Relationship-Based Support

Students are more likely to regulate their behavior when they feel emotionally safe. Want fewer meltdowns? Start with more connection. Peer mentoring, check-ins, and social-emotional learning (SEL) can go further than any physical hold ever could.

What To Do If Your Child Is Restrained Or Secluded

If it happens, you do not have to accept it quietly. Here is what you can do:

1. Request an immediate meeting to review the incident with the IEP or 504 team.

2. Ask for the school's written policy on crisis intervention and behavior support.

3. File a formal complaint if the intervention was used inappropriately or without following the required procedures.

4. If your child has an IEP or 504 Plan, request that it include protective language, such as:

   - "Restraint and seclusion may only be used in cases of imminent serious physical harm."

   - "The team will use proactive, evidence-based strategies to prevent escalation."

   - "Breaks and regulation strategies will be offered regularly and tracked."

★ **You are your child's best advocate.** Do not let anyone convince you that restraint and seclusion are "just part of school." They are not. And you have every right to demand something better.

Final Thoughts: Behavior Is Not the Problem— Misunderstanding It Is

If there is one takeaway from this chapter, it should be this: *Behavior is communication—and it deserves to be understood, not punished!*

Too often, schools respond to challenging behavior with quick fixes, compliance-driven strategies, or outdated discipline tactics. But you know better. And now you have the tools to expect better, too.

Whether your child struggles with emotional regulation, task avoidance, sensory overload, or anxiety, what they need is not a time-out or a take-away—they need support, structure, and people who get it.

This chapter has walked you through the "why" behind behavior, and more importantly, the "how" of building lasting change:

- How to advocate for a quality FBA conducted by someone actually trained to do it.

- How to make sure a BIP is more than a vague wish list.

- How to push back when schools default to restraint and seclusion instead of skill-building and prevention.

You do not have to be a behavior analyst to understand your child. You just have to be their advocate—which you already are.

And if the system does not respond the first time? Do not confuse that with failure. That is just your cue to push again—louder, clearer, backed by data and law.

Because your child does not need to be "fixed."

They need to be seen, supported, and set up to succeed.

Key Takeaways:

✓ **Behavior is communication**—always ask what is driving it, not just how to stop it.

✓ **FBAs should be conducted by trained professionals**, ideally a Board Certified Behavior Analyst (BCBA). You have every right to ask about credentials.

✓ **A strong BIP teaches replacement behaviors**, uses positive reinforcement, and includes consistent progress monitoring.

✓ **Restraint and seclusion are not behavior plans**—they are crisis responses, and should be treated as such.

✓ **You can request an FBA or BIP in writing** at any time if your child's behavior is interfering with learning.

✓ **Do not accept vague language or inconsistent implementation.** Ask for specifics, data, and documentation.

✓ **Safer alternatives exist.** De-escalation training, sensory spaces, and relationship-based strategies should be the norm.

✓ **Your voice matters.** You have the legal right to be involved in every part of your child's behavioral support plan.

◉ *Behavior is not the enemy. Disconnection is. With the right support, every child can build regulation, resilience, and real confidence. Let's stop managing children—and start understanding them.*

CHAPTER 10:
Discipline Protections Under The IDEA

Discipline in schools can often feel like a tightrope walk, especially when your child has a disability. On one side, schools have a responsibility to maintain order and safety; on the other, students with disabilities have the right to fair, individualized, and legally protected disciplinary processes.

The IDEA (Individuals with Disabilities Education Act) ensures that schools cannot just suspend, expel, or repeatedly remove students with disabilities because of behaviors related to their disability. If a child's actions are driven by their disability—or if the school failed to provide the supports outlined in their IEP—then disciplinary consequences must be handled differently.

This chapter will help you navigate your child's legal rights, the Manifestation Determination Review (MDR) process, and alternative placement options so that you can effectively advocate when disciplinary issues arise.

A. Manifestation Determination Review (MDR): Where Discipline Meets Disability

What Is An MDR?

An MDR is not just a meeting—it is a safeguard to make sure children are not punished for disabilities instead of being supported. A Manifestation Determination Review (MDR) is a critical legal checkpoint. It asks: Did the behavior happen because of the child's disability—or because the school did not follow the IEP?

If the answer to either question is "yes," then the school cannot discipline the student the same way they would a non-disabled peer. It is not a loophole; it is a safeguard.

The Two Critical Questions In An MDR:

1. Was the behavior caused by or directly related to the child's disability?

> ➔ **Example:** A student with autism experiences sensory overload and lashes out. Since the behavior is tied to their disability, the solution is not suspension—it is support.

2. Was the behavior the result of the school's failure to implement the IEP properly?

> ➔ **Example:** A student with an anxiety disorder has an outburst after missing scheduled sensory breaks. If the school skipped the break, they share the responsibility.

What Triggers IDEA's Discipline Protections?

IDEA's discipline protections kick in when a disciplinary action results in a "change of placement"—meaning your child is being removed from their regular learning environment for an extended period. This can happen in two ways:

1. A single removal lasting ten or more consecutive school days.

> ➔ **Example:** If a student is suspended for two weeks, this is considered a significant removal.

2. A series of shorter removals that add up to a "pattern of exclusion."

> → **Example:** A student with ADHD receives multiple one- or two-day suspensions throughout the school year, but these add up to more than ten days total.

Even informal removals—like repeatedly being sent home early—can trigger IDEA protections if they form a pattern. Schools cannot use repeated removals as a way to dodge their responsibility to provide appropriate behavioral supports.

What Schools Must Do When IDEA's Discipline Protections Apply

Once a school removes a student beyond the ten-day threshold, it must:

- Notify parents in writing and explain the proposed disciplinary action.

- Hold a Manifestation Determination Review (MDR) within ten school days.

- Ensure the student continues receiving educational services during any removal.

What Happens After An MDR?

If the behavior is a manifestation of the disability:

- No expulsion, long-term suspension, or other harsh penalties.

- The school must conduct an FBA (Functional Behavioral Assessment).

- The BIP (Behavioral Intervention Plan) must be created or updated.

- The student must return to their original placement—unless the parent agrees otherwise (no pressure, right?).

If the behavior is not a manifestation:

- The school may proceed with disciplinary actions.

- But your child must still receive educational services to make progress on IEP goals. Because IDEA does not take a time-out—even if your child is.

Quick Questions for an MDR Meeting:

- "What support failed before the behavior happened?"

- "How will the IEP or BIP be changed moving forward?"

- "How will we track if these changes are working?"

Why MDRs Matter

MDRs prevent students from being punished for things that are not truly "misbehavior"—they are manifestations of disability or unmet needs. It is how we make sure discipline does not become discrimination.

And if the school decides the behavior was not a manifestation? You can challenge it. Due process is your legal safety net—not just for lawyers and courtroom dramas.

B. Patterns Of Removal: One Day Here, Two Days There... Add Up

One-day suspensions might seem harmless—but they add up fast. Schools often count on you not noticing. Like a game of disciplinary Jenga, those removals quietly stack until everything tips—and under IDEA, that triggers serious legal protections.

What Counts As A "Pattern" Under IDEA?

IDEA does not just look at the number of days a student is removed—it considers how those removals occur. A "pattern" happens when:

- The removals total more than 10 school days in a school year,
- The behaviors are substantially similar, and
- The school does not offer adequate behavioral support or services in response.

⚡ **Translation:** If your child is repeatedly sent home for the same kind of behavior—and nothing changes in their supports—that is a red flag.

→ Common (& Sneaky) Examples Of Patterns Of Removal:

- **Suspension Roulette:** One-day suspensions every time your child has a meltdown. Ten suspensions later? You are over the threshold.

- **The "Go Home Early" Shuffle:** Staff calls you at 11 a.m., saying your child is "having a tough day" and should probably leave early, "just this once." Except... it is not just once.

- **Time-Out to Nowhere:** Your child is removed from the classroom to a separate space "for safety" but receives no instruction or support. If it keeps happening, it counts.

Month	Removal Type	Notes
September	1-day suspension	Outburst during math
October	Sent home early (3 times)	"Having a hard day" notes
November	2-day suspension	Fight in cafeteria
Total Days	11	*Pattern triggered!*

Example of a Pattern of Removals Under IDEA

Why Patterns Matter

When there is a pattern, the school is legally required to take action—not just keep removing the student and hoping for the best.

Once a pattern is established, it is treated like a change of placement, which means:

- The school must notify you in writing.

- An MDR must be held within 10 school days.

- Your child must continue receiving services and supports as outlined in their IEP.

This is not optional. It is federal law.

FAPE Still Stands—Even When Behavior Is Hard

Even if your child's behavior is challenging, they are still entitled to:

- Access to the general education curriculum (even during removals),
- Special education services in alignment with their IEP,
- Behavioral supports that are actually designed to address the root of the behavior—not just punish it.

➡ **Pro Parent Move:** Ask for documentation of every removal, formal or informal. If your child has been removed multiple times—even for short stints—request a full review of cumulative days and behavior patterns.

What To Do If You Suspect A Pattern

If your gut says, "this is happening too often," you are probably right. Here is what to do:

1. **Request an MDR**—in writing—if removals exceed 10 days or seem repetitive.
2. **Ask for an FBA** to identify what is really triggering the behavior.
3. **Push for a strong BIP** that is actually implemented—not just written and forgotten.
4. **Document everything**—dates, behaviors, communication, and school responses.

When Schools Try to Dodge the Pattern

Some schools try to avoid reaching the 10-day mark by spacing out suspensions, calling removals "cool-downs," or just sending children home without recording it officially.

✦ **Spoiler:** If your child is missing instruction due to behavior—even without a formal suspension—it still counts.

Do not let semantics override services. If it looks like a duck and quacks like a duck... Well, it probably needs an MDR.

➤ **Bottom line:** IDEA does not just protect against big removals. It protects against repeated removals that add up and deny your child meaningful access to education. And if the school is not tracking those days, you should be.

✦ **NOTE:** If you suspect a removal pattern is developing, it is a good idea to consult a special education attorney. You may not need full legal intervention yet—but if something is not working, you need to know where the line is. Even if it is not time to bring in the big guns, make sure you know when that time *will* be.

C. Alternative Placements: Navigating Detours

Under very specific situations, a school may decide that a student's behavior warrants removal from their current educational setting—even if that behavior is tied to a disability. When that happens, it is called an Interim Alternative Educational Setting (IAES).

Alternative placements are not a loophole for schools to remove students indefinitely. IDEA only allows this kind of move under serious circumstances—and even then, the protections do not go away.

When Are Alternative Placements Used?

In some cases, a school may remove a student to an Interim Alternative Educational Setting (IAES) for up to 45 school days, even if the behavior is a manifestation of their disability. This applies when a student has engaged in serious infractions, including:

- Possession of a weapon on school grounds.
- Use, possession, or sale of illegal drugs at school.
- Threat (or reality) of serious bodily injury to another person.

⚡ **Key Reminder:** These are narrow exceptions. The behavior must meet the legal definitions—vague accusations or school policy violations do not qualify unless they meet one of these specific criteria.

And if these conditions are not met? Then the school must go through the usual MDR process and cannot use an IAES as a shortcut.

But Wait—Does The MDR Still Apply?

Yes. Absolutely.

Even when a school places a student in an IAES for one of these violations, they must still conduct a Manifestation Determination Review (MDR) within 10 school days of the decision to change placement.

- The school can take immediate action to ensure safety.
- But the MDR ensures that the student's rights are still protected.
- It also helps inform the behavioral supports and services the student needs while in the IAES—and when transitioning back.

If the behavior is not a manifestation, the student can remain in the IAES and may face further discipline, as long as they continue receiving educational services.

If it is a manifestation, the student can still stay in the IAES for up to 45 days— but only for those specific infractions. For anything else, the school must return the student to their original placement unless the parent agrees otherwise.

What Should An Alternative Placement Provide?

Even in an alternative setting, the student must still receive FAPE. This includes:

- Access to the general education curriculum.
- Behavioral intervention services to address the underlying cause of the behavior.
- Special education services outlined in the IEP.
- Support to transition back to their regular placement.

✳ **Advocacy Tip for Parents:** If your child is placed in an IAES, ask:

→ "What educational services will be provided to ensure continued learning?"

→ "How will behavioral interventions be implemented to address the root cause of the behavior?"

→ "What is the school's plan for transitioning the student back into their regular placement?"

An IAES is not about removing the student—it is about providing the right support so they can safely return stronger.

Preventing Alternative Placements

The best way to avoid disciplinary removals is proactive intervention:

★ **Request an FBA** (Functional Behavioral Assessment) to identify behavioral triggers before they escalate.

★ **Ensure a strong BIP** (Behavioral Intervention Plan) is in place and followed consistently.

★ **Work closely with the IEP team** to address challenges before they result in disciplinary action.

Final Thoughts: Your Child's Rights Do Not Get Suspended

Let's face it—navigating school discipline when your child has a disability can feel like entering a game where the rules keep changing and nobody gave you the handbook. But IDEA is that handbook. And it is built on one non-negotiable principle: students with disabilities have the right to an education, even when behavior becomes challenging.

Whether it is a single long-term suspension, a pattern of short removals, or a sudden placement in an alternative setting, your child's legal protections do not disappear. Schools are required to ask tough questions—Was the behavior connected to the disability? Did the school follow the IEP?—before they impose consequences. And if they skip those steps? That is where you step in.

You do not have to be a lawyer to be a powerful advocate. You just need to be informed, persistent, and unapologetically focused on what your child needs to succeed—not just academically, but emotionally and behaviorally, too. If the school pushes back, however, it may be time to find a special education attorney to consult.

When parents stand informed, the system has to listen—and change.

Key Takeaways:

✔ **MDRs are required** whenever there is a change in placement, even for serious infractions.

✔ **Behaviors caused by a disability cannot be punished like willful misconduct**—or by the school's failure to support the disability.

✔ **Short-term removals can add up.** Ten scattered days may legally count as a pattern and trigger IDEA protections.

✓ **Even in an alternative placement, your child has a right to FAPE**—that includes curriculum access, IEP services, and a plan to return.

✓ **Proactive support (like an FBA and BIP) is your best defense** against repeated removals and unnecessary disciplinary action.

✓ **You have the power to challenge decisions.** Do not accept removals, placements, or punishments that feel wrong. Request an MDR, call for documentation, and—if needed—pursue due process.

Discipline should never be used to push a child with a disability out of their education. With the right tools and knowledge, you can ensure that discipline becomes a doorway to support—not a dead end.

Now that you know your rights, you are already one step ahead.

CHAPTER 11:
Bullying, Harassment, And Intimidation

Creating A Safe Learning Environment: Turning Concern Into Action

Bullying is not a normal part of childhood. Period. It does not matter what was acceptable when you were growing up, it should never be dismissed as a "rite of passage." It is a significant issue that can cause long-term emotional and psychological harm, particularly for students with disabilities. For these students, bullying can be especially damaging because they may already face challenges in social interactions, communication, and self-advocacy that make it difficult to recognize, report, or respond effectively to bullying.

◇ **Key Point:** When bullying disrupts a child's ability to access education, it is not just a social problem—it is a legal violation under IDEA and Section 504.

Unfortunately, many schools still downplay bullying or treat it like an unavoidable part of growing up. Spoiler alert: it is not. Schools have a legal obligation to ensure a safe and supportive learning environment, and when bullying interferes with a child's ability to learn, parents have every right to demand action.

This chapter will equip you with the knowledge, strategies, and legal protections you need to ensure your child is safe, supported, and able to thrive.

A. Finding Your Way Through A Difficult Landscape

Bullying is not just about physical aggression. It can take many forms—verbal, relational, and even digital (cyberbullying). And while all children are at risk, students with disabilities are often targeted more frequently due to physical, behavioral, or communication differences that may make them stand out.

The Many Faces Of Bullying

Type of Bullying	Examples
Physical	Hitting, pushing, damaging belongings
Verbal	Name-calling, teasing, threats
Relational	Exclusion, rumor-spreading, social manipulation
Cyberbullying	Texting, social media harassment, gaming abuse

Types of Bullying and Their Common Examples

✦ **Why does this matter?** Some children do not even realize they are being bullied—especially if they have social communication challenges or struggle with reading social cues. A child with autism, for example, may not recognize sarcasm or subtle social exclusion until the situation escalates. This is why proactive intervention is critical.

Why Are Students With Disabilities At Higher Risk?

Students with disabilities may be targeted due to:

Bullying, Harassment, and Intimidation

→ **Physical or Social Vulnerabilities** – Children with physical disabilities, speech differences, or reliance on assistive technology may be more visible to potential bullies.

→ **Behavioral or Sensory Differences** – Children with autism, ADHD, or sensory processing disorders may exhibit behaviors that peers do not understand, such as hand flapping, avoiding eye contact, or difficulty with social cues.

→ **Misunderstood Behaviors** – Some children struggle with interpreting social cues, which can lead to unintentional conflicts with peers. Others may express emotions in ways that do not fit the "norm," making them easier targets.

→ **Perception of Isolation** – Students who spend less time in general education settings due to special education services may feel alienated or be viewed as "different."

The bottom line? Children who stand out in any way—whether physically, socially, or behaviorally—are at higher risk of being bullied.

★ **Real Talk:** If your child is frequently coming home upset, withdrawing from school-related activities, or suddenly losing interest in things they once enjoyed, do not dismiss it as just a phase. Ask specific, open-ended questions about their school day—not just "Did you have a good day?" but "Who did you sit with at lunch?" or "What was the best and worst part of today?" These questions open the door for your child to share concerns that they may not think to bring up otherwise.

What Parents Can Do To Reduce The Risk Of Bullying

★ **Advocate for Inclusion** – Push the school to foster an inclusive culture through peer mentorships, buddy systems, and social skills groups. Schools that promote peer understanding see lower rates of bullying against students with disabilities.

★ **Encourage Self-Advocacy** – Teach your child how to speak up for themselves. Role-play different situations and practice assertive communication so they feel more confident reporting problems.

★ **Educate Teachers and Staff** – Schools should provide anti-bullying training that specifically addresses disability-related bullying. Teachers need to recognize the unique ways students with disabilities may experience and respond to bullying.

★ **Keep an Open Line of Communication** – Make sure your child feels safe coming to you with concerns. Let them know it is never their fault if someone is treating them poorly.

Do Not Assume "Zero Tolerance" Means Zero Problems

If your school claims to have a zero-tolerance policy, ask what that actually means in practice—and how it has been enforced.

Some schools talk tough but fail to act when bullying actually happens. Others rush to suspend or expel without addressing the root causes—like emotional dysregulation, trauma, or social skills deficits.

And some rely on "no-contact contracts" or peer agreements that one student may not even be capable of following—especially if they struggle with social awareness, impulse control, or understanding personal boundaries.

You have the right to ask:

- What specific steps does the school take when bullying is reported?

- How are incidents investigated, documented, and followed up on?

- What support is provided to the student who was targeted—and to the student who engaged in the behavior?

- Are FBAs or behavior supports being considered for students who repeatedly bully others?

- Can I review documentation on how previous bullying incidents were handled?

⚡ **Zero Tolerance ≠ Zero Harm:** Automatic punishments often hurt vulnerable students the most—especially those whose behaviors stem from disability-related needs. Always push for supports before suspensions.

Federal law requires schools to track bullying incidents and ensure that all students, including those with disabilities, are protected from hostile environments and given access to appropriate services.

Cross-Reference: If your child is avoiding school, refusing to attend, or showing signs of anxiety or emotional shutdown—**do not assume it's just behavior.** These may be the ripple effects of ongoing bullying. See *Chapter 12: Navigating School Avoidance and Truancy* for how to identify root causes, secure evaluations, and push for proper interventions.

B. Your Rights When Your Child Is Bullied (or The Bully Themself)

Bullying is not just a social issue—it is a legal issue when it interferes with a child's education. Schools are legally required to intervene when bullying prevents a child from learning or creates an unsafe environment.

Legal Protections For Students With Disabilities

There are two primary federal laws that protect students with disabilities from bullying:

1. Individuals with Disabilities Education Act (IDEA)

If bullying prevents a child with an IEP from receiving a Free Appropriate Public Education (FAPE), the school must take immediate action to address it. This could include:

- Conducting a Functional Behavioral Assessment (FBA) to identify supports.

- Adjusting the IEP to include accommodations like a safe place for breaks or social skills training.

- Providing counseling services or assigning an adult mentor to monitor safety.

2. Section 504 of the Rehabilitation Act

If a child does not have an IEP but has a disability that affects their education, they are protected under Section 504. Schools must:

- Investigate bullying complaints and respond appropriately.

- Implement reasonable accommodations to ensure the child's safety.

- Take disciplinary action against students who engage in harassment.

➡ **Pro Parent Move:** If the school brushes off your bullying concerns, respond with this: "Since bullying is interfering with my child's ability to access their education, how does the school plan to meet its legal obligation to provide a Free Appropriate Public Education under IDEA or Section 504?" That sentence alone tends to change the tone of the conversation.

Few things rattle a parent faster than learning your child is involved in bullying. Whether they are the one being bullied—or the one doing the bullying—your gut tightens. Your pulse speeds up. And your brain immediately asks: What do I do now?

The good news? You have rights. And so does your child. The even better news? You do not have to choose between advocating for accountability and advocating for support. You can (and should) do both.

⚡ If Your Child Is Being Bullied

Children with disabilities are at increased risk for bullying. If the school environment becomes unsafe, inaccessible, or emotionally harmful, it is not just a discipline issue—it is a denial of their legal right to a Free Appropriate Public Education (FAPE).

Here is what the school is required to do:

- ✓ Investigate promptly when bullying is reported
- ✓ Document what happened and what steps were taken
- ✓ Take meaningful action to stop the bullying and prevent it from continuing

Ensure your child continues to access education in a safe way, which may include:

→ Changes in schedule or placement
→ Counseling or check-ins
→ Extra supervision or peer supports
→ Updates to the IEP or 504 Plan

If bullying affects your child's ability to concentrate, attend school, or participate in social activities, it must be addressed through their IEP or 504 Plan.

▶ **Two Paths Forward:** Whether your child is experiencing bullying—or engaging in it—the goal is not blame. It is support, accountability, and growth.

⚡ So, What If Your Child Is the Bully?

Take a deep breath. Then another.

Finding out your child has harmed someone else—especially if they have a disability—is difficult, emotional, and often laced with guilt or defensiveness. But this is not about blame. It is about support.

Children with disabilities may engage in bullying behavior for many reasons, including:

▶ **Emotional dysregulation**—reacting impulsively when overwhelmed.

▶ **Difficulty reading social cues**—what seems like teasing to them may feel like cruelty to others.

▶ **Struggles with power and control**—asserting dominance when they feel insecure in other areas.

▶ **Unmet behavioral or sensory needs**—which can lead to aggression or frustration-based responses.

Bullying behavior does not mean your child is "bad." "Good" children (just like adults) can make bad choices. It often means something is going unaddressed—and it is time to dig in.

➜ What The School Should Do

Whether your child is being bullied or is the one doing the bullying, schools have a responsibility to assess, support, and intervene. This is not just about checking boxes—it is about ensuring both safety and growth.

For the child who is targeted:

- ✓ **Revisit their IEP** or 504 Plan to ensure protections are in place.
- ✓ **Add specific services** such as social work check-ins or trauma-informed counseling.
- ✓ **Review data:** How often is this happening? Where? What has been done so far?

For the child engaging in the behavior:

- ✓ **Request** a Functional Behavioral Assessment (FBA) to determine why the behavior is happening.
- ✓ **Develop** or revise the Behavioral Intervention Plan (BIP) to include:
  - ○ Teaching empathy and boundaries
  - ○ Coping strategies and calming routines
  - ○ Support during unstructured times, such as lunch or recess
- ✓ **Consider** counseling, social skills instruction, or peer mentoring.

➡ **Pro Parent Move:** Frame this in the IEP meeting as a learning opportunity, not a punishment. Ask: What supports can we put in place to help my child succeed socially and emotionally—while preventing harm to others?

⚡ When The School Fails to Act

Sadly, some schools respond with punishment alone or try student contracts that have little meaning to the students—or, worse, do nothing at all. Whether your child is being harmed or doing the harming, here is what you can do when the school drops the ball:

- Put everything in writing. Every incident, every email, every meeting. Document it.

- Request an IEP or 504 meeting to formally address the issue.

- File a complaint with the district or the Office for Civil Rights (OCR) if the bullying continues or the school fails to take action.

- Request an Independent Educational Evaluation (IEE) if the school's assessment of your child's behavior seems incomplete or inaccurate.

- Ask about compensatory education if bullying (on either side) has disrupted your child's ability to access learning.

You are not just advocating for safety—you are advocating for services, supports, and long-term success.

⚡ When Bullying Leads To School Refusal

If your child starts missing school, refusing to go, or showing signs of emotional distress tied to school attendance, you may be seeing the effects of bullying— even if they haven't named it yet. This is not school avoidance for no reason.

Bullying that creates fear, anxiety, or isolation often leads to chronic absenteeism. Turn to ***Chapter 12: Navigating School Avoidance and Truancy*** for a full breakdown of school avoidance, how to differentiate it from truancy, and what supports schools are legally required to provide.

C. Taking Action: Steps For Prevention and Resolution

Bullying is not just an unfortunate part of growing up—it is a direct barrier to learning. When bullying affects a child's ability to feel safe and succeed in school, action must be taken. As a parent, you have powerful tools to hold the school accountable, ensure your child's safety, and push for systemic change when necessary.

This section provides a clear, step-by-step roadmap to stop bullying, secure the right supports, and escalate action when the school fails to take action.

Step 1: Document Every Incident (Because If It's Not Written Down, It Didn't Happen)

Before taking action, gather evidence. Schools take complaints more seriously when there is a paper trail. Keep detailed records of every bullying incident (assuming your child tells you), including:

- → Date, time, and location (e.g., "March 10, lunchroom")
- → What happened (exact words used, physical contact, online harassment)
- → Names of any witnesses (peers, staff, bus drivers, etc.)
- → Emotional impact on your child (school avoidance, anxiety, outbursts)
- → Educational impact (drop in grades, refusal to attend school, complaints of illness)

➡ **Pro Parent Move:**

- If bullying happens online, take screenshots of the messages before they disappear.
- If bullying happens in person, ask your child to write down their experience in their own words—this helps keep the details fresh.

Step 2: Report The Bullying In Writing (And Keep A Copy!)

Once you have documented incidents, submit a written report to the school principal, guidance counselor, and teacher. Schools tend to respond faster when complaints are formal and documented.

What To Include In Your Letter Or Email:

✓ A factual account of the bullying incidents (use your records!)
✓ A statement about how this is interfering with your child's education
✓ A request for a meeting to discuss intervention steps
✓ A timeline (e.g., "Please provide a written response within five school days.")

✎ *Sample Email/Letter*

> *Subject: Urgent: Bullying Report for [Child's Name]*
>
> *Dear [Principal's Name],*
>
> *I am writing to formally report bullying incidents involving [Child's Name] at [School Name] on [Dates]. These incidents include [Brief Description] and have impacted my child's ability to attend and focus in school.*
>
> *Since bullying is interfering with [Child's Name]'s education, I request an immediate meeting to discuss interventions. Please provide a written response within five school days.*

Thank you for your prompt attention to this matter.

Sincerely,
[Your Name]
[Your Contact Information]

➡ **Pro Parent Move:** If the school ignores or downplays your concerns, send a follow-up email copying the director of special education or the superintendent. Schools tend to act when district leadership is involved.

Step 3: Request An IEP Or 504 Plan Review (If Necessary)

If bullying affects your child's ability to learn, you have the right to request an IEP or 504 Plan review to ensure safety measures are in place.

◇ Possible IEP/504 Plan Accommodations For Bullying:

- Supervised transitions (hallways, lunch, recess)
- Designated "safe person" to check in with throughout the day
- Social skills training (for self-advocacy, peer interactions)
- Counseling services to help process trauma
- Alternative lunch or recess options (if unstructured time is unsafe)

➡ **What to Say in the Meeting:** "Since the bullying is interfering with my child's ability to access their education, what specific steps will the school take under IDEA or Section 504 to ensure their safety and well-being?"

➡ **Pro Parent Move:** Schools may hesitate to document bullying-related accommodations in an IEP or 504 Plan. If they push back, request a Functional Behavioral Assessment (FBA) to assess the impact of bullying on behavior, attendance, and mental health.

Step 4: Follow Up And Hold The School Accountable

After you report bullying, the school is required by law to take action. Check your state laws for specific bullying statutes—they often go further than federal law in terms of timelines, notification, and documentation.

Even without those specifics, federal laws require schools to do the following at a minimum:

→ Investigate the complaint (interview students and staff, review evidence).
→ Provide a written response explaining findings and any actions taken.
→ Implement protective measures (disciplinary action, safety plan, or student supports).

In addition to federal protections, most states have their own laws that may include:

- Defined timelines for responding to complaints
- Parent notification requirements
- Mandated interventions, safety planning, or follow-up procedures

✱ **Pro Parent Tip:** Visit your state's Department of Education website or search for "[Your State] anti-bullying law" to understand your child's full rights. The more you know, the more powerfully you can advocate.

Do Not Accept Vague Responses

If the school says, "We did not find enough evidence," respond with:

➤ "Can I see a copy of the school's anti-bullying policy?"

➤ "Please provide a record of past bullying investigations." (Schools are required to track complaints—even unresolved ones.)

> "What specific steps will the school take to ensure my child's safety and emotional well-being?" Ask this in writing—and expect a clear plan in return.

Step 5: Escalate If The School Fails To Act

If the school ignores or mishandles the situation, take it to the next level:

1. **The School District Superintendent** – Request district-level intervention.

2. **The Office for Civil Rights (OCR)** – File a formal complaint if the bullying involves discrimination under Section 504.

3. **State Department of Education** – Most states have a special education compliance office that enforces student rights.

➡ **Pro Parent Move:** If you file a complaint, reach out to local disability rights organizations or state education officials - they may be able to support your complaint. Schools move faster when they know more eyes are on them.

Final Thoughts: Safety Is Not Optional

No child should have to choose between getting an education and feeling safe. And no parent should be told to "wait and see" while their child dreads walking into school—or worse, refuses to go at all.

Whether your child is the one being bullied or the one acting out, the solution is never silence. It is action. And yes—sometimes, it is insistence.

Bullying is not a rite of passage. It is a red flag. And in the context of disability, it is often a warning that something deeper is being missed—unmet needs, lack of inclusion, or social-emotional gaps no one has thought to fill.

But here is what is also true: schools have responsibilities, and you have power. You do not need to know every law to speak up. You just need to start asking the right questions—and refuse to settle for vague answers.

The goal is not just to stop the bullying. The goal is to make sure your child is supported, protected, and learning in an environment where they can be exactly who they are—and still feel like they belong.

Key Takeaways

✓ **Bullying is not "normal."** It is a barrier to learning—and schools must act.

✓ **Students with disabilities are at higher risk** of being targeted and misunderstood.

✓ **Both targets and aggressors may need services**—not just consequences.

✓ **Schools are legally required to investigate, respond, and protect.**

✓ **You have the right to call an IEP or 504 meeting** if bullying interferes with your child's learning.

✓ **Documentation is power.** Write it down, follow up, and escalate if needed.

✓ **Parents do not need to be legal experts.** You just need to be persistent.

No matter how difficult or emotional this process becomes, remember this: your advocacy is not just about preventing harm—it is about building something better. A stronger plan. A safer school climate. A child who knows they are worth protecting. When you stand up, ask questions, and push for change, you are not just addressing a moment—you are shaping the future. Keep going. Your child is watching, and they are learning what it means to speak up.

✿ *When parents demand better, schools must do better. And when enough of us refuse to be silent, change becomes unstoppable.*

CHAPTER 12:
Navigating School Avoidance And Truancy

School avoidance and truancy are often treated as the same issue—but they are fundamentally different. While both may involve unexcused absences, the underlying causes and the appropriate responses are not the same. Mislabeling school avoidance as truancy is one of the most damaging—and common—mistakes schools make.

◇ **Why It Matters:** When schools mislabel school avoidance as truancy, they often miss the chance to intervene early—and students can spiral into chronic absence, court involvement, or even dropping out.

Where school avoidance is rooted in emotional distress, trauma, or unmet needs, truancy is often viewed as willful defiance or disengagement. But in practice, the line is rarely that clear. Many students who are labeled as "truant" are, in fact, overwhelmed, unsupported, or silently struggling with issues the system has missed.

Understanding the distinction is the first step in advocating for the right kind of support. When the school misinterprets the behavior, it almost always misapplies the intervention—and that can push students further away from learning, connection, and safety.

A. Understanding School Avoidance And Truancy

Where Avoidance Begins: The Social Layer

Many students begin avoiding school not because of curriculum—but because of classmates. If your child's distress escalated after a conflict, exclusion, or sudden social withdrawal, don't overlook the possibility of bullying or harassment. See ***Chapter 11: Bullying, Harassment, and Intimidation*** for a deep dive on identifying, documenting, and addressing bullying through both advocacy and law.

School Avoidance (School Refusal) vs. Truancy

School Avoidance	Truancy
Rooted in emotional distress (e.g., anxiety, trauma, sensory overload)	Often associated with willful disconnection, peer influence, or boredom
Visible signs of panic, anxiety, physical complaints	May show indifference or deliberate deception about absences
Needs emotional, behavioral, or academic support	Needs re-engagement strategies, not just punishment
Protected under IDEA/504 if disability-related	Still requires understanding—but often treated punitively unless disability is identified

Distinguishing School Avoidance from Truancy

School avoidance and truancy can feel like a relentless battle—leaving parents exhausted, anxious, and wondering what they are missing. One day, your child is dragging their feet to get out the door. The next, they are refusing to leave the house altogether. Maybe they begin each morning with stomachaches or panic attacks. Maybe the school keeps calling about unexcused absences that are starting to stack up.

Here is what matters most: chronic school avoidance is not about laziness or defiance. It is a signal—loud and clear—that something deeper is going on beneath the surface. Whether your child is struggling with anxiety, bullying, trauma, or an undiagnosed learning difference, school refusal is often their way of saying, "I cannot do this."

In my twenty years of practice, I have heard the same advice over and over: *"You must get them to school—no matter what."* I have even followed that advice myself as a parent—for several months. And in all that time, both personally and professionally, I have never seen that approach resolve the problem. What I have seen is that it exacerbates the situation, deepens the distress, and delays meaningful support.

Look Closer: Could Bullying Be The Cause?

Emotional refusal often has a backstory. If your child's school avoidance began suddenly—or worsened after a conflict—don't rule out bullying, exclusion, or peer harassment. These triggers are especially common for students with disabilities or social differences. ***Chapter 11: Bullying, Harassment, and Intimidation*** walks you through how to identify bullying, document it, and push for real school action under IDEA and Section 504.

Before jumping to solutions, it is essential to understand how schools often confuse two vastly different issues: school avoidance and truancy. While they may look similar on paper—missed days, unexcused absences, falling behind— the why behind them matters.

- **School Avoidance (School Refusal):** A child persistently avoids school due to emotional distress—not because they are lazy or indifferent, but because something about the school environment feels overwhelming, unsafe, or unmanageable. This can stem from anxiety, bullying, sensory overload, or undiagnosed learning challenges. The refusal is not a choice; it is a coping mechanism.

- **Truancy:** Traditionally refers to a student deliberately skipping school without a valid reason. It is often viewed as willful defiance or disengagement and may be linked to risky behavior, peer influence, or lack of motivation.

Why This Distinction Matters: In practice, many students who are labeled "truant" are actually experiencing school avoidance. When emotional distress is misinterpreted as misconduct, schools may respond with punishment instead of support—escalating the problem instead of addressing its root.

However, the line is not always clear. While some truancy may appear willful, it can still be rooted in unmet needs—such as undiagnosed learning disabilities, trauma, or a long-standing lack of academic or emotional support. In these cases, what looks like defiance may be a form of quiet disengagement, resulting from years of frustration or failure, which could require the same level of assessment, intervention, and individualized support as more overt school avoidance.

Without addressing the underlying cause, punitive measures often miss the mark—and can further alienate the student from both learning and connection. Whether it is called truancy or refusal, the goal should be the same: understand the "why" and build a path back to school that feels safe, supported, and meaningful.

How School Avoidance Can Manifest

School avoidance rarely starts as full-on refusal. It often builds slowly, showing up in small, easily overlooked ways—until one day, it feels like your child is physically and emotionally unable to walk through the school doors.

⚡ *Common Signs Of School Avoidance:*

- Morning meltdowns or panic attacks about going to school—tears, yelling, or shutting down completely.

- Physical complaints like headaches, stomachaches, or dizziness that magically disappear once school is no longer on the table.

- Avoidance of specific parts of the school day, such as gym, lunch, recess, or classes that feel particularly overwhelming or triggering.

- Sleep issues—either staying up late due to anxiety or struggling to wake up and get ready in the morning.

- Begging to stay home, even when they genuinely enjoy learning or have strong relationships with teachers.

- Extreme distress on Sundays or before school breaks end, also known as anticipatory anxiety.

- Refusal that escalates over time, starting as minor resistance and growing into full-day absences.

✦ **Note:** These behaviors are often driven by internal emotional distress, not manipulation or rebellion. What looks like "acting out" is often really shutting down.

⚡ How Truancy May Present Differently:

- **Skipping** individual classes or full days without informing a parent or guardian.
- **Hiding out in bathrooms,** hallways, or other low-supervision areas during class—even during lunch or free periods.

- **Lying** about attendance or hiding report cards and school communication.
- **Spending time in risky or unsupervised environments** during school hours.
- **Frequent disciplinary action**, including detentions or suspensions for unexcused absences.
- **Lack of emotional distress** about missing school, and in some cases, open defiance or disengagement.
- **Indifference**—or even pride—about missing school.

Why This Distinction Matters

Because if we misunderstand the "why," we will almost always misapply the "how"—especially when it comes to intervention.

- A child avoiding school because of anxiety, trauma, or sensory overwhelm needs connection, safety, and accommodations, not attendance contracts and punishments.

- A teen skipping school out of boredom or disconnection needs re-engagement, not just a stricter consequence.

- And if a child is struggling because of undiagnosed learning challenges, what they need is support and evaluation, not being labeled "noncompliant."

⚡ When school avoidance is treated as truancy, schools may apply punitive measures—like detention, court referrals, or threats of retention—which not only fail to resolve the issue but often make it worse.

B. Root Causes And Legal Protections

School avoidance rarely starts as full-on refusal. It often builds slowly, showing up in small, easily overlooked ways—until one day, it feels like your child is physically and emotionally unable to walk through the school doors.

Common Causes Of School Avoidance

If your child is refusing to go to school, the next step is to identify the reason. Here are some of the most common reasons:

- **Anxiety and Depression** – Fear of failure, social anxiety, panic attacks, or overwhelming pressure.

- **Bullying and Social Challenges** – Fear of being teased, excluded, or physically harassed.

- **Undiagnosed Learning Disabilities or ADHD** – Difficulty with reading, math, or organization leads to frustration and embarrassment.

- **Medical or Sensory Issues** – Chronic illness, sensory overload, or fatigue make school physically draining.

- **Trauma or Family Instability** – Divorce, grief, or sudden life changes can make school feel emotionally unsafe.

A child experiencing any of these factors may begin to avoid school gradually, or the refusal may seem to happen overnight. Some children exhibit clear distress, while others internalize their discomfort, making it harder for parents and educators to spot the problem.

➥ **Pro Parent Move:** If your child suddenly develops school refusal behaviors, document what is happening and look for patterns. Does it happen on test days?

After a rough social situation? In a certain class? The patterns can give clues about the underlying issue.

Even High-Performing Students Can Struggle

One common misconception is that if a student is doing well academically, they cannot be struggling emotionally. This is simply not true. Many students who appear successful on paper—earning good grades or behaving well—may still be silently battling anxiety, depression, or other emotional challenges that interfere with attendance.

Mental health difficulties do not always look like failure. In fact, perfectionism, masking, and people-pleasing behaviors can sometimes hide just how much a student is struggling inside.

When School Avoidance May Indicate A Disability

If your child's difficulty attending school is connected to anxiety, ADHD, autism, trauma, or other emotional or learning challenges, they may qualify for services under IDEA (the Individuals with Disabilities Education Act) or Section 504 of the Rehabilitation Act.

⚡ *If school avoidance is tied to a disability—even one that has not yet been formally diagnosed—the school is legally obligated to evaluate and provide support.*

This support may include:

- A 504 Plan with accommodations like adjusted schedules, breaks, counseling, or home-based learning when needed.

- An Individualized Education Program (IEP) with goals, services, and modifications to help the student access learning.

- A Functional Behavioral Assessment (FBA) to identify triggers and underlying causes of the behavior.

- A Behavioral Intervention Plan (BIP) with strategies to help the student return to school safely and successfully.

⚡ **Important:** The law does not require a student to fail to qualify for services. If your child's emotional, behavioral, or sensory needs are significantly interfering with their ability to attend school, that is enough to initiate a full evaluation.

➡ **Pro Parent Move:** If you suspect your child's school avoidance is disability-related, request an evaluation in writing. Schools must respond within legally required timelines—and cannot deny or delay evaluation solely because your child is missing school.

Category	School Avoidance (School Refusal)	Truancy
Underlying Cause	Emotional distress (anxiety, trauma, sensory overload, etc.)	Disengagement, rebellion, peer pressure, or lack of motivation
Student's Experience	Wants to go to school but feels overwhelmed or unsafe	Chooses not to attend school; may not see value in going
Parent Awareness	Parents are typically aware and involved, often struggling to help	Parents may be unaware of absences or unable to enforce attendance
Emotional Indicators	Crying, panic, somatic symptoms (e.g., stomachaches), meltdowns	Indifference, defensiveness, or even pride in skipping

Category	School Avoidance (School Refusal)	Truancy
Avoidance Patterns	Avoids specific stressors (e.g., tests, lunch, gym, peer conflict)	Skips entire days or classes without pattern
Response to Absences	Feels guilt or shame about missing school	May minimize or justify absences
School's Typical Response	Often misidentified as defiance; may lead to punishment	Typically addressed with disciplinary action or legal consequences
Effective Interventions	Mental health supports, FBA/BIP, IEP/504 accommodations, family-school collaboration	Re-engagement strategies, mentoring, and addressing barriers to motivation
What Makes It Worse	Pressure to attend without support, punitive responses	Ignoring the issue or responding only with consequences
Overlap to Watch For	Emotional distress can sometimes be mislabeled as defiance	Disengagement may stem from unaddressed learning or mental health needs

Comparing School Avoidance and Truancy: Key Differences and Overlaps

✦ **Note:** Even students who earn good grades or appear academically successful can still experience school avoidance. Mental health struggles like anxiety, depression, or perfectionism can be hidden behind high performance—and schools may miss the signs if they only look at attendance data or academic output.

✱ Pro Tip for Parents: If your child is missing school—no matter the reason— keep a written record of what you observe at home and what the school reports. Patterns reveal causes, and causes guide solutions.

⚡ What NOT To Do When Facing School Avoidance

- **Do not force** attendance through threats or punishment—it usually increases anxiety.

- **Do not dismiss** the struggle as "laziness" or "manipulation."

- **Do not delay** asking for help—early intervention matters.

- **Do not accept** a truancy label without questioning the root cause.

- **Do not try to "wait it out"** without a concrete plan—school avoidance typically worsens without action.

➥ **Pro Parent Move:** Approach your child's reluctance with curiosity, not anger. "What is feeling hard today?" opens more doors than "You have to go."

C. Getting Support And Taking Action

If your child's school avoidance is related to a disability—as discussed in the previous section—then schools are legally obligated to act. That means not only providing evaluations and identifying needs, but also following through with meaningful, individualized supports. These might include an IEP, a 504 Plan, a Behavioral Intervention Plan, or accommodations like modified schedules or home-based services.

But understanding what a school can do is only part of the equation. This section focuses on what schools are required to do—and what you can do if they are not following through.

Legal Protections For Students With Disabilities

Here is something many parents do not realize: School avoidance and truancy can be symptoms of an underlying disability. If your child's attendance struggles are connected to anxiety, ADHD, autism, depression, or other emotional or neurological conditions, they may be legally entitled to support—not punishment.

Under the Individuals with Disabilities Education Act (IDEA) and Section 504 of the Rehabilitation Act, schools are required to provide evaluations and accommodations if a child's disability interferes with their ability to attend school regularly.

Supports Schools Can Provide

- **IEPs:** Provide specialized instruction, accommodations, and related services tailored to the student's needs.

- **504 Plans:** Offer accommodations such as modified schedules, counseling, reduced workloads, sensory breaks, or temporary home instruction.

- **FBAs:** Identify the triggers behind school avoidance or refusal.

- **BIPs:** Outline strategies and supports to help the student build coping skills and return to school gradually.

⚡ If your child's school avoidance is disability-related, they cannot be disciplined in the same way as a student without a disability. Federal law requires schools to address the root cause—not just the behavior.

What Schools Are Legally Required To Do

If a child is struggling with school attendance, schools are obligated to do more than issue warnings or assign detention. They must take meaningful, individualized action aimed at understanding and addressing the root cause of the problem.

Before referring a student to truancy court or juvenile services, schools are typically required to implement a series of tiered interventions, such as:

- Referral to a Student Support Team (SST) or consideration for an IEP or 504 Plan

- Access to counseling, mentoring, or regular check-ins

- Development of an attendance improvement plan

- Referral to a School Attendance Review Board (SARB) in districts where one exists

✦ In many states, these early intervention steps are legally required before any punitive action can be taken. Skipping them may violate state education codes or civil rights laws—especially if the student has a disability.

Schools should also take the following actions to ensure they are supporting the student appropriately:

→ **Evaluate** for potential disabilities that may be contributing to the attendance issue. This includes psychological assessments and, when appropriate, psychiatric evaluations—not just academic testing.

→ **Provide interventions** instead of punishment. This may include Functional Behavioral Assessments (FBAs), Behavior Intervention Plans (BIPs), counseling, or tailored accommodations.

➝ **Offer flexible and creative solutions,** such as:

- Partial-day schedules
- Teletherapy or virtual instruction
- Transportation supports
- Scheduled breaks or alternative learning spaces

➝ **Collaborate with families** to develop a plan that is not only legally sound but also realistically supports the child's needs. Open, ongoing communication is essential—and schools should actively invite parents to share what is and is not working at home.

➥ **Pro Parent Move:** If the school resists flexible accommodations, calmly explain what your child needs to begin engaging again. A plan grounded in reality is far more effective than one built around compliance alone.

When Schools Get It Wrong

Unfortunately, not all schools handle school avoidance appropriately. Some see chronic absenteeism and immediately jump to truancy court, threats, or punitive measures.

⚡ Common Misconceptions:

- **"This is a home problem."** (Home problems can also be school problems—if a student cannot get to school, how can it not impact their education?)

- **"The child is just lazy or defiant."** (No, it is more likely they are overwhelmed or struggling.)

- **"If we involve truancy court (juvenile services), that will get the parents' attention."** (But truancy court does not address anxiety, trauma, or learning disabilities—and it rarely solves the root problem.)

If This Happens, Take Action

→ **Request an evaluation in writing.** Ask the school to determine whether your child qualifies for an IEP or 504 plan. Include specific concerns about emotional or behavioral barriers to attendance.

→ **Document all absences, communications, and incidents.** This creates a timeline and paper trail that can help support your case.

→ **If you disagree with the school's evaluation,** you have the right to request an Independent Educational Evaluation (IEE) at the school's expense.

→ **If your child missed significant instruction** due to the school's failure to evaluate or support them appropriately, ask whether they are eligible for compensatory education—additional services to make up for what was lost.

→ **Consider seeking advocacy support** if the school refuses to comply with evaluation timelines, denies services, or continues to default to discipline instead of intervention.

Final Thoughts: From Absences To Answers

School avoidance and truancy are not just attendance problems—they are signals. Signals that something is not working. That a child is in distress. That school may feel overwhelming, unsafe, or emotionally inaccessible. And those signals deserve more than a disciplinary response—they deserve understanding.

As a parent, your job is not to force your child into school at all costs. Your job is to pause and ask, What is getting in the way? What is my child trying to tell me?

And then, to bring that question to the school—clearly, persistently, and without apology—until someone listens.

Because the reality is that when attendance issues are treated as defiance, children are pushed further into isolation. But when they are treated as communication—as a message—we open the door to real solutions. Solutions that involve mental health support, learning assessments, and behavior plans. Solutions that require the school to become a partner, not an enforcer.

Whether your child is missing school due to anxiety, depression, trauma, sensory overload, executive functioning struggles, or quiet disconnection, the path forward is the same: Understand the root. Push for support. Reject shame.

You have the right to expect more than truancy threats and empty calls home. You have the right to expect a plan—one that is proactive, compassionate, and rooted in law.

And most importantly: Your child has the right to be seen, supported, and protected—not punished—for their struggle.

Key Takeaways

✓ **School avoidance is not defiance**—it is distress.

✓ **Truancy can also reflect unmet needs**—not just misbehavior.

✓ **Disability-related attendance challenges are protected under IDEA and Section 504.**

✓ **Punishment does not resolve emotional or learning struggles.** Support does.

✓ **Parents are powerful advocates.** Document everything, ask questions, and push for solutions.

Closing Thought

School refusal can feel like a crisis—but it can also be a turning point. When you step in not with shame, but with strategy, you shift the trajectory. You show your child that their distress is not an inconvenience—it is a message that matters. And you remind the school that attendance is not just about being present; it is about access, equity, and belonging. Your child does not need to be pushed harder. They need to be understood, supported, and seen. And you have every right to demand that they are.

★ *When parents refuse to see attendance as defiance, and instead see distress as a doorway, they change not just outcomes—but lives.*

CHAPTER 13:
Advocating for Your Child

Because no one knows your child—or fights for them—like you do.

Advocacy is the backbone of ensuring that a child with disabilities receives the education they deserve. If you advocate for your child's needs, you do not just open doors—you build bridges that no system can close.

Schools are educational institutions, yes—but they are also bureaucracies. And in that system, without strong, informed parental advocacy, critical services can fall through the cracks. This chapter will equip you with essential advocacy skills, help you build a clear advocacy plan, and show you how to take action—effectively and persistently.

Whether you are brand new to this process or have been navigating the special education system for years, the tools in this chapter will help you communicate clearly, document smartly, and push for meaningful progress in your child's education.

A. Understanding Your Role As An Advocate

Becoming A Confident, Informed, And Sustainable Advocate

Let's start with this: under IDEA, parents are not "invited guests" at the IEP table. You are a required member of the team—and your input is not just valuable, it is protected by law.

Still, schools operate within systems that often prioritize efficiency, budget, and paperwork over individualized support. Educators are juggling large caseloads and competing demands. That does not excuse delays or denials—but it does mean that you are the most consistent, informed, and invested person on the team.

➡ **Pro Parent Move:** If the school tells you, "We don't offer that," or "We don't have the budget for that," remind them: special education services are based on need, not availability. If your child qualifies, they must provide it. Budget issues are their problem—not yours.

Why Your Voice Matters

Services get delayed. Accommodations get skipped. IEP goals get overlooked. Not always out of malice—but often out of inertia. Your advocacy ensures that your child does not fall through the cracks.

Teachers and administrators will come and go. You are the constant. You see the long-term impact. You know when things are working—and when they are not.

⚡ And while schools are required to provide an "appropriate" education, appropriate is not the same as great, best, or ideal. Advocacy is often about pushing that line forward.

Sustainable Advocacy Starts With You

Advocacy is not a sprint—it's a marathon. You cannot help your child thrive if you burn out halfway. Sustainable advocacy starts with taking care of yourself, too.

Try this:

- ✓ Keep a running list of small advocacy wins to remind yourself why you are doing this.
- ✓ Connect with at least one other parent advocate—you are not in this alone.

✓ Take breaks when needed. Resting is not quitting.

➡ **Pro Parent Move:** Advocacy is not about knowing everything. It is about showing up, asking questions, and refusing to be dismissed.

B. Building Collaborative Relationships

How To Communicate Effectively And Get Things Done

IEPs are not created in isolation. They are shaped through emails, phone calls, meetings, hallway check-ins, and yes, sometimes hard conversations. But behind every successful advocacy effort is a foundation of clear communication.

Communicate Clearly And Consistently

- Be concise, respectful, and focused on solutions—not just frustrations.
- Confirm conversations with follow-up emails to create a written record.
- Keep all emails, letters, and notes in one place. If it is not documented, it did not happen.

Build Strategic Relationships

- Schedule regular check-ins with key teachers or staff members.
- Acknowledge educators who go above and beyond—positive relationships build long-term trust.
- Address concerns collaboratively at first. If that fails, escalate strategically.

➡ **Pro Parent Move:** If your emails are ignored, send a formal written request for a meeting—with a deadline. Schools often respond more quickly when a paper trail begins to form.

Know (And Use) Your Rights

Parents have a legal right to:

- Participate in all decisions about their child's services
- Access educational records
- Request evaluations and meetings
- Disagree with decisions and file complaints

If the school refuses a request, ask for Prior Written Notice (PWN)—a powerful tool that requires them to document why they are refusing.

C. Turning Advocacy Into Action

◉ Mini Roadmap: Your First 90 Days Of Advocacy

Getting organized doesn't mean getting it all done at once—it means focusing on what matters most at each stage.

Early Days

Focus: Understand Your Child's Current Plan

- ✓ Read through your child's IEP or 504 Plan in full.
- ✓ Highlight key areas: services, accommodations, goals.
- ✓ Start organizing all records—either in a physical binder or digital folder.
- ✓ Keep track of emails, reports, evaluations, and meeting notes.

➡ **Pro Parent Move:** Ask, "When is our next IEP meeting, and who is the case manager?"

If the team is new, send a short intro email to build rapport early.

Once You Get Your Footing

Focus: Build Your Knowledge And Relationships

- ✓ Learn your rights under IDEA and Section 504 (start with reputable parent-friendly guides).
- ✓ Attend a local workshop or online training on special education basics.
- ✓ Schedule check-ins with your child's teacher, therapist, or case manager.
- ✓ Begin noticing patterns—what's working, what's not.

➡ **Pro Parent Move:** Join a local or national parent advocacy group online. Peer support makes everything feel more doable—and less lonely.

In The Comfort Zone

Focus: Set Advocacy Goals And Monitor Implementation

- ✓ Choose one or two areas to prioritize (e.g., missed services, unclear goals, lack of communication).
- ✓ Track your child's progress and services—keep a simple log.
- ✓ Request a meeting if you see red flags or stagnation.

➡ **Pro Parent Moves:** Submit a Parent Concerns letter before your next IEP meeting. Bring a trusted support person—another parent, therapist, or advocate—to help you feel confident and heard.

You don't need to master everything in 90 days. You just need to start. Advocacy is a muscle—build it one rep at a time.

From Organized To Effective

Being a strong advocate means staying organized, clear about your goals, and prepared to take the next step when needed. This section breaks down how to move from planning to action—and how to keep schools accountable along the way.

Keep The Receipts: Documentation As Advocacy

Good record-keeping is critical for advocating effectively, tracking progress, and holding schools accountable. The more organized your documents, the stronger your case. Whether you prefer digital storage, a paper binder, or both, having a system in place ensures you can access important documents when needed.

What to keep

> - **IEPs & 504 Plans** – Keep all versions to track changes over time.

> - **Progress Reports & Report Cards** – Compare academic and behavioral trends.

> - **Evaluations & Assessment Reports** – Include both school and private evaluations.

> - **Emails & Meeting Notes** – Written communication documents discussions and decisions.

> - **Prior Written Notices (PWNs)** – Essential if the school denies a request or makes changes.

> - **Service Logs & Therapy Notes** – Track whether the school is providing the required services.

Documenting School Decisions

- If the school denies a request, document it. Request Prior Written Notice (PWN) explaining their decision.

- Summarize verbal conversations in writing. If a discussion happens in a meeting or phone call, follow up with an email: "Thank you for discussing [issue] today. Just to clarify, my understanding is [summary]. Please let me know if this is incorrect."

- Keep records of services provided (or not provided). If your child is supposed to receive speech therapy twice a week but only gets it sporadically, document it.

Paper Binder Organization Tips

If you prefer a physical system, a well-organized IEP binder keeps everything accessible. Helpful supplies include a 2–3 inch three-ring binder, dividers or tabs to separate sections, plastic sheet protectors (so you do not have to punch holes in everything), and sticky notes or highlighters for quick referencing. Keep each section organized chronologically—old to new or new to old. Do what works for your brain, but be consistent.

Suggested Sections:

- ☑ **Notices** – whether the notice for the IEP meeting or a change in attendance policy, if it is important, keep it in one place!

- ☑ **IEP & 504 Plans** – Keep the most recent copy in the front, with older versions behind it.

- ☑ **Evaluations & Assessments** – Include all school and private testing.

☑ **Progress Reports & Report Cards** – Helps track academic trends over time.

☑ **Correspondence** – Print emails, meeting notes, and important communications.

☑ **Service Logs & PWNs** – If the school denies or changes services, document it here.

☑ **Advocacy Resources & Notes** – Include legal rights, parent advocacy guides, and important reminders.

➡ **Pro Parent Move:** Before an IEP meeting, gather relevant documents and place them in the front pocket of your binder for easy access during the discussion.

Digital Organization Tips

If you prefer storing records electronically, keeping files organized and easily accessible is key. Use cloud storage or a digital filing system (e.g., Google Drive, OneDrive, Evernote) that automatically organizes files and can be accessed from any device. Use a consistent naming system for files that will sort them automatically. Whether sorting by date or document type, consistency is key.

Sort by Date: Start with the year for easy chronological sorting

> 2025-01-01 IEP.pdf

Sort by Type: If the type is more important, title it accordingly

> IEP 2025-01-01.pdf

➡ **Pro Parent Move:** Store scanned copies of signed IEPs and PWNs so you always have a backup if originals go missing.

Why Organization Matters

- Well-kept records strengthen your advocacy. You will have proof of decisions, services, and agreements.

- A well-organized binder or digital system ensures you can quickly access documents when needed.

- If a dispute arises, detailed documentation provides evidence to support your case.

➡ **Pro Parent Move:** Schools have their records—you need yours, too. Whether in a binder or on a hard drive, a well-organized system keeps you in control.

Communicating With The School: Strengthening Partnerships

Effective communication with your child's teachers, therapists, and IEP team helps ensure consistency, accountability, and collaboration. The more engaged you are, the easier it is to address concerns proactively rather than reactively.

Tips For Effective Communication:

- ✓ **Build relationships early** – Do not wait for a problem to arise; establish rapport with teachers and service providers from the start of the school year.
- ✓ **Stay engaged beyond IEP meetings** – Attend parent-teacher conferences, check in after progress reports, and ask for informal updates.
- ✓ **Be approachable, but assertive** – A cooperative approach fosters trust, but being informed and persistent ensures your child's needs remain the priority.

➡ **Pro Parent Move:** If communication feels one-sided, request regular check-ins (e.g., biweekly email updates) with key staff to stay informed about progress and any concerns.
Follow Up on Concerns: What to Do When Things Are Not Working

Even with a well-written IEP, services do not always get implemented as promised. If something is not right, do not wait—take action immediately.

Steps For Parents To Take

➤ **Document the concern** – Keep a written record of missed services, unaddressed accommodations, or other concerns. Dates, issues, and impact.

➤ **Start with direct communication** – Reach out to the teacher, therapist, or case manager with a polite but firm email or conversation. Often, a polite, firm reminder can get things back on track.

➤ **Request an IEP review if concerns persist** – You do not have to wait for the annual meeting. If something is not working, you can request an IEP meeting at any time.

➡ **Pro Parent Move:** If services are repeatedly missed, ask for compensatory services—this means extra time or services to make up for what was lost. Schools are required to provide them when a failure to implement services has occurred.

Always Ask, Even If You Think The Answer Is No

Schools sometimes assume that if parents do not ask, they do not need to provide certain services or supports. Do not let assumptions dictate your child's education—ask anyway. Ask about all available supports. Schools will not always offer services unless you ask for them.

- **Request explanations in writing** – If a service is denied, ask: "Can you provide that in writing, along with the data used to make this decision?"

- **Know that persistence matters** – Sometimes, schools delay or deny requests, hoping parents will drop the issue. Keep asking.

Know When To Push: From Prep To Escalation

◉ *Set Clear Goals*

While you can always change your route or even your destination, how can you know where you are going without a destination in mind? Make sure you know your own and your child's (if applicable) short- and long-term goals. Even if they are not all in the IEP, it is important to always know what you are striving for. Here are some examples of short and long-term goals

- **Short-term goals:** Improve reading fluency, reduce anxiety, and build social skills.

- **Long-term goals:** Increase independence, prepare for transitions, build self-advocacy.

To ensure you are making progress along your route, ensure goals are measurable—otherwise, how will you know if they are working?

Prepare For Meetings

- Submit a Parent Concerns document 3–5 days before any IEP or 504 meeting.

- Request an agenda—or bring your own.

- Bring someone with you, such as a friend, advocate, therapist, or another parent.

Use A 3-Point Approach:

1. What is the issue?
2. What does the data show?
3. What do you propose?

▶ **Instead of saying:** "I feel like my child is not progressing in reading." Say: "Based on the last three progress reports, my child's fluency has plateaued. I would like to add an evidence-based reading intervention."

⚡ *Escalate When Necessary*

If the school is not responding, delaying services, or denying supports:

- Request mediation with a neutral third party.
- File a state complaint if IDEA is being violated.
- Request a due process hearing for serious issues impacting FAPE.

➡ **Pro Parent Move:** Schools sometimes delay, hoping you will back off. Do not. IDEA has strict timelines—use them.

If informal communication fails, take the next step—each rung builds power.

1. **Direct Communication:** Start with a polite but firm email to the teacher or case manager.

2. **Request an IEP or 504 Meeting:** You do not have to wait for the annual meeting. You can request one at any time.

3. **Request Mediation:** Bring in a neutral third party to help resolve disagreements.

4. **File a State Complaint:** A state complaint can trigger an investigation and force the school to correct IDEA violations—like missed services, ignored timelines, or failure to follow the IEP.

5. **Request a Due Process Hearing:** This is a formal legal process. Use it when serious issues (like denial of services) remain unresolved.

Final Thoughts: The Long-Term Impact Of Advocacy

Advocacy is not a one-time event. It is a long game—a continuous process of showing up, asking tough questions, pushing for clarity, and celebrating the progress, no matter how small.

As your child grows, their needs will evolve. Transitions will come. Services may shift. New challenges will emerge. But the tools you use—documentation, communication, preparation, persistence—will always be relevant.

The most effective advocates are not the loudest in the room. They are the ones who are informed, organized, and unwilling to let the system forget that their child matters.

➡ **Pro Parent Move:** Your voice is the most powerful tool your child has. Use it clearly, consistently, and unapologetically.

Key Takeaways:

✓ **Advocacy is not a phase**—it is a practice.
✓ **Preparation matters**—documents, goals, and data help drive change.
✓ **Communication is your bridge**—follow up, clarify, and document everything.
✓ **Escalation is a right**—when collaboration fails, use the tools IDEA gives you.
✓ **Your persistence is not "too much."** It is the reason your child gets what they need.

You do not have to be perfect to be effective. You just have to keep showing up. Every email you send, every document you organize, every question you ask—it all adds up. Advocacy is not just about fixing problems; it is about building a foundation your child can stand on.

You do not have to move mountains every day. You just have to keep moving—and every step you take is one more your child does not have to take alone.

CHAPTER 14:
Emotional Well-being For Parents

Self Care is not selfish—it is self preservation!

Navigating The Emotional Journey Of Advocacy and Parenting

Advocacy is not just about mastering the process—it is about sustaining yourself along the way. This chapter is not a detour from the work; it is a checkpoint. The demands of special education advocacy can be relentless, and emotional well-being is not a luxury—it is part of the strategy. When parents pause, reset, and reconnect to their own strength, they can show up more clearly and consistently for their child.

Advocating for a child with special needs is not just about IEPs, meetings, and services—it is also about keeping yourself together while doing it all. The relentless push for accommodations, the bureaucratic hurdles, the emotional weight of your child's struggles—it all takes a toll.

And let's not forget the emotional rollercoaster—one minute you are celebrating a small victory (your child finally got that much-needed speech therapy!), and the next, you are banging your head against a wall because the school is suddenly reevaluating whether your child even needs those services. Advocacy can feel like a constant uphill battle, which is why managing your emotional well-being is just as important as understanding special education law.

This chapter offers practical strategies for managing stress, protecting your emotional well-being, and even finding humor in the chaos. Because some moments in this journey are so ridiculous, all you can do is laugh.

Emotional well-being is not one-size-fits-all. There is no formula for what you will need emotionally to sustain this work. What works for one parent might feel irrelevant—or even unhelpful—to another.

Some of you will need therapy. Others will need silence. Some will laugh through the absurdity. Others will cry through the exhaustion. Most will do all of the above, sometimes in the same week. The goal here is not to offer a complete solution—it is to offer a mirror, a few tools, and a reminder that your well-being matters as much as your child's IEP.

This is not a footnote in your advocacy journey. This is part of the plan. If you do not protect your energy, everything else becomes harder. If you do, everything becomes more possible.

A. Coping With Stress And Anxiety

The emotional weight of advocacy is cumulative. This section provides tools not just to survive the hard moments—but to sustain the entire journey ahead.

Understanding The Emotional Toll Of Advocacy

Advocating for a child with special needs is like having a second full-time job, but without the paycheck or vacation days. The stress is not just about pushing for services—it is about staying on top of your child's program while still managing siblings, your full-time job, prescriptions, and organizing extracurricular activities, from therapy to football. Parenting ain't easy! But parenting special needs is nuts.

Over time, this stress accumulates, leading to burnout, anxiety, and even physical health issues if left unchecked.

⚡ Common Sources Of Parental Stress

- **Constant Advocacy Pressure** – Feeling like you always have to fight for basic rights.

- **Uncertainty About the Future** – Worrying about your child's long-term educational, financial, and social outcomes.

- **Navigating the System** – Endless bureaucracy, paperwork, and unresponsive institutions.

- **Social Isolation** – Feeling disconnected from friends and family who do not fully understand the challenges.

- **Emotional Exhaustion** – Facing setbacks, denials, and slow progress, despite all your efforts.

- **Guilt** – That persistent, nagging feeling that you are never doing enough, no matter how hard you try.

And let's not forget decision fatigue—constantly having to research, weigh options, and make critical decisions about your child's education and well-being. Should you push for more therapy? Is that private evaluation worth it? What if the school retaliates if you file a complaint? The mental load is enormous.

Partners and the Emotional Load

In most families, one parent becomes the point person for special education advocacy—or honestly, for everything related to the kids. They become the default contact. The keeper of appointments. The note-taker. The meeting scheduler. The one who remembers which form is due and what the OT said last Tuesday. This happens even in households where both parents work full-time.

If that is you, then you already know how heavy that mental load can be—and how isolating it often is.

You might have a partner who supports you emotionally but is not looped into the day-to-day. Or a partner who simply does not engage, leaving you to carry the entire system on your back. Or the classic: *"You are better at that than I am."*

Maybe you are in lockstep with your partner—able to balance responsibilities like trapeze artists in perfect rhythm. If so, hold onto that and protect it. That kind of coordination is rare, and it makes the hard days more survivable.

But for many, the imbalance leads to resentment, exhaustion, and emotional distance.

◉ *For The Primary Parent: Staying Sane When You Are The One Carrying It*

- **Stop waiting for the other person to take the lead.** That may never happen. You are not failing because they are underperforming.

- **Set boundaries around communication.** You do not need to debrief every meeting or ask for permission to make decisions. Share what matters— but protect your bandwidth.

- **Ask for specific support, not blanket involvement.** *"I need you to handle the next school email thread"* is more effective than *"You never help with anything."*

- **Vent to someone safe**—but not always to your partner. Sometimes the healthiest move is processing your frustration with someone who understands this dynamic, like a fellow parent advocate or a therapist (I highly recommend the latter).

▶ For the partner who wants to step up: how to stop being a bystander

If you are reading this and realizing you have been less involved than you should be—good. Awareness is the start, but action is the fix.

Here is how you can be useful **without making your partner do more emotional labor just to include you:**

- **Do not ask "What can I do?"** That question puts the burden right back on your partner to assign you tasks. They do not need another job.

- **Learn the routine.** Know the teachers' names, the service providers, the acronyms. Figure out where the IEP folder lives. Be able to talk about your child's needs without being handed a cheat sheet.

- **Track the calendar.** Know when the next meeting is. Offer to attend, take notes, or follow up on an action item. Even if you cannot be there, being aware gives your partner a chance to offload some mental stress before it piles up.

- **Jump in without a manual.** If your partner is sick, overwhelmed, or just done, you should be able to step up without needing a step-by-step guide. If you cannot parent without asking 20 questions, it is time to brush up.

- **Carry part of the emotional weight.** This means listening without fixing, validating without judgment, and showing up without being asked. Presence is powerful.

The goal is not to split everything 50/50. The goal is to build shared ownership—so one person is not crushed while the other floats. If your partner only has 80, you bring the other 20. And when they are running at 40, you cover the rest. You do not have to be everything, all the time. But you do have to step up—and step in—when it counts.

I say all of this from experience. And as I have mentioned elsewhere in this book—I did not always get it right. I wish I had followed this advice sooner. But hindsight does not erase the mess. It just gives it shape.

So if you are reading this and feeling like you are already behind, let that go. You are not. Just knowing these patterns exist might be enough to help you make different choices—or at least recognize the weight you are carrying for what it is. That awareness alone is powerful.

✦ And A Note About The Siblings

In many families, the energy around advocacy for one child affects everyone—including the siblings. Sometimes they resent the attention. Sometimes they withdraw. Sometimes they try to overcompensate by being the "easy" one. And in some families, it is even more complicated—blended households, custody schedules, stepparents, estrangement, or just plain chaos.

That is reality. And kids are resilient.

Do not turn this into another source of guilt. You are doing your best. It does not help them if you constantly ask, *"Are you okay? Am I a good parent? Are you happy?"* That just transfers your emotional burden onto them.

What does help is giving them their own tools. And while the last thing you need is another appointment on the calendar, sometimes giving a child their own therapist is one of the best things you can do. Not because something is wrong—but because it gives them a safe space to sort through their own feelings.

Therapy is not about complaining about parents. It is about building emotional vocabulary, learning how to speak up, and understanding that complex feelings are normal. And when those kids grow into teens or adults—and if life ever throws them into crisis—therapy will already feel familiar. It will not be a last resort. It will just be part of their toolkit.

Each of my five children would gladly tell you I am not "Mom of the Year." That award seems to narrowly slip out of reach every single time—usually somewhere between lost permission slips, missed teacher meetings, and "you're on your own" for dinner three nights in a row.

I have not done any of this perfectly. But I have learned—often the hard way—that naming the impact, holding space for each child's experience, and giving them room to have their own emotional process matters. You do not have to fix it all. You just have to stay in the conversation.

And sometimes? Sometimes the most emotionally intelligent thing you can say is, *"You know who would be a good person to talk to about that? Your therapist."*

That is not dismissal (OK, well, sometimes it's dismissal). That is modeling boundaries. That is giving your child permission to process in a space where they can be fully heard—without making you the emotional go-between. That is not failure. That is strategy.

And yes—eventually, it all comes out in the college essays. May as well make it a good story.

Practical Stress-Relief Strategies

→ **Build a Support System** – You cannot do this alone. Lean on family, friends, parent groups, and professional advocates for emotional and logistical support.

→ **Practice Mindfulness** – Daily deep breathing, meditation, or even a short walk can bring mental clarity.

→ **Set Realistic Expectations** – Progress is often slow and unpredictable, but celebrating small victories keeps you going.

→ **Journaling** – Writing about daily challenges and successes helps process emotions and track progress.

→ **Therapy or Counseling** – Seeking professional help is not a sign of weakness—it is a strategy for long-term resilience.

→ **12-Step Programs** – Addiction, burnout, and emotional overload rarely appear all at once—they build slowly, often silently. Whether it is turning to alcohol, food, work, or control as a coping mechanism, these patterns can sneak up on even the most high-functioning, well-intentioned parents. Programs like AA (Alcoholics Anonymous), Over Eaters Anonymous (OA), Al-Anon (for the family and friends of the alcoholic), and CODA (Co-Dependents Anonymous) offer support, structure, and community for those navigating chronic stress, dysfunctional dynamics, or the toll of caregiving. You do not have to hit rock bottom to ask for help—and you do not have to do it alone.

∗ **Pro Parent Tip:** If a school is dragging its feet or delaying services, take a mental health break before responding. Writing a calm, well-structured email will always be more effective than firing off a rage-fueled response.

When to Seek Professional Help

If stress leads to chronic exhaustion, sleep issues, persistent anxiety, physical symptoms, or your life is just plain unmanageable, it may be time to consult a therapist or counselor. Advocacy is a marathon, not a sprint—you need the mental strength to sustain the journey.

B. Self-Care Strategies

Replenishing Your Energy To Continue The Journey

Advocating for your child is demanding. It requires patience, persistence, and a level of emotional resilience that can feel impossible to maintain when you are running on empty. That is why self-care is not a luxury—it is a necessity. You cannot be an effective advocate, parent, or problem-solver if you are constantly overwhelmed, exhausted, or teetering on the edge of burnout.

It is easy to push your own needs aside when there are IEP meetings to attend, services to fight for, and school emails piling up in your inbox. But here's the thing: You cannot pour from an empty cup. Taking care of yourself is taking care of your child, because when you feel balanced, rested, and supported, you can show up as the strong, focused person they need.

Why Self-Care Matters

It is easy for parents to feel guilty about taking time for themselves. But if you do not take care of yourself, you will burn out—and that helps no one.

Self-care is not about neglecting your responsibilities. It is about preserving your ability to keep showing up, day after day, without losing yourself in the process.

Building A Sustainable Self-Care Routine

Many parents believe self-care requires large chunks of time—but even small, daily habits can help reduce stress and improve emotional well-being.

▶ Quick, Actionable Self-Care Routines For Busy Parents

1. **Morning Reset (5 Minutes)** – Take a few deep breaths, set an intention, or stretch to mentally prepare for the day.
2. **Midday Recharge (10 Minutes)** – Step outside for fresh air, listen to music, or write down one thing that went well.
3. **Evening Wind-Down (15 Minutes)** – Engage in a relaxing activity, such as reading, taking a bath, or journaling.

★ *Additional Self-Care Strategies*

- **Exercise** – Movement releases endorphins, which reduce stress and increase energy. Even a short daily walk helps.

- **Prioritize Sleep** – Lack of sleep amplifies anxiety and weakens patience. Aim for at least 7 hours per night.

- **Eat Nutritious Foods** – Blood sugar imbalances affect mood and energy levels. Focus on protein, fiber, and hydration.

- **Engage in Hobbies** – Creative activities like painting, writing, or gardening help process stress in a positive way.

Mid-Journey Reset: Five Rules For The Long Haul

1. You are not your child's entire support system—you are their most consistent advocate.

2. Keep the documents that matter. Let go of what does not.

3. Rest is not retreat. It is preparation.

4. Ask for help early. Ask again if needed.

5. When the system is absurd, allow yourself to laugh. It clears space for perspective.

Use this list anytime you feel stuck or overwhelmed. It is not a solution—it is a reset.

C. Finding Humor In The Chaos

Some days in this journey are so unpredictable, so bureaucratically absurd, or just so exhausting that the only logical response is to laugh. While advocacy for your child's needs is serious work, it does not have to be joyless. Humor can be a lifeline. It creates emotional breathing room, builds perspective, and reminds you that even when things go sideways, you are still standing. When used intentionally, laughter becomes more than a coping tool—it becomes a source of strength.

The Power Of Laughter In Managing Stress

Advocating for your child with disabilities can feel like navigating an endless maze of paperwork, meetings, and unexpected challenges. It is serious work, but that does not mean it has to be devoid of joy. If you cannot laugh at some of the absurdities along the way, the weight of it all can become overwhelming.

Humor is not just a coping mechanism—it is a survival tool. It can turn frustration into perspective, ease tension in high-stress moments, and remind you that not every battle needs to drain your energy. Some days, the best thing you can do is simply laugh, regroup, and try again tomorrow.

The Science Behind Laughter

Laughter is not just about making light of difficult situations—it has real psychological and physiological benefits:

★ **Reduces Stress Hormones** – Laughter lowers cortisol levels, helping parents feel more relaxed and less reactive.

★ **Improves Problem-Solving** – A humorous outlook can reframe frustrating situations, making them feel more manageable. Sometimes, stepping back and finding the humor in a situation can help you approach it from a fresh, less emotional perspective.

★ **Builds Resilience** – Parents who can find joy in small moments tend to handle long-term challenges more effectively. Humor creates emotional distance, allowing you to move forward without carrying every battle on your shoulders.

➡ **Pro Parent Move:** If you find yourself overwhelmed by a situation, ask yourself, "Will this be funny in a year? A month? A week?" If the answer is yes, maybe you can start laughing now.

Finding Humor In The Chaos

★ **Keep a "Ridiculous Moments" Journal** – Document the funniest things your child says, the most absurd school policies you encounter, or the unexpected mishaps that leave you shaking your head. One day, you will look back and laugh.

★ **Share Stories with Other Parents** – Other parents in the special education world understand the unique humor in IEP meetings, school bureaucracy, and sensory-related meltdowns in public. Finding a community that can laugh with you makes the journey feel lighter.

★ **Laugh at Bureaucracy (When You Can)** – Some school policies and procedural delays are so mind-bogglingly inefficient that laughter is the only sane response. If you have ever had to download 4 different apps just to communicate with your child's teachers, you know exactly what this means.

★ **Embrace Imperfection** – There will be days when everything goes completely off the rails. Missed appointments, meltdowns, forgotten paperwork—it happens. Instead of beating yourself up, sometimes the best response is a deep breath, a good laugh, and the knowledge that tomorrow is a new day.

Final Thoughts: Balancing Advocacy And Emotional Well-being

Advocating for your child is not just about knowledge and persistence—it is about sustaining yourself for the long haul. Special education advocacy is not a sprint; it is a marathon, filled with unexpected detours, paperwork pileups, and victories that can feel both hard-won and short-lived. That is why your emotional well-being is not optional—it is foundational.

There will be moments when you feel like you are carrying everything alone. The paperwork, the calls, the emails, the therapies, the meetings, the missed school days, the emotional fallout, the second-guessing. That weight is real. And while it may feel noble to carry it all without complaint, burnout serves no one.

You do not need to fight every battle. You do not have to answer every email within five minutes. You do not have to "do it all" to be a good parent. Sometimes, advocacy looks like taking a breath. Or a walk. Or a nap. Sometimes it looks like saying "Not today." The strongest advocates are not the ones who push nonstop. They are the ones who know when to pause, when to laugh, and when to ask for help.

Humor, rest, and perspective are not detours from advocacy. They are what make advocacy sustainable.

➡ **Pro Parent Move:** When things feel heavy, ask yourself:

- Would I expect my child to keep going like this without support?
- What would I want them to do if they felt this overwhelmed?
- Am I showing them what it looks like to care for yourself while caring for others?

Key Takeaways

✓ **You cannot advocate effectively if you are emotionally depleted.**

✓ **Stress and burnout are real**—and they are not signs of weakness.

✓ **Support systems** (professional or peer) are essential for sustainability.

✓ **Self-care is not indulgent.** It is a strategy.

✓ **Humor is a survival tool.** Use it liberally.

✓ **You do not have to be perfect.** You just have to keep showing up.

You are not just advocating for services—you are building the conditions for your child to thrive. That work is complex, emotional, and often exhausting. But you are not alone in it. This chapter offered strategies to help you pause, recalibrate, and continue with intention.

The road ahead will bring new chapters, new questions, and new demands—and your well-being remains essential in all of it.

CHAPTER 15:
Navigating Field Trips And Extracurricular Activities

Creating Inclusive, Engaging Opportunities Beyond The Classroom

Extracurriculars and field trips are not extras—they are essential. They are where children build confidence, friendships, and lifelong skills. But for students with disabilities, these opportunities are too often inaccessible or withheld entirely. Whether due to physical barriers, staff unfamiliarity, or low expectations, the message is often the same: You are not part of this.

However, for children with disabilities, participating in these activities can be challenging—sometimes frustratingly so. Barriers such as inaccessible facilities, lack of awareness among educators and coaches, and the absence of necessary accommodations can make joining a club or team feel like an uphill battle. Some parents may even hear the dreaded, "We don't have a program for that," or "We've never had a student with those needs before."

Field trips, too, are a critical part of the school experience—offering hands-on learning, social interaction, and community engagement. But like extracurriculars, they can present access barriers for students with disabilities if proper planning and accommodations are not in place.

The bottom line: Your child has the right to participate. And with the right supports and advocacy, they can thrive in extracurriculars just as they do in academics.

Under Section 504 of the Rehabilitation Act, schools receiving federal funds must provide students with disabilities equal access to extracurriculars. This protection also extends to field trips. If a trip is offered to students, it must also be made accessible to students with disabilities. This includes transportation, on-site accessibility, medical supports, and supervision accommodations. If a parent is told their child "cannot attend," that is a red flag—not a reason to give up. IDEA reinforces this obligation by requiring that students receive a Free Appropriate Public Education (FAPE), which includes non-academic and extracurriculars that support the child's overall development.

This chapter will help you identify inclusive programs, advocate for necessary accommodations, encourage your child's participation, and—when needed— push for systemic change to ensure every student has access to a well-rounded and meaningful school experience.

A. Finding Inclusive Programs

Extracurriculars are more than just fun—they are crucial to a child's development. Whether it is playing soccer, performing in a school play, joining a robotics team, or competing in debate, these experiences help children build friendships, gain confidence, develop leadership skills, and explore their personal interests.

But for students with disabilities, participation is not always as simple as signing up. Physical, social, and systemic barriers often limit access to these opportunities. True inclusion in extracurriculars is not just about making space—it is about ensuring every student has the opportunity to participate fully and meaningfully.

Legal Snapshot: Your Child's Right To Inclusion

- **Section 504** guarantees equal access to extracurricular activities for students with disabilities in any federally funded school.

- **IDEA** reinforces that FAPE includes non-academic activities that support development.

❋ Field trips and clubs are not optional add-ons—they must be made accessible.

Your Child's Legal Right To Participate

Under Section 504 of the Rehabilitation Act, schools that receive federal funding must provide students with disabilities equal access to extracurriculars. IDEA reinforces this obligation through FAPE, which includes non-academic opportunities that support the child's overall development.

If a school claims, "We cannot accommodate that," or "We have never done this before," remember: the law protects your child's right to participate—just like in academics.

❋ Pro Parent Tip: If your child expresses interest in a program but the school hesitates, ask: "What accommodations have you used in similar situations?" and "What can we do to make this work?"

The Importance Of Inclusive Extracurricular Activities

Participating in extracurriculars provides invaluable life skills that support a child's overall growth:

★ **Social Skills** – Interacting with peers outside of academics fosters teamwork, communication, and relationship-building. Clubs and sports create natural social opportunities for children who may struggle with peer interactions.

★ **Confidence & Self-Identity** – Finding an activity a child genuinely enjoys can boost self-esteem, independence, and a sense of belonging. Feeling valued in a team or club helps reinforce a positive self-perception.

★ **Physical & Mental Well-being** – Sports, music, drama, and creative activities provide stress relief, promote physical fitness, and encourage emotional expression.

★ **Leadership & Responsibility** – Taking on team roles, organizing events, or mentoring younger students teaches problem-solving, accountability, and collaboration.

★ **Academic & Career Benefits** – Many extracurricular activities enhance critical thinking, discipline, and time management—all skills that translate into academic and professional success.

Despite these benefits, many students with disabilities face unnecessary barriers to participation.

⚡ Field Trips Are Not Optional

Field trips are often treated as "nice-to-haves"—but they are part of a well-rounded education. If your child is excluded because of disability-related needs, this could be a violation of their right to accessible education under IDEA or Section 504.

Access ≠ Optional: Field Trip Inclusion Essentials

- Accessible transportation (including wheelchair lifts, aides, or alternative transit)
- Medical supports (nurse or trained staff, medication plans)
- Sensory and behavioral accommodations
- Advance coordination with families for planning

✱ Pro Parent Prompt: "If this trip is part of the curriculum, what are your plans to make it accessible to my child?"

➡ Pro Parent Move: If the school says the trip "may not be appropriate," ask:

- ➤ "What accommodations would make it accessible?"
- ➤ "What steps can we take to support safe participation?"

If the school responds with "just keep them home," remind them:

- ➤ "Since this trip is part of the educational program, how will you ensure my child has equal access?"

What Schools Must Do:

- Provide accommodations that ensure safety and inclusion.
- Offer accessible transportation and chaperone support.
- Collaborate with parents to anticipate medical, sensory, or behavioral needs.

Common Barriers To Inclusion In Field Trips And Extracurriculars

Students with disabilities are often left out of school activities—not because they lack interest or ability, but because of systemic challenges.

- ✗ **Inaccessible Facilities** – Lack of accessible equipment or wheelchair-friendly spaces.
- ✗ **Staff Unfamiliarity** – Coaches or instructors may lack inclusion training.
- ✗ **Social Exclusion** – Peers may not understand how to include classmates with diverse needs.
- ✗ **Assumptions About Ability** – Adults may underestimate students instead of focusing on supports.

✕ **Scheduling Conflicts** – Activities may overlap with therapy sessions or medical needs.

✱ **Pro Parent Tip:** If your child expresses interest in a program, but the school claims they "cannot accommodate it," push back. Under Section 504 and IDEA, schools must ensure equal access to extracurricular activities—just like academics. The law protects inclusion, even if the school has never worked with a student in that activity before.

How To Find Inclusive Programs

If a school program is not naturally accessible or inclusive, parents may need to get creative in finding (or even creating) opportunities that meet their child's needs.

✓ **Ask Schools About Their Inclusion Policies** – Many schools have policies in place to ensure inclusive participation in extracurricular activities. Ask:

- "What accommodations are available for students with disabilities?"
- "Has the school provided supports for students with similar needs before?"
- "Are there staff members trained in adaptive coaching or inclusive instruction?"

✓ **Look for Adaptive Sports and Activities** – Many communities have inclusive athletic and arts programs, such as:

- Special Olympics (sports programs designed for individuals with disabilities).
- Unified Sports (teams combining students with and without disabilities).
- Inclusive theater groups with accessible roles and performance accommodations.

✓ **Partner with Teachers and Therapists** – Special education teachers, occupational therapists, and school psychologists can recommend extracurriculars that match a child's strengths, sensory needs, and interests.

✓ **Seek Out Peer Support Programs** – Some schools offer buddy systems or peer mentoring to help students with disabilities feel more comfortable joining clubs and sports teams.

✓ **Explore Local and Virtual Options** – Many nonprofits, libraries, museums, and youth organizations offer inclusive STEM, arts, and leadership programs. If local options are limited, consider virtual clubs, esports teams, or online interest-based communities.

✓ **Ask Other Parents** – Local disability organizations and parent networks often have the best recommendations for inclusive programs, whether through schools, community centers, or private organizations.

➡ **Pro Parent Move:** If your child is interested in an activity but is not sure if they will feel comfortable, ask if they can attend a few trial sessions before committing. This allows them to ease into the experience and determine what support they may need.

Advocating For Inclusion In Extracurricular Activities

If a program is not currently accessible, parents can help push for change by advocating for inclusive opportunities.

★ **Request Modifications** – Even if an activity is not fully inclusive yet, small adjustments can make a significant difference:

- Accessible equipment or sensory-friendly supports.
- Extended practice times or alternative participation roles.
- Visual schedules or structured routines for predictability.

★ **Educate Coaches and Leaders** – Many want to be inclusive but do not know how. Schools and clubs may not be intentionally excluding students—they just need guidance on how to support them. Offer training resources on disability awareness or ask if a special education staff member can consult on accommodations.

★ **Suggest New Programs** – If nothing inclusive exists, work with other parents or staff to create one. Schools are more likely to act when they see a shared need.

➡ **Pro Parent Move:** Ask solution-focused questions like, "What changes could be made to help my child participate?" and "What supports would make this program more accessible?" This keeps the conversation solution-focused rather than letting them default to 'no, we cannot.'

Every Child Deserves A Place

Extracurriculars are not "extras"—they are essential. They build confidence, nurture talent, and offer joy and connection. Every child deserves access to that.

Inclusion is not about charity—it is about rights. If the door is not open, you can help unlock it. When your child finds a place where they are welcomed and valued, it changes everything—not just for them, but for everyone watching.

➡ **Pro Parent Move:** If a school or community program is not inclusive today, that does not mean it can't be. Ask, push, suggest, and collaborate. You are not just advocating for access—you are shaping a culture of inclusion.

B. Encouraging Participation

Even with accommodations in place, participation does not always come easily. This section focuses on supporting your child emotionally and socially as they step into new activities—and helping them build confidence, resilience, and a sense of belonging along the way.

Overcoming Barriers And Building Confidence

Even when inclusive programs or field trips are available, some children may still feel hesitant to participate due to...

➤ **Fear of social rejection** – Worries about being left out or not fitting in

➤ **Anxiety about performance** – Concerns about keeping up or not being "good enough"

➤ **Previous negative experiences** – Prior exclusion can make children hesitant to try again

➤ **Sensory or emotional overwhelm** – Large groups, bright lights, or noise can be stressful

Strategies To Encourage Participation

◇ **Start Small** – Introduce the child to low-pressure activities, such as attending a club meeting, before making a full commitment.

◇ **Use Strengths and Interests** – If a child loves music, try choir or band. If they enjoy building things, look into robotics or STEM clubs.

◇ **Preview the Experience** – Use photos, maps, or stories to prepare your child for what to expect on a field trip. A social story or visual schedule can help reduce anxiety.

◇ **Pair with a Buddy** – Having a friend or mentor in the activity can provide encouragement and a sense of security.

◇ **Gradually Increase Independence** – Support initial involvement, but encourage progressive independence over time.

◇ **Frame It as a Fun Challenge** – If a child resists, turn participation into a short-term "trial" rather than a permanent commitment.

✱ **Pro Parent Tip:** If a child struggles with transitions, create a social story or visual schedule that explains what to expect during the activity.

The Role Of Extracurricular Activities In A Child's Growth

Extracurriculars offer opportunities for friendship, self-expression, and skill development. You play a crucial role in:

✓ Finding inclusive programs that meet their child's needs
✓ Encouraging participation while addressing hesitations
✓ Advocating for necessary accommodations when barriers arise
✓ Balancing academic and extracurricular commitments for overall well-being

➡ **Pro Parent Move:** With patience, creativity, and a little advocacy, every child can find a meaningful extracurricular activity that enriches their life.

By ensuring accessibility, encouraging participation, and helping their child build confidence, parents can open the door to new friendships, exciting experiences, and a deeper sense of belonging—all of which are just as important as academic success.

C. Advocating For Lasting Change

Encouragement matters. When your child feels supported—not pressured—they are more likely to explore new activities and take healthy risks.

But here is the thing: you should not have to fight the same fight every year. This section focuses on how to move from one-time problem-solving to systems-level advocacy—so that all students, now and in the future, have equal access to extracurricular opportunities.

Beyond Individual Advocacy: Creating Inclusive Systems

Advocating for your child is essential, but what about the next generation of students with disabilities? Many school extracurricular programs lack consistent policies on inclusion, leaving participation up to the discretion of individual teachers or coaches. While some educators are naturally inclusive, others may hesitate or lack training.

That is why system-wide change matters. By working with other parents, educators, and administrators, you can help push for lasting policies that normalize inclusion in extracurriculars.

➡ **Pro Parent Move:** Schools already have policies for attendance, behavior, and sports participation—why not a policy on extracurricular access and inclusion?

Step 1: Work With Your School To Establish Inclusive Policies

Start by asking the right questions:

→ "Does the school have an official policy on accommodating students with disabilities in clubs, sports, or student organizations?"

→ "Does the school have an inclusion policy for field trips—especially for students with mobility, sensory, or medical needs?"

→ "Are club advisors, coaches, and activity leaders trained on disability inclusion?"

→ "How does the school ensure all students—regardless of disability—know about and feel welcomed in extracurriculars?"

If no policies exist – Work with your school's principal, special education team, or PTA to push for one.

If policies exist but are not enforced – Request accountability measures, such as teacher training or parent input on accessibility improvements.

✱ **Pro Parent Tip:** If your district has a Special Education Parent Advisory Council (SEPAC) or Special Education Parent Teacher Association (SEPTA), these are great places to advocate for systemic improvements to access and inclusion.

Step 2: Push For Disability Training Of Extracurricular Staff

Many coaches, club advisors, and arts directors want to be inclusive but do not know how. A simple disability awareness session for extracurricular leaders can prevent exclusion before it starts.

➡ **Pro Parent Move:** Offer to share resources or connect them with local disability organizations that provide training on working with diverse learners.

What training should include?

- Understanding disability beyond stereotypes
- How to plan inclusive field trips that account for accessibility, supervision, and support
- Common misconceptions (e.g., assuming a child with ADHD "cannot focus" in debate)
- Practical accommodations for different extracurricular settings

Step 3: Connect With Other Parents & Build A Community Of Advocates

Schools respond faster when they hear from multiple parents. If your child has faced barriers to participation, chances are other families have too.

Ways to build momentum:

✓ Start a parent-led advocacy group focused on extracurricular inclusion
✓ Connect with local disability rights organizations to amplify your message
✓ Partner with your school's PTA or parent council to bring inclusion into district-wide conversations

✱ Pro Parent Tip: Local media attention can be a powerful tool. If advocacy efforts stall, reaching out to education reporters can sometimes nudge schools into action.

Whether you are building partnerships or pushing for policy change, remember this: small actions—especially when repeated—can lead to cultural shifts. You are not just advocating for your child; you are paving the way for a more inclusive future.

Final Thoughts: Building A More Inclusive Future

The goal is not just to open doors for your child—it is to ensure that all children with disabilities have access to extracurricular activities that build confidence, foster friendships, and develop real-world skills. Inclusion is not optional. It is not a favor. It is a right.

Whether you are pushing for policy changes, helping staff understand accommodations, or organizing with other parents, your advocacy can spark lasting impact—not just for today, but for the students who come next.

Inclusion does not happen passively. It takes persistence, creativity, and a willingness to challenge, "We have never done that before." But the payoff is undeniable. When a child finds their passion and is welcomed in, everything changes.

Every child deserves a place to belong—to be seen, supported, and celebrated, not just in the classroom, but in every accessible and inclusive part of the school community. Whether it is a robotics team, an overnight field trip, or a weekend competition, every student deserves to participate—and to be included from the start, not added in as an afterthought.

Key Takeaways:

✓ **Inclusion is a right**—not a privilege—and applies to extracurriculars as well as academics.

✓ **Schools should have formal, enforceable policies** ensuring access to clubs, sports, and programs.

✓ **Parent-led advocacy** is one of the most effective drivers of systemic change.

✓ **Your experience**, once documented, can serve as a roadmap for others.

✓ **Every child deserves a place to belong**, grow, and thrive.

➡ **Pro Parent Move:** By asking the right questions, pushing for change, and working collaboratively with educators and organizers, you can help create opportunities—not just for your child, but for others in the future.

When one child is truly included, it does more than open a door—it lights the way for others to follow.

CHAPTER 16:
Building Independence

Empowering Students With Disabilities To Lead Fulfilling, Self-Sufficient Lives

Transitioning from adolescence to adulthood is a major milestone for all young people—but for many students with disabilities, this journey takes more than crossed fingers and a few motivational posters. It requires intentional planning, structured support, and targeted skill-building. Independence does not happen overnight. It is built over time through consistent teaching, real-world experiences, and meaningful chances to take ownership of decisions (and yes, that includes learning from some not-so-great ones).

For parents, this transition can be both exciting and terrifying. One minute, your child is in a structured school environment with clear routines and support systems. The next, they are expected to navigate college, employment, and daily life with significantly fewer safety nets—and a lot more "figure it out yourself" moments. That shift can feel overwhelming, and many parents wonder: Will my child be ready?

The good news? Yes, they can be. But only with the right preparation.

So, how do you ensure they have the skills, confidence, and support to thrive as independent adults?

This chapter explores how parents, educators, and support networks can empower students to develop life skills, build social confidence, and prepare for post-secondary education, employment, and self-sufficiency—without relying on magical thinking or hoping someone else teaches them how to do laundry.

So, hopefully, the only question you need to ask yourself is, "Will *I* be ready?"

A. Teaching Core Life Skills: Building Everyday Confidence

Why Life Skills Matter For Independence

Life skills are the foundation of adult independence. They include everything from personal care and household management to handling finances, navigating transportation, and making informed decisions. While some students naturally develop these skills over time, others need explicit instruction, guided practice, and structured opportunities to build confidence.

Parents play a crucial role in this process—helping their children move from reliance on others to self-sufficiency at a pace that works for them. But sometimes, knowing where to start can be half the battle.

Building Independence Over Time

Elementary

✓ Small chores (laundry, hygiene)
✓ Visual routines

Middle School

✓ Simple meal prep
✓ Tracking spending
✓ Planning outings

High School

✓ Job shadowing
✓ Using public transit
✓ Budgeting & bank cards
✓ IEP transition planning

Post-School Life

✓ Self-advocacy at work or college
✓ Scheduling appointments
✓ Managing money & medication

Core Life Skills For Independence

Mastering independence means focusing on the areas that help students navigate adult life with confidence. These are the building blocks of everyday living, and the earlier they are introduced, the better.

Personal Care & Hygiene

- Establishing daily routines for bathing, dressing, and grooming.

- Managing medications and medical appointments—like knowing when to refill prescriptions and how to talk to doctors.

- Understanding personal boundaries, privacy, and how to advocate for oneself in personal care situations.

➡ **Pro Parent Move:** Start introducing hygiene habits as non-negotiables from an early age. Visual checklists, alarms, and reward systems can help reinforce routines—until they become a habit.

Household Management

- Cooking simple meals and learning basic kitchen safety (Yes, including what happens when you microwave metal).

- Cleaning, doing laundry, and keeping shared spaces organized—because no one wants to inadvertently be that roommate or coworker.

- Learning home safety basics, like locking doors, using appliances, and being prepared for emergencies.

✱ Pro Parent Tip: Do not wait until adulthood to introduce chores. Even young children can start learning simple household tasks. Gradually increasing responsibility makes daily living skills second nature over time.

Financial Literacy

- Understanding budgeting, income, and expenses (aka: "No, you cannot spend your entire paycheck on video games and Uber Eats").

- Learning how to pay bills, use banking services, and manage credit responsibly.

- Spotting scams, financial exploitation, and understanding consumer rights—because "Congratulations! You've won a free trip!" is never actually free.

➡ Pro Parent Move: Set up a bank account with a debit card early. Have your child practice tracking their spending and making small purchases. Learning to manage money in low-stakes situations builds confidence for real-life situations.

Transportation & Mobility

- Navigating public transit—reading schedules, managing fares, and planning routes.

- Practicing pedestrian safety and identifying safe walking paths.

- Enrolling in driver's education or accessing transportation assistance for students who will not drive.

➡ **Pro Parent Move:** If public transit is in your child's future, start practicing together before they have to do it solo. Turn it into an adventure, not a panic-inducing experience.

Life Skills Quick Wins: Start Here If You Feel Behind

- Practice a simple recipe once a week.
- Set up a bank account together and review one statement.
- Pick one chore your child can "own" independently.
- Take one public transit trip together each month.
- Talk through how to refill a prescription or schedule a doctor's appointment.

➡ **Pro Parent Prompt:** "What can we try together this week—not perfectly, just on purpose?"

Making Life Skills Stick: Teaching Strategies That Work

Even the best list of skills means little without a plan to teach them. This section offers practical tools to build real-world independence, one habit at a time.

Start Early & Build Gradually

- Introduce age-appropriate responsibilities over time.
- Elementary students can organize school supplies; teens can plan meals or manage small budgets.
- It is not about a crash course in adulthood—it is about building habits that stick.

Use Visual Supports & Technology

- Picture schedules, step-by-step guides, and apps (like budgeting tools or visual grocery lists) can make learning more accessible—and less overwhelming.

Provide Real-World Practice

- Bring your child to the grocery store and let them make decisions.
- Let them plan and cook dinner, even if it is pasta for the fifth night in a row.
- Use real money and real transactions to teach budgeting and impulse control.

Leverage Community Resources

- **Independent Living Centers (ILCs):** Offer training in daily life and self-sufficiency.
- **Vocational Rehabilitation Programs:** Offer hands-on coaching in job and life skills.
- **Local Disability Organizations:** These groups often host financial literacy and independent living workshops.

➡ **Pro Parent Move:** If your child resists learning certain skills, reframe the task as a way to gain freedom, not a chore. Instead of "You need to learn to cook," try "Imagine being able to make your favorite meal anytime you want—let's figure that out."

⊙ **Want even more?** For a downloadable, detailed breakdown of life skills by domain and age, check out resources from <u>The Autism Life Skills Lady</u> (https://lifeskillslady.com/), who offers visual tools, IEP-ready templates, and family-centered strategies to support independent living.

B. Encouraging Social Independence

Developing The Confidence To Navigate The World

Social skills are just as essential as life skills when it comes to independence. Many students with disabilities struggle with things like starting conversations, setting boundaries, or navigating unwritten social rules. These skills do not always come naturally—but they can be taught, modeled, and reinforced over time.

Key Social Skills For Independence

Self-Advocacy

- Communicating personal needs, preferences, and accommodations.
- Practicing how to speak up in IEP meetings, classroom settings, or everyday situations.

Interpersonal Communication

- Engaging in conversations and practicing appropriate eye contact.
- Reading body language, tone of voice, and other social cues (yes, even the subtle ones adults do not always get right either).

Friendship & Relationship Building

- Learning how to initiate and maintain friendships.
- Understanding healthy relationships, consent, and how to set (and respect) boundaries.

Workplace & Digital Communication

- Navigating workplace etiquette—whether in person, over the phone, or in email.
- Using technology (text, email, social media) responsibly and with awareness of tone and audience.

✱ **Pro Parent Tip:** If your child struggles with small talk or unstructured conversations, try practicing scripts or role-playing common social scenarios ahead of time. This is not "cheating"—it is scaffolding for success.

The Journey Toward Independence

Building independence is not a checklist—it is a process. It takes time, practice, and a lot of real-world trial and error.

- Start early and build gradually.
- Encourage self-advocacy in daily decisions, IEP meetings, and personal choices.
- Create structured opportunities to practice both social and life skills.
- Lean on community resources, peer programs, and vocational supports.

And remember, "independence" looks different for every student. Progress is progress—even if it does not follow a straight line or arrive on someone else's timeline.

➡ **Pro Parent Move:** Let your child take risks. Let them make mistakes. Let them fail, learn, and try again. It is hard to step back—but real independence does not come from avoiding failure. It comes from surviving it and growing in the process.

With the right foundation, support, and opportunities, every student— regardless of ability—can build the confidence and skills to lead a fulfilling, self-sufficient life.

C. Preparing For Employment & Post-Secondary Opportunities

The Road To Employment & Higher Education

Becoming independent is not just about knowing how to cook a meal or balance a budget—it is also about figuring out what comes next after high school. For many students with disabilities, that means transitioning into college, vocational training, supported work programs, or direct employment.

✓ Some students thrive in four-year colleges, while others prefer trade schools, apprenticeships, or direct employment.

✓ IEPs end when a student exits the K–12 system. 504 Plans may continue in college or the workplace—but only if the student discloses their disability and requests accommodations. Nothing happens automatically.

✓ Many students struggle to find jobs because they were never taught workplace skills in high school.

So, how do we fix this? By planning early, using real-world experiences, and ensuring students have the right tools for success.

➡ **Pro Parent Move:** The best transition plans do not just talk about careers— they create real-world experiences before high school graduation.

Step 1: Exploring Career & Education Pathways

Some students dream of college. Others want a job that gets them out of a classroom and into the real world. The key is finding the right fit—based on strengths, interests, and support needs.

Post-Secondary Education Options:

- **Four-Year Colleges & Universities** – Most have a disability resource center, but students must self-identify and register for accommodations. (Unlike K–12, nothing is automatic.)

- **Community Colleges** – Flexible, affordable, and often include certificate programs and tutoring or academic coaching.

- **Vocational Training & Apprenticeships** – Hands-on training in high-demand fields like IT, auto repair, culinary arts, and healthcare.

- **Trade Schools** – Short-term programs that prepare students for careers like electrician, HVAC tech, or dental assistant.

- **Work-Based Learning Programs** – Internships, apprenticeships, and job training can give students a head start in the workforce.

✱ **Pro Parent Tip:** College is not the only path to success. Skills-based training, certifications, and apprenticeships are equally valid—and often better aligned with student strengths.

Step 2: Teaching Workplace Readiness Skills

Employers care about soft skills just as much as technical ability. A great mechanic will not keep a job if they cannot show up on time. A talented graphic designer will not last long if they ghost the client.

Essential Workplace Skills For Students With Disabilities:

- **Professional Communication** – Email, phone calls, in-person etiquette, and when not to use emojis in a cover letter.

- **Time Management** – Showing up on time, meeting deadlines, and staying on task without constant reminders.

- **Teamwork & Social Skills** – Navigating coworkers, conflict resolution, and asking for help when needed.

- **Problem-Solving & Decision-Making** – Knowing how to request accommodations and troubleshoot when things go sideways.

- **Financial Literacy** – Understanding paychecks, taxes, budgeting, and how not to blow your first paycheck on Uber Eats (again).

➡ **Pro Parent Move:** Many states offer Pre-Employment Transition Services (Pre-ETS) through vocational rehab. These include resume help, job coaching, and career exploration—and they are often free. Look into it early.

Step 3: Self-Advocacy In College & The Workplace

Whether it is requesting extra test time in college or asking for a modified schedule at work, your child needs to know how to speak up—and who to talk to. This is not just a life skill—it is a survival skill.

Requesting College Accommodations:

- **Register with the Disability Services Office** – This is not automatic. Students must initiate the process.

- **Provide Documentation** – Colleges require medical or psychological documentation for approval.

- **Request Specific Accommodations** – Examples include extended test time, assistive tech, note-taking support, or reduced course loads.

✱ **Pro Parent Tip:** Professors may not understand disability laws. If accommodations are denied, your student should go straight to the disability office—not just the professor—for backup.

Requesting Workplace Accommodations:

Under the Americans with Disabilities Act (ADA), employees have the right to reasonable accommodations. These might include:

- Flexible schedules
- Modified job duties
- Assistive tech or communication supports
- Physical workspace adjustments

➡ **Pro Parent Move:** Role-play workplace conversations before your child starts a job. Practicing how to ask for accommodations builds confidence and helps them advocate effectively when it counts.

Step 4: Connecting With Employment & Transition Support Services

Key Employment & Transition Support Programs:

- **Vocational Rehabilitation Services (VR):** Career counseling, job placement, coaching, and workplace support.

- **Independent Living Centers (ILCs):** Training in budgeting, transportation, communication, and daily life skills.

- **Supported Employment Programs:** Help students with disabilities secure—and keep—jobs with ongoing support.

- **Social Security & Medicaid Waivers:** Programs like SSI and Medicaid Waivers can provide financial and healthcare support after graduation.

➥ **Pro Parent Move:** Some of these services have long waitlists. Apply early—ideally in the last year or two of high school, while your child still has IEP support to back them up.

Final Thoughts: Setting Up For A Successful Future

Transitioning into adulthood is not a single step—it is a process. One that requires preparation, practice, and a whole lot of patience. For students with disabilities, independence does not just "click" one day. It takes intentional planning, skill-building, and real-world experience to help them meet the challenges of college, employment, and daily life with confidence.

The key? Start early.

The sooner students begin developing workplace skills, financial literacy, and self-advocacy strategies, the more capable they will feel when navigating life beyond high school.

This journey will not always be smooth. There will be setbacks. Mistakes. Frustrating days and "Why didn't anyone teach me this?" moments. But that is part of the process. The goal is not to create a flawless plan—it is to give your child the tools, experiences, and resilience they will need when life does not go according to plan (because, spoiler alert, it rarely does).

Key Takeaways:

✓ **Start planning early** – Transition planning should begin by age 14 (or earlier).

✓ **Encourage work experience** – Internships and job shadowing offer essential real-world learning.

✓ **Teach workplace and financial skills** – These are just as critical as academics.

✓ **Promote self-advocacy** – Students need to learn how to request accommodations in college and at work.

✓ **Use available resources** – Vocational rehab, independent living centers, and support programs can make all the difference.

➡ **Pro Parent Move:** Let your child fail safely. Forgetting to set an alarm for work now teaches responsibility in a low-stakes way—before it becomes a job-losing moment. Let them mess up. Let them recover. That is how confidence is built.

With structured planning, community support, and lots of hands-on learning, students with disabilities can step into adulthood with courage—and build the self-sufficient, fulfilling lives they deserve.

◉ *Not just laundry. Not just job skills. Not just college applications. This is how independence is built.*

CHAPTER 17:
Celebrating Milestones–Honoring Growth, Grit, And The Journey

---

Progress is not a straight line. It is a spiral—slow, messy, and full of detours. And every inch forward deserves to be recognized.

Acknowledging Every Victory In The Special Education Journey

One day, you look back and realize: your child just did something they could not do six months ago. It may not have come with confetti or a report card sticker, but it was big—because it took effort, support, and persistence to get there.

The special education journey is a marathon, not a sprint. There is no single "lightbulb moment" where everything suddenly clicks. Progress unfolds gradually—sometimes so slowly that you do not see it until you stop and reflect. But make no mistake: every step forward matters.

That is why celebrating milestones—both big and small—is essential. Whether it is a first full sentence, completing homework without help, advocating for themselves, or reaching an IEP goal that once felt out of reach, every win deserves to be acknowledged.

This chapter is about honoring the journey. You will learn how to recognize growth, celebrate in meaningful ways, and document progress—not just as a keepsake, but as a testament to everything your child (and you) have accomplished.

A. Recognizing Progress

◉ Milestone Moments That Matter

Examples:

✓ First time completing a task independently
✓ Initiating a conversation with a peer
✓ Advocating for their own needs in an IEP meeting
✓ Showing emotional regulation after a tough moment
✓ Independently handing in homework on time
✓ Meeting a long-standing goal (even if it took 3 years)

Why Small Wins Matter Just As Much As Big Ones

One of the most challenging parts of the special education journey is that progress often moves at a slow, steady pace—not in giant leaps. As a parent, it can be hard to see growth when you are living in the day-to-day. But then one day, your child does something they could not do before—and you realize just how far they have come.

Only a bit of progress... is still progress.

Celebrating the small wins can:

★ **Boost Motivation** – Recognizing progress helps children see that effort pays off—and encourages them to keep trying.

★ **Build Confidence** – Small wins reinforce a growth mindset and show children that their abilities are expanding.

★ **Encourage Self-Advocacy** – As children see what is working, they become better at naming their strengths and needs.

★ **Validate the Whole Team** – Progress is not just a student win—it reflects the effort of parents, teachers, and therapists, too.

➨ **Pro Parent Move:** Feel like you are stuck in a "no progress" loop? Step back and compare where your child was six months—or even a year—ago. Growth does not always show up in the moment, but zooming out can reveal how far they have really come.

How To Track Progress Effectively

Monitoring and documenting progress ensures that even the smallest wins do no get lost in the noise. Here is how to do it:

✓ **Progress Monitoring Reports** – Schools provide quarterly or annual updates on IEP goals.

✳ **Pro Parent Tip:** Do not settle for vague phrases like "making progress." Ask for specifics—work samples, data, or examples.

✓ **Performance Data & Work Samples** – Keep early and recent assignments to compare and highlight growth over time.

✓ **Behavioral Logs & Checklists** – For students working on regulation or social skills, tracking positive behavior reveals gains that testing may not always show.

✓ **Parent & Teacher Observations** – Informal notes from both home and school can offer a fuller picture of how your child is growing across environments.

✓ **Student Self-Reflection** – Older students can track and reflect on their own progress, boosting motivation and ownership.

✓ **IEP Meeting Notes** – Keep copies of past goals, teacher feedback, and updates on accommodations. This creates a roadmap of what is working and what still needs support.

Strategies For Celebrating Progress

✳ **Acknowledge Effort, Not Just Outcomes** – "I see how hard you are working" can be just as powerful as "You nailed it!" Effort deserves applause.

✳ **Use Reflection Prompts** – Help children recognize their own growth:

> ➤ "What did you do today that made you feel proud?"
> ➤ "What is one thing you have improved at this week?"

✳ **Let Children Help Set Goals** – When children help choose their own milestones, they stay more engaged and motivated to reach them.

✳ **Celebrate the Whole Support Team** – Teachers, therapists, and family members all contribute to a child's progress—recognize their efforts too.

✱ **Pro Parent Tip:** If your child feels uncomfortable with verbal praise, try non-verbal recognition—like a sticker, high-five, favorite snack, or a quiet moment together. The meaning matters more than the method. Some children prefer low-sensory or solo recognition. A calm car ride, a note on their pillow, or a quiet shared laugh might be the most meaningful celebration of all.

B. Creative Ways To Celebrate

Making Recognition Meaningful, Not Pressure-Filled

Not every child wants a standing ovation—and not every win needs a banner and balloons. Some children thrive on public recognition, while others prefer quiet, personal moments. The goal is not fanfare—it is meaning. Choose ways to celebrate that feel authentic, motivating, and pressure-free.

Everyday Recognition Strategies

Small wins deserve celebration too—and sometimes it is the smallest gestures that stick.

✓ **Verbal Praise** – A simple "I saw how hard you worked on that!" can go a long way. Keep it specific and sincere.

✓ **Sticker Charts or Token Rewards** – Younger children often respond to visual trackers that reinforce effort and build momentum.

✓ **Special Rituals** – Create traditions like a Friday victory dance, a "You Did It!" whiteboard, or a "high-five wall" with sticky notes of encouragement.

✓ **Personalized Certificates** – Think beyond grades: "Bravery in Trying Something New" or "Master of Multiplication" are fun and empowering.

✓ **Pick-the-Activity Reward** – Let your child choose a favorite activity—like movie night, playground time, or their go-to dinner—when they reach a milestone.

Milestone Celebrations

For major accomplishments—like reaching an IEP goal, showing a significant behavior shift, or advocating for themselves—consider turning up the celebration dial just a bit.

✳ **Achievement Parties** – Keep it small or go big, but gather loved ones to say: This mattered. You did it.

✳ **Community Recognition** – Some schools host ceremonies or feature student stories in newsletters. Advocate for your child's wins to be seen.

✳ **Social Media Shoutouts** – With your child's consent, share the moment online. It not only affirms their success, but it also inspires other families.

✻ **Educational Outings** – Turn a celebration into a learning opportunity. A museum trip, science exhibit, or bookstore visit can be both fun and meaningful.

School-Based Recognition

Some schools already have structures in place to celebrate progress. If they do not—this is your moment to advocate.

✓ **IEP Progress Awards** – Monthly or quarterly recognitions for students meeting personal goals.
✓ **Classroom Acknowledgments** – Morning shoutouts, "student of the week" features, or praise during circle time.
✓ **End-of-Year Reflections** – Celebrations that honor growth, not just grades.

➡ **Pro Parent Move:** If your child's school does not already recognize IEP progress, speak up. Request a system that includes and honors all students—and the unique paths they are walking.

C. Documenting Your Child's Journey

Creating A Record Of Growth For Advocacy And Memories

Looking back at a child's progress over time is both a motivational tool and a valuable record for advocacy. Documentation helps families track growth, demonstrate patterns of progress, and celebrate successes in a tangible way.

Ways To Document Progress

▶ *Progress Portfolios*

- Keep a binder or digital file with IEPs, progress reports, and work samples.

- Include "before and after" examples to highlight improvements over time.

▶ Journals & Reflection Logs

- Keep a personal journal to track significant moments and achievements.
- Encourage children to record their own reflections on challenges and successes.

▶ Memory Books & Scrapbooks

- Create a scrapbook filled with artwork, photos, and school projects.
- Include notes from teachers, therapists, and family members.
- Not into crafts? No problem. Create a "Progress Folder" on your phone with photos, scanned work, or milestone notes. Even one saved moment can become a powerful reminder of how far your child has come.

▶ Video & Photo Documentation

- Record short videos showcasing milestones like learning a new skill or completing a project.
- Create a digital slideshow of progress over the years.

▶ Letter To The Future

- Have your child write (or dictate) a letter to their future self about the challenges and achievements they have had.

✱ Pro Parent Tip: Look Back to Move Forward. When preparing for an IEP meeting, start by reviewing your child's last big win. Lead the meeting with it. Set the tone with growth, not deficits.

Final Thoughts: Embracing The Journey

Special education is not just about reaching milestones—it is about acknowledging the terrain your child has crossed and the resilience it took to get here.

You have fought for evaluations, rewritten IEP drafts, showed up at hard meetings, and probably cried in your car more than once. And yet, here you are. Still standing. Still advocating.

Let that count for something.

Key Takeaways:

✓ **Celebrate the wins**—especially the quiet ones no one else sees.
✓ **Personalized praise is not fluff**; it builds confidence and stamina.
✓ **Tracking progress is not just data**—it is a record of growth and proof of your advocacy.
✓ **Every messy step forward deserves acknowledgment.**

This chapter, and this book, are your reminder: **You are doing a phenomenal job**. Not a perfect one—but an extraordinary one.

Take the win.

Mark the progress.

Celebrate the child in front of you—not the one in someone else's data set.

✱ *Here is to every messy step, quiet win, and all the milestones yet to come. You are not just tracking progress—you are making it possible.*

CHAPTER 18:
Staying Informed

This is not about politics. It is about survival. The systems meant to protect your child may be eroding—but your power to push back is not.

Empowering Parents Through Knowledge And Advocacy In Uncertain Times

Navigating special education has never been easy—but today's families face a new challenge: federal efforts to dismantle the very agencies meant to protect their children with disabilities. With budget cuts and defunding efforts targeting the U.S. Department of Education and other key disability rights agencies, the special education landscape is at risk of massive upheaval.

Here Is What That Means For You:

➤ **Your State Is Now the Front Line.** Federal oversight may shrink—but your state's education laws, timelines, and dispute procedures remain. Learn them. Use them. Push for their enforcement. This is where the next fight will be won.

➤ **Laws like IDEA, Section 504, and FAPE still exist—but without enforcement, accountability becomes much harder.**

➤ **Special education funding could be drastically reduced,** forcing schools to scale back on support staff, therapy services, and accommodations.

➤ **Complaints may lose federal oversight,** leaving parents to pursue legal action on their own rather than through agencies like the Office for Civil Rights (OCR).

➤ **States already struggling to fund education may use federal rollbacks as an excuse to further cut special education budgets**—disproportionately affecting students with disabilities.

So, what can parents do in this uncertain time? **Stay informed. Stay engaged. And be ready to advocate—especially at the local level.** Right down to your school board.

This chapter will walk you through the tools, networks, and updates you need to stay ahead of policy shifts and protect your child's rights—no matter what happens in Washington.

A. Your Advocacy Toolkit

Resources To Stay Ready When Systems Fall Short

In a time when federal protections may be weakened, parents must double down on using every available resource to advocate for their child's education. If agencies like the DOE's Office for Civil Rights (OCR) or the Office of Special Education Programs (OSEP) are understaffed, defunded, or dismantled, the responsibility to hold schools accountable will fall even more on families.

Trusted Online Resources For Special Education

There is no shortage of information online—but not all of it is accurate or parent-friendly. The following sources are trusted, advocacy-focused, and built for families navigating the complexities of special education law.

◆ *Council of Parent Attorneys and Advocates (COPAA)*

A national organization that trains parents, attorneys, and advocates to protect the rights of students with disabilities. COPAA (https://copaa.org) offers legal resources, submits amicus briefs, and connects families with professionals who know how to fight—and win. If IDEA enforcement weakens, the role of COPAA will become even more essential.

◆ *Wrightslaw*

The go-to site for understanding special education law and how to apply it. Wrightslaw (https://www.wrightslaw.com/)offers step-by-step guidance on IEPs, dispute resolution, filing complaints, and legal advocacy—written in language that parents can actually understand.

◆ *Center for Parent Information and Resources (CPIR)*

A clearinghouse for state-specific special education resources. CPIR (https://www.parentcenterhub.org/) supports Parent Training and Information Centers (PTIs) (https://www.parentcenterhub.org/find-your-center) and Regional Parent Technical Assistance Centers, providing tools and training for families nationwide.

◆ *Understood.org*

Designed for parents of children with learning and attention challenges, the Understood (https://www.understood.org/) site delivers practical tips, videos, and toolkits for navigating school supports and working with educators.

◆ *National Disability Rights Network (NDRN)*

A network of federally mandated legal advocacy agencies offering free or low-cost legal services to families. If you need help enforcing disability rights protections, NDRN (https://www.ndrn.org/) is a good place to start.

⚡ **What Could Change:** If the DOE is dismantled or defunded, these organizations will likely become even more essential—but also more overwhelmed. Start building relationships with them now, before you are in crisis mode.

Government Agencies Offering Support (For Now...)

While federal enforcement agencies are still in place, parents should use them fully. But if their roles shrink or disappear, families will have to turn to state-level protections and private legal support.

◆ *State Departments of Education*

With the potential weakening of federal enforcement, your state's education department may become your first line of defense. Some states offer stronger protections than federal law—but others may not maintain those protections without oversight.

◆ *Office of Special Education Programs (OSEP)*

If funded, OSEP (https://www.ed.gov/about/ed-offices/osers/osep) monitors how states implement IDEA and offers guidance to parents and schools. If eliminated, oversight of district compliance would be left to the states—or no one at all.

◆ *Office for Civil Rights (OCR)*

This federal agency handles discrimination complaints, including disability-based harassment and denial of FAPE. If OCR (https://www.hhs.gov/ocr/index.html) is dismantled, families would need to rely on private legal action instead of filing complaints with the federal government.

⚡ Enforcement On The Edge: What May Be Lost

→ Federal oversight of IEP compliance (OSEP)
→ Civil rights investigation of disability discrimination (OCR)
→ Federal accountability for IDEA violations
→ Reliable complaint mechanisms for parents

⚡ What To Do?

→ Parents may have to shift advocacy from federal agencies to state complaints and lawsuits.
→ Legal action may become the only way to hold districts accountable in some areas.

Just Getting Started? Here's Your Fast-Track Toolkit:

Feeling overwhelmed? That is normal. You do not have to do all of this at once. Save this list. Choose one action. Come back to the rest when you can. Advocacy is not a race—it is a return trip.

- Find your Parent Training and Information Center (PTI).

- Bookmark Wrightslaw and sign up for COPAA's newsletter.

- Learn your state's dispute resolution timeline.

- Identify your local school board representative and state legislator.

- Write down your child's top 3 advocacy needs—it is your elevator pitch.

B. Joining Support Networks

The Power of Community and Connection in Uncertain Times

With federal protections under attack, parent advocacy groups will become more critical than ever. Special education has always been a fight, but if enforcement agencies disappear, local and state-level advocacy will be the last line of defense.

Types Of Support Networks To Prioritize

➤ **State-Based Parent Advocacy Organizations** – Some states will step up and strengthen their protections even if the federal government backs off. Parents should immediately contact local advocacy organizations if they need legal support.

➤ **Disability Rights Groups** – National disability advocacy groups, such as The Arc (https://thearc.org), Autism Speaks (https://www.autismspeaks.org), and CHADD (https://chadd.org), will likely increase their legislative lobbying efforts to protect the IDEA and Section 504.

➤ **Legal Aid Organizations** – If the USDOE's enforcement power is removed, parents may have to rely more on disability rights attorneys to force compliance through lawsuits rather than federal complaints.

➤ **State and Federal Representatives** – Call and email your elected officials about education issues—even (and especially) when they already agree with you. The more constituent voices they can point to, the stronger their position becomes when it is time to vote or push back. Numbers matter. So do your words.

⚡ If the doe is dismantled, support networks will:

→ Shift from federal agencies to private advocacy organizations.
→ Become more overwhelmed with requests, meaning parents must act fast when seeking help.
→ Potentially push for state-level protections, meaning parents should get involved in local policy advocacy.

C. Engaging In Policy And Legislative Advocacy

Why Parents Must Get Involved In Education Policy

Special education protections do not exist by accident. Every safeguard—from IEP rights to Section 504 accommodations—was hard-won by parents, advocates, and disability rights organizations.

But those protections are not guaranteed to last. In times of budget cuts, legal challenges, and shifting priorities, parents must step in not just to react—but to shape what happens next.

⚡ What This Means for Parents:

→ Federal agencies like the Office for Civil Rights (OCR) and the Office of Special Education Programs (OSEP) may no longer enforce IDEA with the same strength.

→ State laws may weaken or strengthen, depending on leadership and legislation.

→ Parents will play a critical role in defending—and defining—the future of special education.

★ The good news? You do not need to be a policy expert to make an impact. You just need to know where to look, who to contact, and how to make your voice heard.

Advocacy Action Map

- **FEDERAL** – Contact Congress, monitor U.S. Department of Education, follow COPAA/NDRN

- **STATE** – Monitor your legislature, attend budget hearings, join local disability councils

- **LOCAL** – Attend IEP meetings, follow school board agendas, write letters to the editor

Step 1: Stay Informed On Legislative Changes

Most changes to special education happen at the state or federal level, but they always trickle down to impact your local school. Staying informed is the first line of defense.

Resources For Tracking Policy

- **COPAA (copaa.org)** – Offers updates on legal trends, policy threats, and advocacy strategies.

- **Wrightslaw (wrightslaw.com)** – Breaks down what legal shifts actually mean for families.

- **U.S. Department of Education (ed.gov)** – Tracks proposed rule changes, funding shifts, and enforcement priorities.

- **National Center for Learning Disabilities (ncld.org)** – Focuses on IDEA and learning disability-specific policy.

- **Your State's Department of Education** – Look here for state bills and special ed policy updates.

➡ **Pro Parent Move:** Sign up for email alerts from disability rights orgs so you hear about policy changes before they are finalized—not after.

Step 2: Speak Up And Contact Your Legislators

Laws do not change in a vacuum. They change when people speak up—and lawmakers listen when parents do the talking. Even if your representative is already on your side, they need backup. Your calls and emails give them cover, credibility, and the power to say, "This is not just me. I have constituents behind me."

How To Contact Lawmakers Effectively

★ **Direct Action Tool:** Want to quickly find your elected officials? Use My Reps (https://myreps.datamade.us/)to locate contact info for your federal, state, and local representatives. Your voice matters—make sure they hear it.

> 1. **Find Your Reps** – Use https://www.house.gov/ and https://www.senate.gov/ to find your federal representatives, or visit your state's legislative website for state-level officials.
>
> 2. **Make It Personal** – Example: "My child with autism relies on IDEA protections. Weakening these laws would hurt students like them."
>
> 3. **Request Action** – Example: "I urge you to oppose cuts to the Office for Civil Rights. Without OCR, families like mine have no recourse when schools violate the law."

➡ **Pro Parent Move:** Call the local office, not just the D.C. line. Constituents who appear on local radars tend to get more attention.

Step 3: Join Forces With Advocacy Organizations

Individual voices are powerful. Organized voices are unstoppable. Advocacy groups help coordinate messaging, train parents, and provide the legal and political muscle to move change forward.

Where To Get Involved

- **COPAA** – Supports parents and attorneys who work to uphold the IDEA.

- **National Disability Rights Network (NDRN)** – Protects civil rights at the national and state level.

- **Your State's SEPTA (Special Education PTA)** – Focuses on school district-level advocacy.

- **Parent Training and Information Centers (PTIs)** – Offer free training and support on state-specific advocacy.

➡ **Pro Parent Move:** Look for town halls or legislative listening sessions run by local coalitions. Show up. Bring your story. These moments move policy more than you think.

Step 4: Attend Public Hearings And School Board Meetings

Whether it is a district meeting or a state-level hearing, decisions are made by the people who show up.

How To Prepare:

- Check the agenda in advance. Look for keywords like "special education funding" or "student services."

- Bring a brief statement. Two minutes is plenty.

  ➡ **Example:** "My child's speech therapy was already cut last year. Further reductions to IDEA funding would make an already difficult situation worse."

- If you cannot attend, submit written testimony or ask another parent to share your statement for you.

➡ **Pro Parent Move:** Bring a printed copy of your statement and email it to the board or committee afterward—your words are harder to ignore when they are on record.

⚡ Policy Watch: Red Flags To Track

- Budget proposals that remove or freeze IDEA or 504 enforcement staff

- State-level bills that shift funding away from special education services

- Local school board budget changes, cutting paraprofessional staff or therapies

- Guidance memos from your district reducing compensatory services post-pandemic

Final Thoughts: Parents Are The Frontline Of Advocacy

Advocacy is not just about protecting your child today—it is about defending the rights of all children tomorrow. Every protection students have now exists because parents refused to stay silent. Now, it is our turn.

Key Takeaways:

✔ **Stay informed** – Track changes to IDEA, Section 504, and state-level education policy.

✔ **Engage with legislators** – Your story can shape laws and protect rights.

✔ **Join advocacy groups** – Collective voices lead to lasting change.

✔ **Show up** – School board meetings and public hearings need your voice in the room.

The laws that protect students with disabilities exist because families showed up—loudly, persistently, and together. Now, it is our job to keep them strong—and to show the next generation what true advocacy really means.

You are not alone. You are part of a movement—a lineage of parents who never stop pushing for what is right.

You did not ask for this fight. But you are here. And that matters. Your voice is powerful. And your child is watching.

APPENDICES

APPENDIX 1:
Understanding What Evaluations Cover (Expanded But Not Exhaustive List)

A comprehensive evaluation is more than a battery of tests—it is a roadmap to understanding your child's strengths and struggles. These evaluations form the foundation for IEPs, 504 Plans, intervention strategies, and instructional decisions.

Schools often refer to their standard battery as a "psychoeducational evaluation" or "psych-ed," which typically includes cognitive testing, academic achievement testing, and behavior rating scales when concerns about attention, behavior, or emotional functioning arise. Additional assessments—such as speech-language, occupational therapy, or social-emotional evaluations—may be included based on the child's needs.

Unless there is a compelling reason to take a stepwise approach, all necessary evaluations should be conducted at the same time as part of a comprehensive initial evaluation. If the school suspects a disability in a particular area but does not assess it, they do not get a second chance to circle back and address it later during the IEP meeting. If they chose not to evaluate that area in their initial review, and parents disagree, the proper next step is for parents to request an Independent Educational Evaluation (IEE). *See **Chapter 3: Identifying your Child's Needs**.*

These assessment can be used to track progress over time. Each domain below explains how difficulties may present in the classroom and outlines common tools used to assess that specific area of need.

1. Cognitive Abilities

Cognitive evaluations assess how a student thinks, reasons, remembers, and processes information. This is where we get the IQ score, often referred to as the Full Scale IQ (FSIQ). However, a single number does not capture the full picture. Many students have uneven profiles—strengths in some areas and weaknesses in others—that the FSIQ may mask. Understanding the pattern of cognitive abilities is far more useful than relying solely on the composite score.

Classroom Impact:

- Performs inconsistently across subjects or tasks
- Struggles to complete multi-step directions or sustain focus
- Works slowly or becomes easily frustrated with complex material
- Shows strong verbal abilities but weak memory, attention, or processing speed
- Has difficulty organizing thoughts or shifting between tasks

Common Tools Used:

- **WISC-V (Wechsler Intelligence Scale for Children – Fifth Edition)** – Measures verbal comprehension, working memory, processing speed, visual-spatial and fluid reasoning
- **Woodcock-Johnson IV** – Cognitive Subtests, also offers an alternative cognitive profile
- **Differential Ability Scales (DAS-II)** – Another option for young or lower-functioning students

1.a. Cognitive Assessments for Younger Children

For younger children (typically ages 2.5 to 7), developmentally appropriate tools are used in place of or alongside standard cognitive tests. These assessments are tailored to capture emerging reasoning, memory, and problem-solving skills in early learners.

Classroom Impact:

- Struggles to follow directions or routines
- Has difficulty learning letters, shapes, or simple patterns
- Avoids puzzles, blocks, or early problem-solving tasks
- Shows limited attention span or persistence during learning activities
- Has trouble with expressive or receptive language during structured play

Common Tools Used (For Younger Or Lower-Functioning Children):

- **WPPSI-IV (Wechsler Preschool and Primary Scale of Intelligence – Fourth Edition)** – For ages 2.5 to 7 years, assesses verbal and nonverbal reasoning, working memory, and processing speed in young children, especially useful for preschoolers or kindergartners.
- **Differential Ability Scales** – Second Edition (DAS-II): Suitable for ages 2.5 to 17 years, often used with young children, nonverbal learners, or students with lower cognitive functioning, breaks cognitive skills into clusters (verbal, nonverbal, spatial), flexible administration based on age and language skills

2. Academic Skills

Academic evaluations assess foundational and advanced skills in reading, writing, and math. These help identify specific learning disabilities, such as dyslexia, dysgraphia, or dyscalculia.

Reading

Classroom Impact:

- Avoids reading aloud
- Reads slowly or haltingly
- Has difficulty summarizing or answering questions about what they read
- Skips or substitutes words
- Appears disengaged or lost during literacy activities

Common Tools Used:

- **Woodcock-Johnson IV (WJ-IV)** – Assesses decoding, fluency, and comprehension
- **WIAT-4 (Wechsler Individual Achievement Test)** – Covers basic reading, reading comprehension, and fluency
- **Gray Oral Reading Tests (GORT)** – Evaluates rate, accuracy, and comprehension
- **Comprehensive Test of Phonological Processing (CTOPP)** – Assesses phonemic awareness and memory
- **WISC-V (Working Memory Subtests)** – Supports identification of memory-related reading difficulties

Writing

Classroom Impact:

- Disorganized or incomplete written work
- Struggles with grammar, punctuation, and spelling
- Avoids writing assignments
- Poor handwriting or letter formation

- Takes longer than peers to express ideas in writing

Common Tools Used:

- **WIAT-4** – Evaluates spelling, sentence composition, and essay writing
- **Test of Written Language (TOWL)** – Assesses mechanics, organization, and vocabulary use
- **Woodcock-Johnson IV (Written Expression subtests)**
- **Beery VMI** – Measures visual-motor integration linked to handwriting
- **WISC-V** – Assesses underlying cognitive contributions to writing challenges

Mathematics

Classroom Impact:

- Struggles to memorize math facts
- Avoids word problems or multi-step tasks
- Has difficulty understanding abstract math concepts
- Frequently misaligns numbers or reverses digits

Common Tools Used:

- **WIAT-4** – Measures math problem-solving, fluency, and numerical operations
- **Woodcock-Johnson IV** – Evaluates applied math and basic calculation skills
- **KeyMath-3 Diagnostic Assessment** – Provides an in-depth math profile
- **WISC-V (Working Memory, Visual-Spatial)** – Supports understanding of problem-solving breakdowns

2.a. Achievement Assessments For Younger Children

Academic assessments for younger or developmentally delayed children must be developmentally appropriate and sensitive to early learning milestones. These tools help identify emerging strengths or delays in foundational academic skills, even before formal instruction begins.

Classroom Impact:

- Difficulty recognizing letters, numbers, or basic shapes
- Avoids drawing, coloring, or pre-writing tasks
- Struggles to follow along with group learning activities
- Limited vocabulary or difficulty expressing ideas verbally
- Becomes easily frustrated or disengaged during structured tasks

Common Tools Used:

- **KTEA-3 (Kaufman Test of Educational Achievement – Third Edition)** – Suitable for Pre-K through Grade 12; assesses early reading, math, written language, and oral language; appropriate for lower-functioning or young children

- **WIAT-4 (Wechsler Individual Achievement Test – Fourth Edition)** – Can be used with children as young as age 4, but is most effective for students in Grade 1 and up; includes reading, math, and written expression subtests

- **Woodcock-Johnson IV Tests of Achievement** – Offers subtests for children as young as age 2; highly adaptable for assessing foundational academic skills across reading, writing, and math in young learners

3. Executive Functioning

Executive functioning skills are the brain's self-management system. These include the ability to plan, organize, initiate tasks, manage time, regulate emotions, and monitor one's own behavior. Weaknesses in these areas can significantly impact academic performance, classroom behavior, and social interactions.

Classroom Impact:

- Misses deadlines or forgets to bring materials
- Has trouble starting tasks without prompting
- Struggles to switch between activities or follow changes in routine
- Becomes overwhelmed by multi-step directions
- Loses track of time or fails to complete work within limits
- Reacts emotionally to frustration or unexpected challenges

Common Tools Used:

- **Behavior Rating Inventory of Executive Function – Second Edition (BRIEF-2)** – Parent and teacher rating scales that assess inhibition, shifting, emotional control, working memory, planning, and self-monitoring
- **Delis-Kaplan Executive Function System (D-KEFS)** – Performance-based tasks that evaluate skills like cognitive flexibility, inhibition, problem-solving, and abstract thinking
- **WISC-V (Wechsler Intelligence Scale for Children – Fifth Edition)** – Working Memory and Processing Speed subtests provide insight into core executive processes such as attention, task persistence, and mental organization

4. Adaptive Behavior

Adaptive behavior refers to how well a child adjusts to their environment, handles frustration, and performs tasks that are age-appropriate.

Classroom Impact:

- Meltdowns when routines change
- Refuses to participate in unfamiliar activities
- Avoids group work due to poor coping or social problem-solving skills
- Struggles to manage personal belongings or follow through with routines

Common Tools Used:

- **Vineland Adaptive Behavior Scales** – Measures communication, daily living, and social skills
- **Adaptive Behavior Assessment System (ABAS-3)** – Assesses functional independence and adaptability
- **Teacher and parent rating forms**

5. Behavior And Emotional Functioning

These evaluations examine emotional regulation, attention, and behavioral patterns that can affect learning and relationships.

Classroom Impact:

- Overreacts to minor frustrations
- Meltdowns, aggression, or withdrawal
- Appears anxious, depressed, or emotionally shut down
- Frequent disciplinary incidents or task refusal

Common Tools Used:

- **Behavior Assessment System for Children (BASC-3)** – Broad view of emotional and behavioral functioning
- **Conners 4** – Assesses inattention, hyperactivity, impulsivity, and executive functioning
- **Achenbach System of Empirically Based Assessment (ASEBA)** – Includes parent and teacher behavior ratings
- **Autism Rating Scale (ARS)** – Screens for social-emotional or behavioral traits linked to autism

6. Assistive Technology Needs

These evaluations determine whether a student would benefit from tools that support writing, communication, organization, or focus.

Classroom Impact:

- Illegible handwriting
- Struggles with organization, planning, or note-taking
- Avoids verbal or written tasks due to expressive challenges
- Becomes frustrated when trying to keep up with classwork

Common Tools Used:

- **SETT Framework (Student, Environment, Tasks, Tools)** – Evaluates need for assistive tech
- Team-based assessments involving OT, SLP, and special educators

  → *Examples of tools recommended:*
  - Speech-to-text software
  - Word prediction tools

- Graphic organizers
- AAC devices (for significant speech/language challenges)

7. Auditory Processing

Auditory processing difficulties affect how a child interprets spoken information, especially in noisy or fast-paced environments.

Classroom Impact:

- Frequently asks for instructions to be repeated
- Mishears similar-sounding words
- Appears inattentive during lectures
- Difficulty following conversations in groups

Common Tools Used:

- **Test of Auditory Processing Skills (TAPS)** – Measures auditory memory, discrimination, and sequencing
- **SCAN-3 for Children** – Screens for auditory processing disorders
- **Speech-language pathologist (SLP) evaluations**

8. Functional Skills

Functional skill assessments examine a student's ability to independently manage the basic daily tasks required in school settings. These evaluations are especially relevant for students with developmental delays, intellectual disabilities, or executive functioning challenges.

Classroom Impact:

- Needs reminders or assistance to pack materials or organize supplies
- Forgets steps in familiar routines like lining up or transitioning between classes
- Requires adult prompting to complete basic classroom tasks
- Struggles with independence during unstructured times (e.g., arrival, lunch, dismissal)

Common Tools Used:

- **Vineland Adaptive Behavior Scales** – Measures communication, daily living, and socialization skills across home and school settings
- **Adaptive Behavior Assessment System (ABAS-3)** – Assesses functional independence in areas like self-care, communication, and community use
- **Observational Checklists and Teacher Interviews** – Help capture how skills are demonstrated in naturalistic settings across the day

9. Motor And Physical Skills

Motor skill evaluations look at how a child moves and controls their body, both in precise, small movements and in larger, whole-body tasks. **Fine motor skills** involve the use of small muscles—particularly in the hands and fingers—for tasks like writing, cutting, and manipulating objects. **Gross motor skills** involve larger movements that use the arms, legs, and core for balance, coordination, and strength. Challenges in either area can affect a student's participation in both academic and physical aspects of the school day.

Fine Motor Skills

Classroom Impact:

- Messy or illegible handwriting
- Trouble using scissors, drawing, or manipulating small objects
- Avoids fine motor tasks like coloring, puzzles, or keyboarding

Common Tools Used:

- **Beery-Buktenica Visual-Motor Integration (Beery VMI)** – Assesses how well a child integrates visual information with fine motor control; often used to identify handwriting and copying challenges.
- **Peabody Developmental Motor Scales (PDMS-2)** – For children birth to age 5; measures grasping, hand use, and object manipulation to identify early motor delays.
- **Occupational Therapy (OT) Evaluations** – Assess grip strength, coordination, and dexterity through hands-on tasks; tailored to classroom needs.

Gross Motor Skills

Classroom Impact:

- Poor balance or posture
- Clumsy movements
- Difficulty in PE, sports, or playground activities

Common Tools Used:

- **Bruininks-Oseretsky Test of Motor Proficiency (BOT-2)** – Assesses balance, coordination, strength, and agility; useful for identifying motor delays that impact PE, playground, or physical classroom tasks.
- **Physical Therapy (PT) Evaluations** – Examine gait, strength, posture, and coordination through observation and structured tasks; used to determine how motor issues affect school participation and mobility.

10. Sensory Processing

Sensory integration challenges affect how a child experiences and reacts to sensory input (e.g., noise, light, touch, movement).

Classroom Impact:

- Overreacts to textures, sounds, or bright lights
- Constantly moving, fidgeting, or touching items
- Avoids messy activities or noisy environments
- Meltdowns or withdrawal triggered by sensory overload

Common Tools Used:

- **Sensory Profile** – Caregiver and teacher questionnaire that identifies patterns of sensory sensitivity, avoidance, or seeking.

- **Sensory Processing Measure (SPM)** – Rates sensory responses across settings like home and school; includes subscales for vision, touch, movement, and body awareness.

- **Occupational Therapy (OT) Assessments** – Observe how a child reacts to sensory input and how it affects regulation, focus, and classroom participation.

11. Social Skills And Pragmatic Communication

These assessments measure a child's ability to interpret social cues, engage in reciprocal conversation, and adapt to social norms.

Classroom Impact:

- Struggles to make or keep friends
- Misinterprets jokes, tone, or body language
- Interrupts or dominates conversations
- Reacts poorly to social feedback or correction
- Appears awkward or rigid during group activities
- Shuts down or becomes frustrated during peer interactions

Common Tools Used:

- **Social Language Development Test (SLDT)** – Measures a student's ability to understand and apply social language skills, including making inferences, interpreting perspective, and navigating conversational norms
- **Social Skills Improvement System (SSIS)** – Evaluates cooperation, empathy, self-control, and peer interaction through rating scales completed by teachers, parents, and students
- **Teacher Observations and Structured Interaction Tasks** – Provide insight into how a student interacts in naturalistic and guided settings, often used as part of a speech-language or psychological evaluation
- **Autism Rating Scale (ARS)** – Screens for social-emotional behaviors and communication patterns associated with autism spectrum disorder, often used in conjunction with other tools for differential diagnosis

12. Transition Assessments (For Older Students)

Yes—transition evaluations are essential for students aged 14 and up under IDEA, and they are often overlooked in evaluation guides. These assessments help plan for post-secondary goals, including education, employment, and independent living.

Classroom Impact

Postsecondary Education/Training:
- Struggles to ask for help or express learning needs
- Avoids discussing accommodations or support with teachers
- Does not use available supports (e.g., extended time, notes)
- Has trouble identifying strengths, interests, or goals
- Disengages from future-planning tasks
- Lacks social confidence or connection with peers

Employment:
- Misses deadlines, forgets materials, or arrives unprepared
- Struggles with teamwork or peer conflict
- Needs constant reminders to stay organized or on task
- Has difficulty following directions or adapting to changes
- Avoids job-prep tasks or becomes easily overwhelmed
- Reacts poorly to feedback or frustration

Independent Living:
- Struggles with time management and daily routines
- Inconsistent use of tools like planners or schedules
- Needs help making decisions or anticipating consequences
- Does not self-advocate for basic needs or clarifications
- Has difficulty managing stress or emotional reactions
- Relies heavily on adult support to stay functional

Tools Used

- **Transition Planning Inventory** – Second Edition (TPI-2): Assesses strengths and needs in areas like employment, further education, daily living, and community participation, input from student, parents, and school staff
- **Enderle-Severson Transition Rating Scales (ESTR-J and ESTR-III)** – Used for students with mild, moderate, or severe disabilities, focuses on functional skills needed for post-school success
- **AIR Self-Determination Scale** – Measures student involvement in goal setting, problem-solving, and future planning, often used as a baseline for building self-advocacy skills
- **Casey Life Skills Assessment** – Evaluates daily living and independent living readiness, popular with older teens transitioning out of special education or foster care systems
- **Work-Based Learning Evaluations** – Often customized based on internships, job placements, or vocational training programs, focuses on job skills, attendance, professionalism, etc.

APPENDIX II:
Is It Time To Request An Evaluation Checklist

Is It Time to Request an Evaluation?

Use this checklist to identify whether it may be time to request a formal special education evaluation for your child. Trust your observations, and use this as a conversation starter with your child's teacher or care team.

Check all that apply:

☐ My child is consistently struggling in reading, writing, or math compared to peers.

☐ My child receives frequent disciplinary actions at school (suspensions, detentions).

☐ Teachers report attention or focus concerns that interfere with learning.

☐ My child has difficulty regulating emotions—frequent meltdowns, shutdowns, or anxiety.

☐ Sensory issues (noise, touch, lights) seem to affect my child's participation in school.

☐ My child avoids school, frequently complains of illness, or has school-related anxiety.

☐ Social interactions are limited, difficult, or absent altogether.

☐ I suspect a learning disability, ADHD, autism, anxiety, or another condition is involved.

☐ I have raised concerns, but the school has not taken formal action.

☐ My gut says something is wrong, but I cannot quite explain what.

What To Do Next

If you checked two or more boxes—or even just one that deeply concerns you—consider writing a formal request for evaluation. You have the legal right to request this at any time.

See ***APPENDIX III: Sample Email Template to Request an Evaluation*** for Special Education next.

APPENDIX III:
Sample Email Template To Request An Evaluation For Special Education

✏. *Sample Email/Letter*

> *Subject: Request For Special Education Evaluation*
>
> *Dear [Special Education Coordinator],*
>
> *I am formally requesting a comprehensive special education evaluation for my child, [Child's Name], who is in [Grade] at [School Name]. I suspect that my child may have a disability that is impacting their ability to learn, specifically in the areas of [reading, writing, math, attention, social skills, etc.].*
>
> *Under the Individuals with Disabilities Education Act (IDEA), I understand that my child has the right to a free, appropriate public education (FAPE) and an evaluation to determine if they qualify for special education services. I am requesting that this evaluation include assessments in the following areas:*
>
> - *Cognitive [measures intellectual abilities and problem-solving skills]*
>
> - *Achievement [measures academic achievement—reading, writing, and math skills—and compare them to grade-level expectations]*
>
> - *[List additional specific concerns: reading comprehension, literacy, fine motor skills, executive functioning, speech and language, attention, sensory processing, etc.]*

I request that the school provide me with the necessary consent forms and a timeline for the evaluation process. I also request Prior Written Notice (PWN) if the school refuses to evaluate my child, as required under IDEA.

Please confirm receipt of this request as soon as possible. I look forward to working with the school to support my child's learning needs.

Sincerely,
[Your Name]
[Your Contact Information]

⚡ **Important:** The school has 60 days (or less if your state's timeline is shorter) to complete the evaluation and hold an IEP meeting to discuss it once you sign the consent forms.

APPENDIX IV:
IEP/Eligibility Meeting Checklist

✳ **Pro Parent Tip:** Walking into meetings prepared shifts the power to YOU.

Essentials:

☐ Latest copy of your child's IEP or 504 Plan (if available)
☐ Recent evaluations (school and private)
☐ Written concerns and goals you want to address
☐ Progress reports or report cards
☐ Meeting notice and agenda (if sent by school)
☐ Questions list to ask during the meeting
☐ A folder or binder to keep documents organized

If Available:

☐ Any private medical diagnoses or provider notes
☐ Copies of behavior charts or work samples
☐ Parent observations from home (strengths, struggles)
☐ Letters or notes from outside therapists or tutors

Optional (but Powerful):

☐ Support person (friend, advocate, or note-taker)
☐ Notebook or laptop to take notes
☐ Water and snack (meetings can run long)

Pro Tips for the Meeting:

☐ Arrive early so you can settle in.

☐ Take notes—names, promises, timelines.

☐ Ask for clarification if terms are confusing.

☐ Stay calm but firm—you are the expert on your child.

☐ Request Prior Written Notice if services are denied or reduced.

APPENDIX V:
IEP Goals Checklist For Parents

Use this checklist to review your child's annual IEP goals and short-term objectives. Do not settle for vague promises—insist on clarity, accountability, and purpose.

✔ Individualization

☐ Does the goal reflect my child's current strengths and challenges—not just generic language?
☐ Is this goal different from last year's, or does it show meaningful progress and development?

✔ Clarity

☐ Is each goal written in plain language that I can understand?
☐ Does the goal clearly describe what skill or behavior my child is expected to improve?
☐ Can I explain the goal to someone else without having to guess what it means?

✔ Specificity

☐ Is the goal specific to my child's needs, based on recent evaluations or observations?
☐ Does it say exactly what will be taught, not just a general subject area like "reading" or "social skills"?

✔ Measurability

☐ Can progress be tracked clearly and objectively—with data, not just vague impressions?
☐ Does the goal include measurable criteria (e.g., 80% accuracy in 4 out of 5 trials), and is the method for tracking progress clearly explained?
☐ Will I receive regular progress updates—not just once a year?
☐ Is there a plan in place if progress is not happening as expected?

✔ Achievability

☐ Is this goal realistic based on my child's current performance and available supports?
☐ Does it challenge my child appropriately—without being so hard it sets them up to fail?
☐ Is the goal attainable within one school year, given the instruction and services provided?

✔ Relevance

☐ Is the goal connected to an identified area of need in the PLAAFP?
☐ Does it support my child's access to and progress in the general education curriculum?
☐ Does it promote functional, behavioral, or social-emotional growth, if those areas are impacted?

✔ Timeframe

☐ Is there a clear timeline?
☐ Do the short-term objectives break the goal into meaningful steps across the year.

APPENDIX VI:
Age-Appropriate Ways For Kids To Join The IEP Process

A quick-reference guide for helping your child meaningfully participate in their IEP— at any age or ability level. Not every child will do all these things—which is okay. Use what fits their personality, needs, and comfort level.

See **_Chapter 4: The IEP Process_** for more on student roles in IEP meetings and how to decide when (and how) your child should participate.

Student Voice Matters

Involving your child in their IEP fosters confidence, ownership, and self-advocacy. The approach should grow with your child's age and communication style.

✱ **Pro Parent Tip:** The law requires that students be invited to their own IEP meeting by age 16, but you do not need to wait. Student involvement can begin as early as preschool—with the right support.

Ages 3-7: Introduce the Basics

- Use picture schedules, social stories, or roleplay to help your child understand what school supports are for.

- Let them help pick tools (like fidgets, headphones, or breaks) that support their learning.

- Encourage simple choices: "Would you rather have a quiet corner or noise-canceling headphones?"

Ages 8–12: Practice Self-Expression

- Help them name strengths and challenges (e.g., "I am good at math, but writing is hard for me.")

- Let them write or draw a short "About Me" letter to share with the team.

- Practice IEP meeting roleplay at home: "What would you want your teacher to know?"

Ages 13–15: Build Self-Advocacy & Future Readiness

- **Invite them to part of the IEP meeting**—especially during the goals section. Begin connecting these goals to their own interests, values, or future dreams (even if those dreams change).

- **Teach them how to ask for accommodations** and explain what helps them thrive—not just at school, but in life. This builds lifelong communication skills.

- **Help them prepare 2–3 talking points** to share in the meeting (with coaching if needed), and link those points to something they want—more independence, better support, a goal they care about.

✱ **Pro Parent Tip:** Teens are far more likely to engage when they see how the IEP connects to *their* life—not just compliance. Talk about real-world scenarios, future goals, or "what's in it for me" moments. Self-advocacy becomes a lot more meaningful when it moves beyond school paperwork and toward personal possibility.

Ages 16+: Lead the Process

- The student should be involved in transition planning, postsecondary goals, and service discussions.

- Encourage them to chair part of the IEP meeting or present their own goals.

- Support them in learning their rights under IDEA and ADA, especially as they approach adulthood.

➜ **Remember:** Participation can be verbal, written, drawn, or supported by technology. The goal is not perfect articulation—it is voice, choice, and agency.

APPENDIX VII:
Your IEP Team Map

Key Members of the IEP Team and How Parents Can Collaborate

Role	What They Do	When to Contact Them	Pro Parent Tip
You **(The Parent)**	Expert on your child. Your insight shapes every decision.	Always—you are a required IEP team member.	Keep a notebook of concerns, progress, and questions.
General Education Teacher	Describes classroom expectations, tracks daily performance.	When classroom behavior, assignments, or participation are a concern.	Ask for classwork samples or patterns they observe.
Special Education Teacher	Implements IEP goals, monitors progress, adjusts instruction.	For service delivery updates or problem-solving around goals.	Maintain an open email thread for ongoing updates.
School Psychologist	Leads evaluations, explains test results, supports behavioral planning.	During or after the evaluation process.	Ask them to walk you through assessment data one-on-one.
Therapists (SLP, OT, PT)	Deliver related services like speech, sensory integration, or mobility support.	When services are missing or progress is unclear.	Request quarterly updates or logs.
Behavior Specialist	Designs and monitors behavior intervention plans; coaches staff.	When behavior plans are unclear,	Ask to review the Behavior

Role	What They Do	When to Contact Them	Pro Parent Tip
		inconsistent, or ineffective.	Intervention Plan (BIP) regularly.
School Counselor/ LSW	Supports emotional wellness, coping strategies, and social-emotional learning.	When anxiety, friendships, or mental health needs impact school.	Ask about small-group supports or check-ins written into the IEP.
Advocate or Attorney	Supports you during IEP meetings or disputes.	When facing conflict, pushback, or legal concerns.	Vet credentials—training and ethics matter in advocacy.

APPENDIX VIII:
Parent Concerns And Prep Guide

✎ Sample Email/Letter

Subject: Parent Input & Concerns For Upcoming IEP Meeting – [Student's Name]

Dear [Case Manager / Special Education Coordinator / Teacher's Name],

I'm writing to share some parent concerns and input in advance of our upcoming IEP meeting for [Child's Name] on [Date]. My goal is to ensure the meeting is as productive and focused as possible, and that we're all aligned in supporting [Child's Name]'s continued progress.

I have noticed the following strengths at home:

- *[List 2–3 strengths or interests – e.g., "Strong memory for facts," "Creative storytelling," "Compassionate with siblings and peers"]*

I'd love to hear from the team whether you're seeing the same strengths at school. This not only helps us all stay aligned, but also reminds us to build from what's working.

I have the following concerns:

[⚡ Note: Please see the PARENT PREP GUIDE below for help narrowing down your top 2–4 concerns.]

1. *[Insert Academic/Behavioral/Functional Concern] → For example: "[Child] continues to struggle with reading comprehension,*

particularly when asked to make inferences or summarize text independently."

2. *[Insert Social-Emotional or Peer Interaction Concern]* → *For example: "I've noticed increased anxiety before school and a reluctance to participate in group work."*

3. *[Insert Service or Support Concern]* → *For example: "It's unclear if speech and language services are targeting both expressive and pragmatic communication. I'd like to better understand the goals and progress monitoring."*

I/we would appreciate input on:

- *Any areas you would like their input such as, "How the current goals are being measured and whether [Child] is on track to meet them," "Whether any accommodations or supports might need adjusting based on recent challenges," and, "If additional assessments are recommended in light of new concerns."*

Thank you for your collaboration and continued support. Please let me know if you'd like to discuss any of this before the meeting. I look forward to working together to create a plan that truly supports [Child]'s growth.

Warmly,
[Your Name]
[Contact Info]

Parent Prep Guide: What To Share Before The IEP Meeting

Use this guide to reflect on how things are going across key areas. Then identify your top 2–4 priorities to share with the team.

1. Academic Progress

What subjects are going well? What areas are still hard?

- Is your child making expected progress in reading, writing, or math?
- Are they able to complete assignments with support?
- Do you feel their current goals and services are effective?

✎ Notes:

2. Social Connection

How is your child doing with peers?

- Are they making or keeping friends?
- Are there signs of exclusion, bullying, or isolation?
- Do they enjoy group activities or avoid them?

✎ Notes:

3. Emotional Wellbeing

How does your child feel about school?

- Do you see signs of anxiety, stress, or dread before school?
- Are there emotional outbursts, shutdowns, or avoidance behaviors?

✎ Notes:

4. Behavior and Self-Regulation

Are there any behavioral concerns at home or school?

- How does your child handle frustration, feedback, or redirection?

- Are they easily overwhelmed, impulsive, or checked out?

✎ Notes:

5. Independence and Daily Functioning

Can your child manage routines and tasks without constant prompting?

- For 7th grade and up: Can they get themselves up and ready on time in the morning?

- Are they able to follow classroom routines, keep track of materials, and advocate for help?

- Do they manage transitions, locker use, and navigating the school day independently?

✎ Notes:

6. Homework And Assignments

How does your child manage work outside the classroom?

- Are they remembering to write down assignments and bring materials home?

- Are long-term projects being completed on time?

- How much adult support is required at home?

✎ Notes:

7. Strengths And Interests

- What are your child's strengths and passions?

- What activities do they enjoy and excel in—either in or outside of school?

- What motivates them or helps them feel confident?

✎ Notes:

8. Communication With The School

- Are you getting the information you need?
- Do teachers or staff provide consistent updates on progress, behavior, or services?

- Have there been delays or breakdowns in communication?

- Are you unsure who to go to with questions or concerns?

✎ Notes:

✓*Next Step: Narrow It Down*

From the sections above, choose your top 2–4 priorities to share in your Parent Concerns email or during the IEP meeting. Focus on what is most urgent, unclear, or meaningful right now.

✱ **Pro Parent Tip:** Your input does not have to be perfect—it just needs to reflect what you are seeing and what your child needs. The team can help problem-solve from there.

APPENDIX IX:
Sample Email Template To Report Bullying

✎. *Sample Email/Letter*

Subject: Urgent: Bullying Report for [Child's Name]

Dear [Principal's Name],

I am writing to formally report repeated bullying incidents involving my child, [Child's Name], at [School Name]. These incidents occurred on [Dates] and include [Brief Description]. My child has expressed fear about attending school, and this has negatively impacted their ability to focus in class.

Since bullying is interfering with my child's ability to access their education, I am requesting an immediate meeting to discuss intervention strategies. I would appreciate a written response outlining the school's plan to address this issue within five school days.

Thank you for your prompt attention to this matter.

Sincerely,
[Your Name]
[Your Contact Information]

➡ **Pro Parent Move:** If the school ignores or downplays your concerns, send a follow-up email copying the director of special education or the superintendent. Schools tend to act when district leadership is involved.

APPENDIX X:
Advocacy Quick Start Checklist

Small steps. Big impact. Start here.

Stay Informed

☐ Sign up for email alerts from advocacy orgs (COPAA, NCLD, Understood, Wrightslaw)
☐ Follow your state's Department of Education for policy updates
☐ Join one disability rights or parent-led organization in your state

Speak Up

☐ Identify your state and federal representatives
☐ Send one email or call to share how special education laws impact your child
☐ Save a template you can reuse for future outreach

Join Forces

☐ Attend a webinar, town hall, or training hosted by a local or national advocacy group
☐ Connect with at least one other parent advocate—you do not have to do this alone
☐ Bookmark the Parent Training and Information Center (PTI) in your state

Show Up

☐ Check your local school board meeting calendar
☐ Prepare a 2-minute public comment about a special education issue
☐ If you cannot attend in person, submit written testimony or find someone who can speak on your behalf

➜ **Pro Parent Reminder:** You do not need to do everything. Start with one action. Then another. Advocacy is not about perfection—it is about persistence.

⭐ **Direct Action Tool:** Want to quickly find your elected officials? Use myreps.datamade.us to locate contact info for your federal, state, and local representatives. Your voice matters—make sure they hear it.

APPENDIX XI:
Life Skills Readiness Checklist

Use this checklist to assess your child's independence skills. You don't need to check every box at every age—this is a tool, not a test. The goal is progress, not perfection.

Elementary School (Ages 5–10)

Focus: Early routines, confidence-building, and foundation skills.

☐ Brushes teeth independently

☐ Packs backpack with reminders

☐ Identifies daily schedule (home and school)

☐ Helps with basic chores (laundry sorting, setting table)

☐ Uses visual or written checklist to complete routines

☐ Can explain personal likes/dislikes

☐ Asks for help when confused or unsure

✱ **Parent Pro Tip:** Introduce one "solo" chore they can own—like feeding a pet or clearing the table.

Middle School (Ages 11-13)

Focus: Emerging independence and decision-making.

☐ Prepares simple meals (sandwiches, toast, microwave use)

☐ Tracks small spending (allowance or gift money)

☐ Understands personal hygiene routines without prompting

☐ Plans simple outings (e.g., bike ride to a park, packing for a sleepover)

☐ Knows how to use a phone to contact parents or guardians

☐ Practices expressing needs in class (e.g., asking to use a break pass)

* Parent Pro Tip: Open a student checking account together and practice checking balances.

High School (Ages 14-18)

Focus: Daily living, advocacy, and future planning.

☐ Participates in IEP or 504 meetings with support

☐ Cooks full meals with a recipe

☐ Tracks appointments and/or assignments on a calendar

☐ Uses public transportation with assistance or practice

☐ Manages personal hygiene and laundry routines

☐ Has practiced self-advocacy (e.g., "I need extra time" or "This isn't working for me")

☐ Understands basic budgeting (income vs. expenses)

✱ **Parent Pro Tip:** Arrange a job shadow day or paid/unpaid work experience.

Post-School/Young Adult (Ages 18+)

Focus: Self-management, employment, and long-term independence.

☐ Schedules own appointments (doctor, therapist, DMV)

☐ Manages medication independently (timing, refills, tracking)

☐ Handles personal banking (bills, deposits, online banking)

☐ Understands rental basics (leases, utility bills, tenants' rights)

☐ Communicates needs to employers, professors, or service providers

☐ Manages a daily or weekly routine without outside prompting

✱ **Parent Pro Tip:** Meet with vocational rehab or an Independent Living Center for coaching and supports.

Bonus: Planning Questions—Ask Yourself:

- What is one life skill my child is already great at?

- Which 2–3 skills feel most urgent for the next 6 months?

- What support (tools, modeling, coaching) does my child need to learn those skills?

- Who can help us teach or reinforce these skills (teacher, sibling, OT, support worker)?

More Resources:

For printable tools, IEP integration guides, and domain-specific life skills strategies, visit The Autism Life Skills Lady (https://lifeskillslady.com/). Her Life Skills Cheat Sheet is especially helpful when preparing for IEP transition planning.

APPENDIX XII:
Advocacy & Special Education Resource Guide

List here are the resources referenced in the book. It includes national organizations, funding resources, legal supports, and where to find help in your state.

★ National Advocacy & Parent Support

✓ **The Arc**
Support for individuals with intellectual and developmental disabilities.
✳ https://thearc.org

✓ **The Autism Life Skills Lady**
Providing information and tools for parents about transition and life skills.
✳ https://lifeskillslady.com/

✓ **COPAA (Council of Parent Attorneys and Advocates)**
Legal and advocacy training, including the SEAT program.
✳ https://copaa.org

✓ **Parent Training and Information Centers (PTIs)**
Free training and support in every state.
✳ https://parentcenterhub.org/find-your-center

✓ **NCLD (National Center for Learning Disabilities)**
Advocacy, research, and family resources.
✳ https://ncld.org

✓ **OSEP (Office of Special Education Programs)**
IDEA regulations and policy guidance.

✳ https://sites.ed.gov/idea

✓ **OCR (Office for Civil Rights)**
To file disability discrimination complaints.

✳ https://www.ed.gov/about/ed-offices/ocr

✓ **Understood.org**
Tools for learning and attention issues.

✳ https://www.understood.org

✓ **Wrightslaw**
Special education law, advocacy, and training.

✳ https://wrightslaw.com

✪ Financial Assistance & Grants

✓ **UnitedHealthcare Children's Foundation**
Medical-related grants for children.

✳ https://www.uhccf.org

✓ **The Christopher & Dana Reeve Foundation**
Resources and grants for mobility and access.

✳ https://www.christopherreeve.org

✓ **National Autism Association**
Safety tools, grants, and advocacy.

✳ https://nationalautismassociation.org

✓ **Easterseals**
Education, employment, and community services.

✳ https://www.easterseals.com

✓ **Vocational Rehabilitation (VR)**
State programs for post-secondary and employment support.

✳ rsa.ed.gov/about/states

✓ **SSI (Supplemental Security Income)**
Financial aid for children with disabilities.

✳ https://www.ssa.gov/ssi

✓ **Medicaid Waivers**
Search: "Medicaid Waiver + [Your State]"

✳ https://www.medicaid.gov

✳ Legal Help & Policy Advocacy

✓ **Disability Rights Education & Defense Fund (DREDF)**
Legal strategies and civil rights protections.

✳ https://dredf.org

✓ **COPAA (Council of Parent Attorneys and Advocates)**
Special education legal resources and advocate/attorney locator.

✳ https://copaa.org

✓ **Special Needs Alliance**
Legal services and planning for families of children with disabilities.

✳ https://specialneedsalliance.org

✓ **ADA National Network**
Information on disability rights and protections in schools.

✳ https://adata.org

✓ **Office for Civil Rights (OCR)**
For filing disability discrimination complaints in education.

✳ ed.gov/about/ed-offices/ocr

✓ **OSEP (Office of Special Education Programs)**
Federal guidance on IDEA, IEPs, and dispute resolution.

✳ https://www.ed.gov/about/ed-offices/osers/osep

✓ **Find Your Representatives**
Use this tool to contact federal, state, and local officials.

✳ https://myreps.datamade.us

✦ How to Search for Local Support

Use these phrases with your state/region:

☑ "Special education advocacy [Your State]"
☑ "Medicaid waiver for children with disabilities [Your State]"
☑ "Special education PTA [Your State]"
☑ "Disability rights [Your State DOE]"
☑ "Educational advocate near me"
☑ "Parent training center [Your State]"
☑ "Transition programs near me"
☑ "Assistive tech grants [Your State]"
☑ "Special education attorney near me"

About the Author

DANA & HER FAMILY

The Author Dana Jonson Dana Jonson is a civil rights attorney based in Connecticut, focused exclusively on special education law. Through her private practice, she fights for the legal rights of children with disabilities—advocating for them at every stage, from IEP meetings to due process hearings and even Federal Court.

In addition to her legal work, Dana hosts the podcast Special Ed on Special Ed, where she and fellow experts break down vital topics to inform and empower special education parents. She also conducts workshops for parents and educators, equipping them with the knowledge to understand their rights and responsibilities within the special education system.

Before becoming a lawyer, Dana worked as a special education teacher and administrator in Boston. She previously held a K–12 certification in Intensive Special Needs, and that classroom experience continues to shape her legal advocacy. Her educational background includes a JD from Northeastern University School of Law, a Master of Science in Education from Simmons College with a focus on Intensive Special Needs, and a Bachelor of Science in Psychology from Fairfield University, concentrating on Developmental Psychology.

Dana is admitted to the Connecticut State and Federal Bar and the United States Supreme Court. Her personal experience as a mother to five children with various special education needs—and as a foster parent to many more—adds a profound layer of empathy and insight to her professional work. Her commitment to special education shines not only in the courtroom but also through her podcast and community outreach, making her a vital voice in the field.

She lives in Connecticut with her husband, children, three dogs, and two cats.